LEGAL SCHOLARSHIP FOR THE URBAN CORE

The problems of entrenched poverty and economic underdevelopment in American urban cores involve multiple overlapping challenges that have stymied consistent and long-term progress for many decades. Although inadequate and misguided laws are not solely responsible for this state of affairs, good laws – and good lawyering – can contribute enormously to overcoming the challenges of the urban cores. By showcasing a range of scholarly analyses, covering a broad spectrum of legal issues and methodologies, this book demonstrates how law and lawyers can and do respond to the challenges of the urban cores. It provides paths forward at the local level in the face of federal political paralysis and inattention and lays a foundation for new paradigms and new approaches to intransigent problems. Modeling engaged legal scholarship as a pragmatic response to contemporary challenges, this book is for anyone concerned about the current state of American urban cores.

PETER ENRICH is Professor of Law at the School of Law, Northeastern University, Boston. He is a leading authority on state and local government law and state and local tax policy, with a focus on issues of fiscal and interjurisdictional dynamics, including education funding and state tax policy.

RASHMI DYAL-CHAND is Professor of Law at the School of Law, Northeastern University, Boston. She is the author of *Collaborative Capitalism in American Cities: Reforming Urban Market Regulations* (Cambridge, 2018) and her article, "Human Worth as Collateral," won the 2006 Association of American Law Schools scholarly papers competition for new law teachers.

Legal Scholarship for the Urban Core

FROM THE GROUND UP

Edited by

PETER ENRICH

Northeastern University

RASHMI DYAL-CHAND

Northeastern University

CAMBRIDGE
UNIVERSITY PRESS

CAMBRIDGE
UNIVERSITY PRESS

University Printing House, Cambridge CB2 8BS, United Kingdom

One Liberty Plaza, 20th Floor, New York, NY 10006, USA

477 Williamstown Road, Port Melbourne, VIC 3207, Australia

314–321, 3rd Floor, Plot 3, Splendor Forum, Jasola District Centre, New Delhi – 110025, India

79 Anson Road, #06–04/06, Singapore 079906

Cambridge University Press is part of the University of Cambridge.

It furthers the University's mission by disseminating knowledge in the pursuit of education, learning, and research at the highest international levels of excellence.

www.cambridge.org
Information on this title: www.cambridge.org/9781108499125
DOI: 10.1017/9781108615181

First published 2019

Printed and bound in Great Britain by Clays Ltd, Elcograf S.p.A.

A catalogue record for this publication is available from the British Library.

Library of Congress Cataloging-in-Publication Data
NAMES: Dyal-Chand, Rashmi, 1970- editor. | Enrich, Peter D., editor.
TITLE: Legal scholarship for the urban core : from the ground up / edited by Rashmi Dyal-Chand, Northeastern University, Boston; Peter Enrich, Northeastern University, Boston.
DESCRIPTION: Cambridge, United Kingdom ; New York, NY, USA : Cambridge University Press, 2019. | Includes bibliographical references and index.
IDENTIFIERS: LCCN 2018061721 | ISBN 9781108499125 (hbk : alk. paper) | ISBN 9781108713146 (pbk : alk. paper)
SUBJECTS: LCSH: Community development–United States. | Social justice–United States. | City planning and redevelopment law–Economic aspects–United States. | Community development–Law and legislation–United States. | United States–Social policy–1993-
CLASSIFICATION: LCC HN90.C6 L44 2019 | DDC 307.1/40973–dc23
LC record available at https://lccn.loc.gov/2018061721

ISBN 978-1-108-49912-5 Hardback

Contents

Editors and Contributors

TONYA L. BRITO is the Jefferson Burrus-Bascom Professor of Law at the University of Wisconsin Law School and a faculty affiliate with the Institute for Research on Poverty (IRP) at the University of Wisconsin. During the 2018–19 academic year, she was a visiting scholar at the Russell Sage Foundation. An award-winning scholar, Professor Brito's work critically examines the intersection of family law and poverty law, focusing on how the welfare state regulates the family relationships of the poor. More broadly, her research interests include family law and policy, law and inequality, socio-legal studies, critical race empiricism, and qualitative research methods. She is the lead principal investigator of a multi-year, multidisciplinary, NSF-funded empirical study examining how the provision of counsel and more limited forms of legal assistance shape access to justice for low-income civil litigants in child support enforcement proceedings. Professor Brito received her AB with honors from Barnard College and her JD cum laude from Harvard Law School.

SCOTT CUMMINGS is Robert Henigson Professor of Legal Ethics and Professor of Law at UCLA School of Law, where he teaches and writes about the legal profession, public interest law, law and social movements, and community economic development. He is the faculty director of Legal Ethics and the Profession (LEAP), a program that promotes research and programming on the challenges facing the contemporary legal profession. He is also a long-time member of the UCLA David J. Epstein Program in Public Interest Law and Policy, a specialization training students to become public interest lawyers. Professor Cummings is coauthor of the first public interest law textbook, *Public Interest Lawyering: A Contemporary Perspective* (with Alan Chen) (2012), and coeditor of a leading legal profession casebook, *Legal Ethics* (with Deborah Rhode, David Luban, and Nora Engstrom) (7th ed., 2016).

RASHMI DYAL-CHAND is a professor of law at Northeastern University School of Law, where she teaches and writes about property law, poverty, local economic development, and consumer law. She is the author of *Collaborative Capitalism in American Cities: Reforming Urban Market Regulations* (Cambridge University Press, 2018). Professor Dyal-Chand was the principal investigator of a multi-year clinical and research initiative at Northeastern Law School funded by the US Commerce Department's Economic Development Administration. She is currently a coprincipal investigator of an NSF study on engineering the sharing economy. Before becoming a law professor, she served as an associate general counsel for The Community Builders, Inc., a major nonprofit affordable housing developer.

Peter Enrich is a professor of law at Northeastern University School of Law. He teaches courses in Contracts, State and Local Government, and State and Local Taxation, and for a number of years served as a faculty supervisor for the school's Legal Skills in Social Context course's Social Justice Project program. He writes about issues of state and local fiscal, tax, and education policy, and serves as a policy and legal adviser to state governments and progressive advocacy organizations. Before becoming a law professor, he was a philosophy professor at University of North Carolina – Charlotte and served as general counsel for the Massachusetts Executive Office for Administration and Finance.

Daanika Gordon is an assistant professor of sociology at Tufts University. Her scholarship explores the role of legal institutions in constructing race- and place-based inequalities. She earned her PhD and MS from the University of Wisconsin-Madison and her BA from the University of California, Berkeley.

Kathleen S. Morris is a professor of law at Golden Gate University School of Law, where she specializes in State and Local Government Law, Federal Constitutional Law, State Constitutional Law, Public Lawyering, and Legal Education. She has also taught at Rutgers and Yale law schools, and in 2006 she cofounded the San Francisco Affirmative Litigation Project at Yale Law School. Her publications include *Uncooperative Localism* (forthcoming); "Cities Seeking Justice: Local Government Litigation in the Public Interest," in *How Cities Will Save the World* (2016); *Expanding Local Enforcement of State and Federal Consumer Protection Laws*, 40 Fordham Urban L.J. 1903 (2013); *The Case for Local Constitutional Enforcement*, 47 Harv.C.R.-C.L. L. Rev. 1 (2012); and "San Francisco and the Rising Culture of Engagement in Local Public Law Offices," in *Why The Local Matters: Federalism, Localism, and Public Interest Advocacy* (2010).

David J. Pate, Jr. is an associate professor of social work and department chair at the University of Wisconsin-Milwaukee, Helen Bader School of Social Welfare, and an affiliated associate professor in the Department of African and African Diaspora Studies, and an affiliated associate professor at the Institute for Research on Poverty at the University of Wisconsin-Madison. His scholarship examines the life course events of Black adult males through the use of qualitative research methods. He earned his PhD in Social Welfare at the University of Wisconsin-Madison, his BA from the University of Detroit, and his MA from the University of Chicago, School of Social Service Administration.

PETER PITEGOFF is a professor of law at the University of Maine School of Law, where he was Dean from 2005 to 2015, and previously was a professor and vice dean at the State University of New York (SUNY) Buffalo Law School. He has taught, worked, and written extensively in the areas of community economic development, labor and industrial organization, corporation and nonprofit law, employee ownership, and legal ethics. Pitegoff served for ten years on the board of directors of Coastal Enterprises, Inc., a national leader in community development finance. Prior to his academic career, he was legal counsel for the ICA Group, a Boston firm that assists worker-owned enterprises and related economic development initiatives. He is a graduate of Brown University and New York University School of Law, where he was a Root-Tilden scholar.

ROBERT SOLOMON is a clinical professor of law at the University of California, Irvine School of Law, where he teaches Community and Economic Development. His writing is informed by his years as a legal services attorney in Pennsylvania and Connecticut, Executive Director of the Housing Authority of the City of New Haven, and clinical teacher. He earned his BA at Rutgers University and JD at George Washington University School of Law.

1

Introduction

This book of essays responds to the intersection of two failures, in the hope that approaches with the promise to address one of these failures may also have promise in addressing the other. The first failure is the dismal inability of American urban policy, over at least the past half century, to significantly improve the lot of the low-income populations that are concentrated in pockets of most American cities. The second failure is the increasingly recognized inability of the American legal academy to find models of legal scholarship that achieve relevance for audiences that can have real impact on real problems.

The failure of much legal scholarship to deliver insights of value to those seeking to confront urban problems certainly does not bear primary responsibility for the continuing problems of the urban cores. Those problems have deep roots, not only in law but also in economics, politics, sociology, and history. Nonetheless, the structures and dynamics of multiple bodies of law are major contributors to our cities' present dysfunction, and are critical tools for any significant reforms. The challenges of the urban core, like many of the challenges confronting contemporary America, involve law as one vital thread in a complex web of forces that together sustain the problems. The challenge of legal scholarship is, in significant measure, the challenge of finding a way to tease out the legal dimensions of these tangled webs and to address those legal dimensions in ways that potentiate change.

What is exciting to us is that we are beginning to see glimmers of hope for legal scholarship with this capacity – often in the form of qualitative research that suggests alternatives to established legal concepts and to familiar legal strategies. Our goal is to showcase some of these examples of engaged and efficacious legal scholarship, both to advance analysis and action that address the challenges of the urban cores and to exemplify the prospects of a newly revitalized legal scholarship.

The hope behind this collection is that some of the promising new scholarship addressing the intractable problems of the urban cores may offer valuable paths forward on both of these problems. In times of paradigm failure, examples of useful work may provide clues about the elements of an effective new paradigm. In particular, if the question is what kinds of scholarly approaches can restore the practical efficacy of legal scholarship, and can revive the interest of communities beyond the legal academy (and, indeed, the interest of the legal academy itself) in engaging with such scholarship, then where better to look but to scholarly writings that show those capacities? In this chapter, we explicate the two failures that this volume seeks to explore. We begin by examining the current crisis in legal scholarship. We then examine the problems of the urban cores. Our purpose is to provide a context for the scholarly work that follows in the remainder of this book.

THE CHALLENGES FACING LEGAL SCHOLARSHIP

In recent decades, a growing chorus of voices, both inside and outside the legal academy, has expressed concerns about the diminishing relevance of legal scholarship to the interests of judges, policy makers, and practicing lawyers. These concerns have not focused specifically on scholarship relating to the challenges of the urban core, or to any particular field of legal scholarship, but much of the critique is as applicable to this field as to many others. Indeed, in several respects, the gap between legal scholarship and the needs for urban transformation may be a particularly vivid example both of the problem and of the potential for a more productive future.

One influential early statement of the concerns about scholarship's disconnection from the world of practice came from Judge Harry Edwards, a distinguished law professor and jurist on the federal court of appeals for the District of Columbia Circuit, in a 1992 article in the *Michigan Law Review*.[1] Judge Edwards observed that legal scholarship has become increasingly detached from the concerns of judges, legislators, and legal practitioners, because an increasingly academic orientation of law professors had shifted scholarship's focus to "abstract theory" (typified by critical legal theory and law-and-economics) at the expense of "practical" scholarship (characterized by a prescriptive focus on legal doctrine).

This critique of the trajectory and relevance of legal scholarship is widely shared, both inside and outside the legal academy. Supreme Court Chief Justice John Roberts famously observed, "Pick up a copy of any law review that you see and the first article is likely to be, you know, the influence of Immanuel Kant on evidentiary approaches in 18th-century Bulgaria, or something, which I'm sure was of great interest to the academic that wrote it, but isn't of much help to the bar."[2] The American Bar Association's MacCrate Commission on Legal Education

[1] Harry T. Edwards, *The Growing Disjunction between Legal Education and the Legal Profession*, 91 MICH. L. REV. 34 (1992).

[2] A *Conversation with Chief Justice Roberts* (C-SPAN television broadcast June 25, 2011), www.c-span.org/video/?c4545488/john-roberts.

reported a widespread sense among practicing lawyers that "law professors are more interested in pursuing their own intellectual interests than in helping the legal profession address matters of important current concern."[3] Professor Robin West decries the legal academy's growing distaste for what she characterizes as "normative" scholarship, which strives to "make the law better" by seeking to "mold, or shape, or reshape, or reform, or radically alter law," and the academy's increasing focus on descriptive scholarship that observes the legal system from an external, often empirical, perspective.[4]

Many factors have contributed to the changing relationship – and the changing perceptions of the relationship – between legal scholarship and potential nonacademic audiences. But one important dimension is surely the evolving nature of legal scholarship itself over the past century. In large measure, the critique of legal scholarship's diminished relevance has focused on the turn away from emphasis on what Robin West refers to as "normative" scholarship, or what Judge Edwards refers to as "practical" scholarship. The suggestion is that legal scholarship in recent decades has become increasingly focused on critical, theoretical, and interdisciplinary perspectives, at the expense of a focus on how the substance of the law, its rules, principles, and doctrines, can be clarified, refined, or reformed to serve recognized societal needs and ends.

One of many possible versions of the story of that evolution goes like this: Once upon a time, perhaps a century ago, legal scholarship was predominantly concerned with the clarification and refinement of legal doctrine, in furtherance of Langdell's vision of law as science. The work of the scholars involved in the American Law Institute's Restatement projects and in crafting the grand treatises of that era was paradigmatic. This model of the legal scholar's role rested on an ideal vision of law as stable, systematic, and apolitical, and a view of scholarship's goal as moving the body of law toward that ideal state, just as empirical scientists' task was to move scientific theory ever closer to truth. And, happily, the legal scholar's task under this vision – clarifying and refining legal doctrine – aligned closely with the concerns of practicing lawyers and judges, and with the scholars' role as teachers of future practicing lawyers.

But, in the early decades of the twentieth century, this vision of law, and of the role of legal scholarship, came under withering and devastating attack from the legal realists. Reacting to profound economic and social change and the resulting stresses on legal norms and principles, the realists convincingly exposed law to be

[3] *Amer. Bar Ass'n Sect. of Legal Educ. & Admission to the Bar, Legal Education and Professional Development – An Educational Continuum* 5 (1992).

[4] Robin West, *The Contested Value of Normative Legal Scholarship*, 66 J. Legal Educ. 6, 7 (2016). West acknowledges, *id.* at 11, the continuing prevalence of normative scholarship in legal journals, but sees it as under attack from a range of perspectives, and argues that these attacks devalue such scholarship and favor other forms that she sees as less valuable in shaping or improving the law.

historically and socially contingent, grounded not on foundational principles but on competing interests, and as inherently political and contested. This transformed understanding of law did not, of course, foreclose legal scholars from a continued focus on the clarification and improvement of legal rules and doctrine, but it stripped such efforts of the veneer of scientific methodology or of progress toward objective truth. Efforts at normative or practical legal scholarship were revealed to be inherently perspectival and political.

What, then, was a legal scholar to do, if she aspired to the norms of objectivity and knowledge advancement that prevail in the academy (and particularly in the social sciences, which are naturally seen as law's nearest academic kin)? Over the ensuing decades, several different paths emerged and assumed prominence in the legal academy, but each of them drew legal scholarship away from its traditional orientation toward doctrinal development, and each of them diminished the direct relevance of legal scholarship to the concerns of practicing lawyers and policy makers.

One path is to reframe the legal scholar's inquiry as an investigation into the actual workings and evolution of law in its practical contexts, drawing on the methods of the empirical social sciences. The law-and-society approach asks not what legal doctrine is or should be, but rather how the law actually plays out in the various social contexts in which it is deployed ("law on the ground" not "law in the books").[5] The focus is on empirical description of the workings of legal institutions and of the role of lawyers and of various actors' understandings and deployments of legal norms in the actual functioning of the social structures that law purports to govern. Such empirical observations are, of course, highly relevant to the practical choices of practicing lawyers and policy makers, and some of the insights generated by the law-and-society movement have had valuable impacts both on the ways that lawyers understand their work and on efforts to reform the structure of legal institutions.

But, to the extent that these audiences are looking to legal scholarship for insight and guidance about the content of "the law" – about legal rules and principles, about the arguments that lawyers can make before legal tribunals, about the ways that law-makers should frame their pronouncements – this scholarship can seem beside the point, or at best of only indirect relevance. Indeed, it often serves to deepen skepticism about the utility of more traditional doctrinal scholarship, by exposing how modest an impact articulated legal rules and principles have on real-world outcomes.

Another path draws on the tools and methodologies, not of sociology and anthropology, but of economics, and seeks to explicate, analyze, and critique legal rules and practices as elements in a system governed by the laws of economic theory. The

[5] For a couple of classic statements of the law-and-society approach, *see* Stewart Macaulay, *The New versus the Old Legal Realism: "Things Ain't What They Used to Be"*, 2005 Wis. L. Rev. 365 and Lawrence M. Friedman, *The Law and Society Movement*, 38 Stan. L. Rev. 763 (1986).

law-and-economics approach, like the law-and-society approach, aims to understand the law as one functioning part of a larger whole, assessing the extent to which legal rules redress or exacerbate imperfections in the larger system that distort the efficient operations of a market economy, and the ways in which economically rational actors' responses to legal rules affect the practical operation of those rules.[6] As with law-and-society scholarship, work in the law-and-economics tradition has certainly exerted considerable influence, modeling and legitimating a new set of arguments that have become highly influential in certain judicial and policy contexts.

But, this approach, too, has largely tended to widen the gulf between academic work and practitioner and policy maker concerns. In part, this is the consequence of the increasingly technical and specialized character of the economic analysis deployed particularly by interdisciplinary law-and-economics scholars, accentuated by growing doubts about whether the asserted laws of economic theory accurately depict the ways that actual human agents and institutions behave. And in part, it reflects skepticism about whether the economists' touchstone of market efficiency is the primary normative standard for assessing legal rules and practices, in the face of a range of other compelling norms for assessing societal outcomes. Moreover, as with much of the law-and-society scholarship, significant segments of law-and-economics analysis, particularly those drawing on Coase's theorem or on public choice theory, tend to minimize the utility of legal analysis and argumentation as sources of practical consequences.

A third prominent path builds on the legal realists' critique of the coherence and the objectivity of legal doctrine by deploying the tools of critical theory to more carefully and thoroughly unpack the logical indeterminacy of legal argumentation and the often unarticulated biases and assumptions that shape legal texts and legal doctrine. The many threads of the critical legal studies movement draw on a wide range of interpretive approaches, from Marxism and postmodern deconstructionism to critical race and critical gender theory, to diagnose the societal forces that shape legal discourse. At its core, the critical legal studies approach uses the analytic tools developed by a range of interpretive disciplines to expose the dependence of legal doctrine and argumentation, not on its purported objective rationality, but on powerful, though typically unstated, underlying societal dynamics and power relationships.

Like the law-and-society approach, the critical approach takes an external perspective on legal content; it does not seek to engage in legal argument or exposition, but rather seeks to explicate the law by placing it in its broader societal context. But where the law-and-society approach focuses on the practical consequences of the legal system, the critical approach focuses on explanation of the legal discourse itself. The resulting scholarship, again, may shed valuable light on the functioning

6 For the classic statement of the law-and-economics approach, *see* Richard A. Posner, *Economic Analysis of Law* (9th ed. 2014).

of legal doctrines and processes, but not in ways that connect to the needs and interests of those who actually engage in legal discourse and practice. Instead of suggesting ways to use or improve the law in practice, critical legal studies serve primarily to cast doubts on the utility and the legitimacy of doctrinal analysis and argumentation by revealing that such practices are a mere superstructure serving to mask the real underlying drivers of legal outcomes.

In sum, according to this story of the evolution of contemporary approaches to legal scholarship, each of these dominant methodologies builds on the realists' insights by turning to non-lawyerly paradigms that shed light on the workings of the law by placing legal doctrine and discourse in their broader societal context. Undoubtedly, when well executed, each of these approaches (and a range of other law-and-xxx approaches drawing on other academic disciplines) can offer invaluable insights into the legal system. But they offer little help – or, at best, only very indirect help – to those who are actually seeking to advance and deploy the tools of legal doctrine and discourse to pursue practical outcomes. And, in fact, the more seriously the insights of these post-realist approaches are taken, the more doubt they cast on the practical relevance or utility of legal doctrine or principles or of efforts to elucidate or improve them. Little wonder, then, that practicing lawyers, judges, and policy makers find so little of practical value – and so much to disdain – in these veins of scholarship.

But how accurately does this story describe the actual path of legal scholarship over the past century? Have we really seen a trend away from doctrinal, normative, practical scholarship and its replacement by the various post-realist approaches described previously? Is it this trend that accounts for the widening gulf between legal scholarship and its potential audiences in the world of practice and policy? Preliminary results of an empirical review of prominent legal scholarship suggest that the story mistakes, or at least greatly exaggerates, actual trends, as reflected in the pages of leading law reviews, and instead tend to confirm the observation of several recent commentators that traditional doctrinal scholarship continues to dominate the legal academy.[7]

With the assistance of a team of research assistants, we are surveying the articles published in a dozen prominent student-edited law journals at intervals over the past century, and classifying those articles in categories intended to capture the trends envisioned in the narrative just described. This project is only partially completed, but the sampling reviewed so far strongly suggests that contemporary legal scholarship, at least what is published in leading student-edited journals, is overwhelmingly doctrinal scholarship of a relatively traditional form, and that the frequency of more

[7] *See, e.g.*, West, *supra* Note 4, at 7; Richard A. Posner, *Symposium: Law, Knowledge, and the Academy: Legal Scholarship Today*, 115 HARV. L. REV. 1314, 1317, and sources cited in n.7 (2002); Robert Ellickson, *Trends in Legal Scholarship: A Statistical Study*, 29 J. LEGAL STUD. 517, 523–24 (2000); Robert W. Gordon, *Lawyers, Scholars, and the "Middle Ground"*, 91 MICH. L. REV. 2075, 2099–100 (1993).

"external" perspectives on law has not changed markedly over the decades, although the particular styles and methodologies of such scholarship have certainly evolved.

More specifically, we identified ten different categories that characterize various threads of legal scholarship[8] and asked our research assistants to identify the categories into which articles published in several different year-long windows fell, recognizing that many articles would fall in more than one category. Of the eighty-two articles reviewed to date in the most recent time period (the 2014–15 academic year), the vast majority of the articles fell into either the doctrinal (forty-three) or normative (fifty-eight) category (with many falling into both). Only eight articles of the eighty-two were classified as neither doctrinal nor normative.[9] Our samples from earlier time periods are not yet as extensive, but the dominance of doctrinal and normative approaches appears relatively constant back to 1914–15.

So, perhaps the problem is not (or is not primarily) that legal scholarship has abandoned the project of examining and attempting to improve legal doctrine, but rather that such doctrinal or normative scholarship, at least in its contemporary forms and in its contemporary contexts, also fails to connect to the needs and interests of practicing lawyers and policy makers. Several factors may contribute to that disconnection.

First, and perhaps foremost, is the fallout from the realists' recasting of the nature of doctrinal discourse. If statements of legal rules or principles are recognized to be assertions of political preferences, and not descriptions or explications of a system of normative standards subject to validation through an agreed methodology, then the doctrinal pronouncements of legal scholars have no particular authority. They simply express one more opinion about what someone would like the rules to be.

Professor West is surely right that there is no cause for complaint that doctrinal discourse and doctrinal scholarship are inherently normative. After all, the very function of legal rules is to provide a structured framework for governing social interactions that commands broad acceptance due to its grounding in acknowledged norms of justice or fairness or social utility. Legal analysis is, as West says, normative "all the way down."[10] And, while we can recognize, with Justice Holmes, the possibility of a legal system grounded on nothing more than the dictates of "an emperor with despotic power and a whimsical turn of mind,"[11] it is the grounding of legal rules and principles on a normative foundation – and their accessibility to normative critique and evolution – that allows law to serve its crucial legitimating function.

[8] The ten categories are: Doctrinal, Normative, Historical, Comparative, Law-and-Economics, Law-and-Society, Critical Legal Studies, Law-and-XXX, Empirical/Quantitative, and Case Studies.

[9] The remaining eight were scattered over the various other categories, with no more than two of them falling in any category.

[10] West, *supra* Note 4, at 14.

[11] Oliver W. Holmes, Jr., *The Path of the Law*, 10 Harv. L. Rev. 457, 465 (1897).

Still, the fact that the mainstream of legal scholarship is inherently normative and therefore contestable, that it focuses not on how things are but on how they ought to be, puts it on a very different footing than the descriptive and empirically testable content of most of the scholarship in medicine or engineering or education or other professional fields. In most other professions, much of the academic work, while not immune to methodological dispute and evolution, provides practitioners with factual information about the world in which they practice, information that helps them to know what results their actions in their practice will produce. So, they turn to scholarly findings because they guide their practice.

If legal scholarship similarly described what the law is, that is, if it described how the legal system would respond to possible behaviors of lawyers and their clients, then practicing lawyers might find such scholarship crucial to their practice. That was at least one face of the classical vision of legal scholarship, the vision put forth by Langdell and persisting into the early twentieth century. But the realist revolution left that vision shattered and discredited. So, post-realist practitioners may occasionally turn to scholarship as a place to find the sources on a particular topic conveniently collected. And litigators may occasionally cite to supportive scholarly writings – at least some of which are recognized to have been written for precisely that purpose – to buttress their arguments. But, in the post-realist world, no practitioner is likely to think of normative scholarship as a source of knowledge, needed for its predictive insights into underlying legal reality.

Other factors also conspire to widen the gap between normative scholarship and the lawyers, policy makers, and others who use and shape law on the ground. For one, normative scholarship is primarily focused on the role that legal rules, principles, and doctrine play in the context of judicial development and application of the law. It is particularly in the context of appellate courts' reasoned elaboration of legal concepts and rules that normative scholarship is most at home, both as elucidation of, or commentary on, what the judges are doing and as intended guidance for their efforts.

In some areas of law, this may be where a good bit of the action is. West's field of constitutional law is perhaps a prime example. But much of the work of practitioners and policy makers, including much of the work of those tackling the challenges of the urban core, is not centered in the appellate courts. Much of it is transactional; much is engaged with regulatory or administrative bodies, not courts; even the portions that do involve litigation are often in settings where no one anticipates that there will ever be a judicial decision, not to mention an appeal. And, to the extent that legal rules are important factors in these settings, they are often very fine-grained rules, resting on technical statutes or regulations or on less formal standards that have become accepted guides to practice. Normative scholarship could, and occasionally does, dive into these quotidian and highly contingent bodies of law, but normative scholarship's norms of reasoned elaboration and of argument to and from principle are often not a natural fit in these contexts – for either the scholars or the practitioners.

Finally, the forms and norms of legal scholarship are anything but practitioner or policy-maker friendly. To state the obvious, law review articles are very long, and often very slow to get to their points. They often seem to reflect the author's need to tell the entire story about a topic, even if most of it has been told repeatedly by others, before coming to their distinct contribution. And this apparent need is quite understandable. For newer scholars, their primary audience is their future tenure reviewers and the scholarly community in which they are seeking to carve a niche, and their primary guidance about what these audiences expect are the models that they see in leading law reviews. Even post-tenure, for most legal scholars the primary audience remains the fellow scholars within their field, and the primary measures of successful scholarship are a prominent law review placement and frequency of citation by other academic writers. Meanwhile, law review editors (third-year law students) bring little expertise, are in their posts for very short terms (while much of their focus is elsewhere), and are hardly likely to see their role as reforming or transforming the nature of legal scholarship, or to have the authority or skill to do so if so inclined.

For all these reasons, it is entirely unsurprising that the kinds of scholarship that fill the pages of the vast array of law journals and that consume much of the time and energy of law school faculty are rarely read widely by those who use law in practical settings. Although lawyers may be conversant with the types of content and argumentation in the law reviews, they cannot reasonably expect that what they find there will be directly useful in their work, unless their work is in the rarefied context of path-breaking appellate litigation. And, for non-lawyers in policy-making or institution-guiding roles, the approach of typical legal scholarship – from its magisterial tone to its extensive use of footnotes and of the arcana of citation form as parts of the exposition of its arguments – often appears foreign and forbidding. Both the lawyers and the non-lawyers who spend their time dealing with time-sensitive, practical matters are likely to experience their challenges as too urgent – and too fluid – to wait for, or to wade through, the legal scholarship.

We don't pretend to have a firm or simple diagnosis for legal scholarship's disconnection from the world of practice or a confident prescription for bringing the legal academy's rich resources into more effective connection with the real-world problems that so many academics see as their concerns. Our hope for this book is that, by sharing and examining some promising examples of what some scholars are producing, we can derive some insights and test some hypotheses about the challenges and the paths forward.

But first, it may be helpful to focus on the specific challenges in the field of our concern – the role of law in addressing the profound dysfunction in many American urban cores.

LAW, ACTIVISM, AND SCHOLARSHIP IN THE URBAN CORES

Although they remain pressing, the legal and policy challenges presented by American urban poverty are not new. For many decades, urban cores across the country have suffered from deep and persistent concentrations of unemployment, economic underdevelopment, and immobility. The paradigmatic image of these areas has been the densely populated and geographically discrete "inner city," where access to housing, consumer goods, financial services, health care, schools, public safety, and other basic amenities is lacking. In the vast majority of urban cores, this image has also been distinctly racial. Experts across a range of disciplines have demonstrated that the stunningly high level of segregation in American cities by the middle of the twentieth century contributed to public and private disinvestment in the urban cores, many of which are still disproportionately populated by African-Americans, immigrants, and other communities of color.

Policy and Activism in the Urban Cores: A Very Brief History

This is not to say that the problem of urban poverty has been ignored. From the turn of the twentieth century onward, beginning with Booker T. Washington and W. E. B. DuBois, prominent African American leaders have engaged in active discussions about strategies for addressing urban challenges.[12] These discussions spawned numerous competent and dedicated private organizations, many of them nonprofit, which deployed a broad range of strategies to address urban underdevelopment. The activism and engagement of these organizations produced meaningful change on the ground, and it also eventually spurred governmental engagement.

While the history of policy making in and about the urban core during the last century is complex and varied, it can be described in three main stages. In the first stage, which began during the New Deal, the federal government explicitly recognized the unique concerns of the urban cores. The socialization of loss that occurred after the Great Depression included a core recognition of a basic "right" or "need" to work, and at least an aspiration to achieve for all Americans a basic standard of living. The policies that followed were developed and promulgated in a top-down approach, whereby federal funding and policy making determined ideological principles, programmatic development, and ground-level implementation. In important respects, the New Deal–era efforts paralleled the development of social and economic policy in post-war Europe, although American initiatives were significantly impeded by the willful failure of federal policy to address (and regularly the active contribution by federal agencies to) the problem of segregation. During this stage, state and local agencies eventually began to recognize and attempt to

[12] Scott L. Cummings, *Community Economic Development as Progressive Politics: Toward a Grassroots Movement for Economic Justice*, 54 Stan. L. Rev. 399, 410–12 (2001).

redress the intransigent problems of urban cores, and these initiatives hued closely to the programmatic choices made at the federal level.

The second key stage occurred from approximately the 1960s to the 1980s, beginning with Lyndon Johnson's Great Society initiatives. In this stage, the so-called War on Poverty took up urban underdevelopment as a central issue, including the recognition of racial segregation as a core part of the problem. Thus, the 1968 report of the Kerner Commission on Civil Disorders described the reality of an urban America composed of "two societies, one black, one white – separate and unequal."[13] At the same time that the federal government explicitly prioritized the alleviation of poverty in the urban cores, however, its involvement shifted significantly from a top-down approach to one that encouraged bottom-up thinking. This shift in strategy produced two distinct (and for a time, complementary) paths, as Scott Cummings describes in his seminal 2001 article, "Community Economic Development as Progressive Politics: Toward a Grassroots Movement for Economic Justice."

On one path, Johnson's War on Poverty catalyzed a series of initiatives, including the Community Action Program, the Model Cities Program, the Community Development Block Grant Program, and the Urban Development Action Grants Program, that sought to empower marginalized communities and promote economic self-sufficiency through local community control at the neighborhood level.[14] While the source of funding was federal, these programs, in contrast to the New Deal-era programs, sought to produce a much more decentralized system of city- and neighborhood-specific programmatic development.

Meanwhile, *law* reform and legal action occurred in and through the development of a wide array of federally funded legal services organizations that served discrete communities, typically at the municipal or county level. These specialized offices of legal action and activism for low-income individuals contributed increased attention and resources to the urban cores. They also contributed to bottom-up activism by focusing on the often unique issues and challenges in the neighborhoods they served.

On the other path described by Cummings, such nationally prominent nonprofit organizations as the National Welfare Rights Organization (NWRO) and the Association of Community Organizations for Reform Now (ACORN) developed grassroots campaigns to support welfare recipients in accessing the welfare benefits they were owed while helping them to politically organize at the local and national levels.[15] Over the course of the next decade, these groups, along with the Southern Christian Leadership Conference's (SCLC) Poor People's Movement and others, organized campaigns on a broad range of issues, including health care access, tax

[13] *Kerner Commission, Report of the National Advisory Commission on Civil Disorders* (1968).

[14] Cummings, *supra* Note 12, at 414–16.

[15] *Id.* at 417–21.

reform, school funding, and employment protections.[16] Although they may not have been explicit about it, SCLC's advocacy for an economic Bill of Rights, NWRO's campaigns for welfare rights, and other activism and rhetoric in these politically engaged efforts again paralleled postwar European efforts to organize around the protection of a set of fundamental human rights. Thus, during the decades between 1960 and 1980, both governmental and nongovernmental programs worked increasingly at a neighborhood level, encouraging innovation and development in and by local communities.

By the early 1980s, however, US urban policy – and activism – took a marked turn. Cummings shrewdly captures this third major stage of urban core policy making and activism in his 2001 article:

> Forged at the intersection of neoliberal economics and postmodern micropolitics, market-based CED rose to prominence in a political and intellectual environment hostile to the social welfare programs and large-scale reform strategies that formed the foundations for earlier mass-based movements for economic justice. By the mid-1990s, a strong consensus had formed around market-based CED precisely because of its broad ideological appeal–resonating both with conservative proponents of free market principles and progressive advocates of localized empowerment strategies. The model of market-based CED that has emerged reflects its diverse ideological lineage, integrating the principles of market expansion, localism, and community empowerment into a conceptual framework for redressing poverty.[17]

Perhaps the most frequently cited definition of community economic development is that provided by William Simon in his 2002 book, *The Community Economic Development Movement*:

> the core definition of CED embraces (1) efforts to develop housing, jobs, or business opportunities for low income people, (2) in which a leading role is played by nonprofit, nongovernmental organizations and (3) that are accountable to residentially defined communities.[18]

Almost a decade later, in 2009, leading CED scholars and practitioners Susan Jones and Roger Clay defined CED as focusing on the "creation and expansion of neighborhood businesses" as well as larger commercial enterprises, the development of affordable housing and health care, and "community building."[19]

While Cummings is most explicit about it, all three of these descriptions of this latest phase of policy and activism in and about the American urban cores describe

[16] *Id.* at 419–22.

[17] *Id.* at 437–38.

[18] William H. Simon, *The Community Economic Development Movement: Law, Business, and Social Policy* (2002).

[19] Roger A. Clay, Jr. & Susan R. Jones, What Is Community Economic Development?, *in Building Healthy Communities: A Guide to Community Economic Development for Advocates, Lawyers, and Policymakers* 3 (Roger A. Clay, Jr. & Susan R. Jones eds., 2009).

an accelerated process of decentralization. This third stage of urban core development was defined by a convergence toward private practices and public policies that sought to leverage the market to revitalize the urban cores. Community empowerment at the extremely local level was an important part of the vision. So too was poverty alleviation for those at the bottom of the economic ladder. But these pieces were ancillary to, and in support of, the ideal of the market as catalyst. As we will discuss, these scholarly descriptions were attempts to capture what had already occurred in practice. They were reactions to, rather than prescriptions for, development in the urban cores.

This third major stage also saw a shift in *legal* practice that accompanied the shift in activism and policy. As a matter of legal strategy, the most significant feature of this shift was the move from litigation to transaction. In paradigmatic terms, the Charles Reich-ian vision of litigating to expand the "new property" rights of welfare recipients was replaced by the work of transactional lawyers leveraging contracts, business organizational forms, spreadsheets, and good will to access new markets and thereby create more (though not necessarily new) wealth.[20] In this sense, the convergence produced a revitalization in legal practice as well as market behavior. It was an opportunity for an entirely new cast of lawyers to contribute their expertise, creativity, and power to the cause of poverty alleviation in the urban cores.

This then, was the moment in which the community economic development movement became the central force in urban policy and activism. It was a moment in which economic and social policy initiatives in the urban cores took a turn away from any meaningful recognition of social democratic principles and toward a neoclassical or neoliberal economic ideal. It was a moment in which the ideology of human rights, particularly social and economic rights, was replaced by an ideal of increased market access and opportunity. It was a deep affirmation of private capital, initiatives, and energy over public investments and indeed public trust. Partly as a result of the disinvestment by policy makers especially at the federal level in the more rights-oriented ideologies and campaigns of organizations like NWRO and ACORN, by the 1990s CED ascended to its place as the predominant policy focus in the urban cores.

The Multiple Challenges of Urban Core Development Today

Yet, despite decades of investment and genuine effort, the problems of the urban cores show few signs of improvement. Poverty and unemployment levels in the inner cities remain much higher than both the national average and the levels in the central cities that surround them.[21] Housing for the urban poor has become

[20] Charles A. Reich, *The New Property*, 73 YALE L.J. 733 (1964).

[21] The Initiative for a Competitive Inner City (ICIC) maintains detailed information about the state of American inner cities. The statistics cited here can be found at ICIC's website, at

increasingly tenuous. The majority of poor tenants pay more than half their incomes in rent, and serial evictions and homelessness have become commonplace.[22] Financial access has taken the pernicious forms of predatory mortgages, payday lending, and similar "alternatives" to mainstream banking that strip impoverished individuals of their savings and hinder any attempts they undertake to save for the future. These problems of economics, employment, financial access, and housing are compounded by multiple overlapping challenges ranging from urban education to crime and policing to environmental and public health inequities. Indeed, the economic stagnation in many American urban cores has been lamentably stable for the last fifty years. Over the decades, American cities have passed through cycles of decline and revival. But across these cycles, the challenges of the impoverished urban core have persisted. As Adam Gopnik has observed, when cities are faring poorly, "they are cesspools of hopelessness," whereas when they are faring well, they are "citadels of inequality."[23]

Certainly, the current cycle of urban core degradation involves even deeper inequality gaps between rich and poor. The current cycle also exhibits more extreme versions of long-existing concerns such as the loss of blue-collar work to increasing mechanization and high tech, the exacerbation of segregation's harms resulting from the subprime crisis, and the widening of the school-to-prison pipeline. These new depths of preexisting troubles have produced a new set of coping mechanisms with their own varieties of predation and loss. One example is the development of the "gig economy" in service sectors as a replacement for more stable (even unionized) blue-collar work.

It is also right to cite gentrification as one particularly significant manifestation of the growing inequality gap today. In many cities, waves of urban renewal have transformed some urban core neighborhoods by displacing one population with another. The resulting dislocation scatters impoverished individuals to other parts of the city and inner suburbs, with corresponding losses of communities and social ties that are immeasurable. Partly as a consequence, even the geographical focus of the modern community economic development movement has become more fragmented.

The response by the current presidential administration to issues in the urban cores has been cartoonishly out of touch with this reality. Trump's vision of the urban cores lumps them together as sites of "carnage,"[24] from which everyone would

http://icic.org/blog/key-battlegrounds-war-poverty/; www.icic.org/connection/blog-entry/blog-in-americas-war-on-poverty-inner-cities-remain-the-front-line.

[22] *See* Matthew Desmond, *Evicted: Poverty and Profit in the American City* (2016).

[23] Adam Gopnik, *Naked Cities: The Death and Life of Urban America*, The New Yorker, Oct. 5, 2015, www.newyorker.com/magazine/2015/10/05/naked-cities.

[24] Remarks of President Donald J. Trump – As Prepared for Delivery, Inaugural Address (Jan. 20, 2017).

wish to escape.[25] His policy responses to such carnage have thus far been to defund programs addressing urban core issues and to place more of the financial burden on residents in the urban cores. A recent initiative by Housing and Urban Development Secretary Ben Carson, for example, seeks to increase rents paid by tenants in federally subsidized affordable housing (sometimes to as much as triple what they paid before) and by imposing work requirements as a precondition for such housing.[26] Similarly, Education Secretary Betsy DeVos has undertaken several initiatives to limit remedies for students defrauded by for-profit colleges, a move that has disproportionately harmed low-income individuals.[27]

Meanwhile today, almost thirty years after CED's ascendance, many of CED's core principles still endure – even in the face of ever fiercer challenges. CED's market focus still holds enormous power. One key example is the increased reliance on public–private partnerships, as evidenced by the primacy of the Low Income Housing Tax Credit (LIHTC) program as a source of affordable housing development and the comparable power of the New Market Tax Credit (NMTC) program in supporting business and real estate development. Another example is the increasing interest in charter schools as a solution to the problem of underperforming public schools in urban cores.

Indeed, perhaps the most noteworthy development in urban core policy, activism, and legal practice over the last three decades is that the basic strategy is fundamentally the same – but, as Pitegoff observes in this volume, the work is increasingly larger in scale and more sophisticated. The LIHTC and NMTC programs are prime examples, but there are many others. In the field of income and job development, the best-developed example, especially of public–private partnership, is the work of the Initiative for a Competitive Inner City (ICIC). This massive nonprofit started by Harvard Business School Professor Michael Porter leverages enormous foundation and other private resources to support investment in and by large businesses to

25 "The Democrats have failed completely in the inner cities. For those hurting the most who have been failed and failed by their politician – year after year, failure after failure, worse numbers after worse numbers. Poverty. Rejection. Horrible education. No housing, no homes, no ownership. Crime at levels that nobody has seen. You can go to war zones in countries that we are fighting and it's safer than living in some of our inner cities that are run by the Democrats. And I ask you this, I ask you this – crime, all of the problems – to the African Americans, who I employ so many, so many people, to the Hispanics, tremendous people: What the hell do you have to lose? Give me a chance. I'll straighten it out. I'll straighten it out. What do you have to lose?" Jenna Johnson, *Donald Trump to African American and Hispanic voters: "What do you have to lose?*, The Wash. Post (Aug. 22, 2016), www.washingtonpost.com/news/post-politics/wp/2016/08/22/donald-trump-to-african-american-and-hispanic-voters-what-do-you-have-to-lose/?noredirect=on&utm_term=.813cc5897234.

26 Brakkton Booker, *HUD Unveils Plan to Increase Rent on Millions Receiving Federal Housing Assistance*, NPR Morning Edition (Apr. 25, 2018), www.npr.org/2018/04/25/605900171/hud-unveils-plan-to-increase-rent-on-millions-receiving-federal-housing-assistance.

27 Heidi Przybyla, *DeVos Goes Deep with Anti-Regulatory Mission at Education Department*, NBC News (July 3, 2018), www.nbcnews.com/politics/politics-news/devos-agenda-higher-education-new-front-democratic-resistance-n888421.

relocate in the inner cities, thereby opening up markets for consumer goods and ideally also jobs for low-income residents of those areas.[28] Grounded in Porter's scholarship on the "competitive advantage" of the inner city, as well as such concepts as business clusters, incubators, and anchor institutions, ICIC is a premier source of research, data, and investment in and about the inner cities. Community benefits agreements are another compelling set of examples of large-scale CED efforts. These have often involved powerful community development corporations leveraging community engagement and media attention to enter into soft contracts with stadium developers and other large entities to create jobs, provide funding for local nonprofits, and improve local infrastructure.

What really stands out in these examples of large-scale urban development programs is the robustness of the public–private partnerships, particularly in channeling private sources of financing into urban core revitalization. Looking across the diverse array of experiments in housing development, income development, and banking, it is apparent that the financial disinvestment by governmental sources has been replaced by complex private financing sources and structures. This in turn has kept many lawyers, accountants, and other experts busier and busier, leveraging their skills to support an increasingly complicated structure for local support.

However, in prioritizing public–private partnerships, private investment, and social entrepreneurialism, these efforts have failed to fully address the multiple negative externalities that they have regularly produced.[29] Examples abound, but perhaps the most obvious is again in the field of affordable housing. There, the development of mixed income housing, hueing to the values and approaches of New Urbanism, has resulted in extensive displacement of public housing residents who are replaced by mixed income communities. In the housing arena, and in other core areas of CED practice, there appears to be little consensus on whether the resulting gentrification is an acceptable – even desirable – consequence of CED interventions.

This disconnect suggests that the contemporary problems of the urban cores, though they may seem obvious, are not well defined. Even more starkly, the very goals of contemporary CED are not well defined. While poverty alleviation, economic development, and desegregation are all imperatives of CED, it is increasingly clear that first-generation CED interventions have produced conflicts among these goals. When such conflicts surface, it appears that different constituencies prioritize

[28] Michael E. Porter, *The Competitive Advantage of the Inner City*, HARV. BUS. REV., May–June 1995, 55–71; Michael E. Porter, *New Strategies for Inner-City Economic Development*, 11 ECON. DEV. Q. 11 (1997); Michael E. Porter, *Clusters and the New Economics of Competition*, HARV. BUS. REV., Nov. 1998, 77–90; Michael E. Porter, *Location, Competition, and Economic Development: Local Clusters in a Global Economy*, 14 ECON. DEV. Q. 15 (2000).

[29] There are clearly important exceptions to this statement, and these have been the subject of important research. Cooperative Home Care Associates in New York and the Dudley Street Neighborhood Initiative in Boston are two well-studied examples.

different goals. And this in turn produces a muddle in which members of the same movement disagree about some of the most prominent interventions. In addition to debating whether gentrification is a positive or negative outcome, CED participants regularly disagree about whether to seek out "big box" stores and stadiums to locate in the inner city. They hotly debate the values of self-employment and homeownership. They place quite different levels of faith in institutions such as McDonalds, Bank of America, and Uber.

It is reasonable also to ask whether the failure to answer those deeper questions has contributed to the repeated failures within CED even to achieve effective community participation. Part of the reason may be the incoherence involved in emphasizing process, at times over substance. Emphasis on process can be a very positive thing and at times has produced great success. However, the last several decades of robust experimentation with community participation, neighborhood control, and other efforts to ensure and protect a community voice may well reveal that while important, these initiatives do not suffice, especially when constraints on investment and more expensive forms of support translate these efforts into a bootstrapping mentality that presumes the need for only temporary investment. For this reason, it is important to ask whether the consensus in favor of ensuring community participation is a distraction from the imperative to answer deeper and more difficult questions.

Scholarship for the Urban Core

Legal scholars writing about community development in the urban cores thus are operating in a context rife with fundamental disagreements about the basic goals and values of contemporary urban development and about the law's role in this context. For example, in a recent roundtable discussion among CED legal scholars from across the United States, one participant described the disagreement as a difference in priorities between the "community" and "economic" pieces of community economic development.[30]

The scholarly debate over worker cooperatives is one among many examples. Both CED scholars and practitioners have discussed the value of worker cooperatives as a tool for poverty alleviation and economic development. But one question that has been raised consistently and never satisfactorily answered is why worker cooperatives have not proliferated in American urban cores. If, as a scholarly and

[30] Some of the papers and issues discussed during that roundtable were published in a symposium issue of the Journal of Affordable Housing and Community Development Law. For the introduction to that discussion, *see* Peter Pitegoff, *Community Development Law, Economic Justice, and the Legal Academy*, 26 J. Affordable Housing & Community Dev. L. 31 (2017).

policy matter, there is a clear and compelling case for such a business form, what are the obstacles in urban America that prevent that form from succeeding? Our inability to answer this question results partly from our failure to test the conditions for successful cooperatives. And this in turn results from a failure to agree on the goals that do or do not prioritize cooperatives.

The basic lack of agreement between and among CED practitioners and scholars about goals and priorities markedly differentiates CED from law and development efforts in other parts of the world. In this other context, scholars and practitioners rely on a relatively well-established set of metrics and priorities, including the United Nations Millennium Development Goals and the Universal Declaration of Human Rights, to organize and prioritize their work.

The lack of basic cohesion at the core of CED has a number of troubling ramifications, some of which legal and other scholars have tried to address. Some of the most productive CED scholarship has openly engaged with difficult questions involving ill-defined goals, systemic failures, and meaningful distributional repercussions. Much of this work has warned against the over-focus on the private market as a systemic or comprehensive solution. Among the authors in this volume alone, Cummings has called, since 2001, for CED to become more politically engaged in the hope partly of producing alliances across race and geography.[31] Pitegoff has analyzed sectoral approaches to local development that seek to stabilize employment conditions across industrial sectors with the goal of achieving work access and stability.[32] Pitegoff and Cummings have also led a crucial inquiry into the viability of worker cooperatives in American cities.[33] Solomon has incisively decried the regulatory disinvestment in, and resulting loss of, community banks, set in a context that devalues financial access for entire populations of individuals.[34] Many other well-known CED scholars have raised similarly foundational questions. Susan Jones has evaluated the systemic potential of small business development in revitalizing urban cores.[35] Susan Bennett has explored the value of public–private partnerships in

[31] Scott L. Cummings, *supra* Note 12; Scott L. Cummings, *Law and Social Movements: Reimagining the Progressive Canon*, 2018 WISC. L. REV. 441 (2018).

[32] Peter Pitegoff, *Worker Ownership in Enron's Wake – Revisiting a Community Development Tactic*, 8 J. SMALL & EMERGING BUS. L. 239, 252 (2004).

[33] David Ellerman & Peter Pitegoff, *The Democratic Corporation: The New Worker Cooperative Statute in Massachusetts*, 11 N.Y.U. REV. L. & SOC. CHANGE 441 (1983); Peter Pitegoff, *Organizing Worker Cooperatives*, 7 LAW & POL'Y 45 (1985); Peter Pitegoff, *Unions and Worker Ownership*, 18 POL'Y STUDIES J. 357 (1990); Scott L. Cummings, *Developing Cooperatives as a Job Creation Strategy for Low Income Workers*, 25 NYU REV. LAW & SOCIAL CHANGE 181 (1999).

[34] Bob Solomon, *The Fall (and Rise?) of Community Banking: The Continued Importance of Local Institutions*, 2 UC IRVINE L. REV. 945 (2012).

[35] Susan R. Jones, *Small Business and Community Economic Development: Transactional Lawyering for Social Change and Economic Justice*, 4 CLINICAL L. REV. 195 (1997).

affordable housing development.[36] Michael Diamond has examined the relationship among lawyering, social movements, and power.[37]

Beyond CED scholarship, one prominent set of scholarly interventions has occurred in scholarship about state and local government law. In this field, there has been a continued focus on doctrinal questions that influence development in the urban core. An important recent example is the scholarship on federal and state preemption of municipal initiatives such as living wage ordinances.[38] Another line of research has involved municipal bankruptcies and the effect on urban cores.[39] Many, though by no means all, of these interventions include more traditional doctrinal analyses and prescriptions, and many are promising for purposes of pushing forward key pieces of law reform and development that have potential for fixing some of the intransigent problems of the urban cores. There has also been productive scholarship outside of the law that is indispensable to our understanding of urban core issues.[40] One relatively common characteristic of this range of diversity of scholarship about the urban core is its ground-clearing effect. Contemporary legal and non-legal scholars have provided a rich and sophisticated understanding of the failures in the most recent phase of urban policy, and in so doing, they have provided a foundation for new thinking, activism, and policy making.

A critical question that we intend to explore, however, is that of scholarly impact. Here, we have examples of scholarship that has raised some of the most important questions for urban development moving forward. Who is listening? Who is our target audience and to what extent are we affecting their decision-making on the ground? How can we use our scholarship to make meaningful progress in American urban cores?

36 Susan Bennett, Constructing the Social Impact Statement to Measure the Full Cost to Public Housing Tenants of Urban Renewal Affordable Housing and Public-Private Partnerships, *in Affordable Housing and Public-Private Partnerships*, 129–67 (Nestor M. Davidson & Robin Paul Malloy eds., 2009).

37 Michael Diamond, *The Transposition of Power: Law, Lawyers, and Social Movements*, 24 GEO. J. POVERTY L. & POL'Y 319 (2017).

38 *See, e.g.*, Clayton P. Gillette, *Local Redistribution, Living Wage Ordinances, and Judicial Intervention*, 101 NW. U. L. REV.1057 (2007); Richard Schragger, *City Power: Urban Governance in a Global Age* (2016); Nestor M. Davidson, *The Dilemma of Localism in an Era of Polarization*, 128 YALE L.J. (forthcoming 2019).

39 Michelle Wilde Anderson, *The New Minimal Cities*, 123 YALE L.J. 1118 (2014); Clayton P. Gillette & David A. Skeel, Jr., *Governance Reform and the Judicial Role in Municipal Bankruptcy*, 125 YALE L.J. 1150 (2016); Bernadette Atuahene & Timothy R. Hodge, *Stategraft*, 91 S. CAL. L. REV. 263 (2018).

40 Renowned sociologists such as William Julius Wilson and Douglas Massey continue to inform our understanding of key legal and nonlegal developments in urban cores, while newer voices such as Deborah Becher's on eminent domain provide insights about overlapping predicaments involving access, rights, inequality, and justice. William Julius Wilson, *Combating Concentrated Poverty in Urban Neighborhoods*, 7 J. APPLIED SOCIAL SCIENCE 135 (2013); Douglas S. Massey et al, *Climbing Mount Laurel: The Struggle for Affordable Housing and Social Mobility in an American Suburb* (2013); Debbie Becher, *Private Property and Public Power: Eminent Domain in Philadelphia* (2014).

A Brief Overview

This, then, is our starting point. We seek partly to answer these questions through our choice of contributions. It appears that many of the primary actors on the ground, the "changemakers" in urban core development, are still self-described members of the community economic development movement. These surely must be key members of the audience for this book, and more broadly for legal scholarship about the urban core. Accordingly, they must also be a core subject of study for this volume. Given the centrality of CED in urban core development today, approximately half of this volume is devoted to work by CED scholars, and about core CED issues. At the same time, some of the most constructive discussions about urban core issues – ranging from racial disparities to unequal work to local policy making to legal access – are occurring outside the field of CED by those who do not self-identify as CED activists or scholars. In an effort both to avoid unnecessary silos and to benefit from wisdom shared across micro-disciplinary specializations, approximately half of this volume includes contributions by legal scholars who do not claim to be working within the community economic development field.

In order to capture the breadth and diversity of productive scholarship on the urban core, we have divided this book into three main sections. In the first section, we feature a methodological approach that we believe is particularly efficacious for taking the necessary next steps in urban core policy and development. The case study methodology is a form of qualitative empiricism in which the researcher intensively and systematically studies a person, group, or community in its natural setting as a means of better understanding a complex phenomenon.[41] Both chapters in this section use this approach as a means of studying discrete, yet foundational, issues in urban core development and law. Cummings examines contemporary forms of urban core lawyering by studying a complex campaign in which lawyers supported a coalition of community groups seeking to raise wages of drayage truck drivers in the ports of Los Angeles and Long Beach, and also to decrease the pollution produced by those trucks. Dyal-Chand studies a single worker cooperative in Philadelphia to understand the forms of democratic participation available to workers in such businesses.

The second section consists of two chapters that reimagine law for the next generation of urban core development. Pitegoff undertakes a broadly historical evaluation of community development finance as a key programmatic undertaking in community economic development. Solomon proposes an innovative and valuable set of law reforms, linked with legal practices, as a means of increasing the development of affordable housing. Both authors draw from their own experiences

[41] For descriptions of the case study methodology, *see* Svend Brinkmann & Steinar Kvale, *InterViews: Learning the Craft of Qualitative Research Interviewing* (3rd ed. 2015); Michael Patton, *Qualitative Research* (2005).

as practitioners and participants in the forms of community development practice that they describe and seek to improve.

In our third section, we showcase three contributions that propose new approaches to legal scholarship for the urban core and/or new pedagogy for teaching about urban core issues. Whereas the chapters in the book's first two sections demonstrate scholarly innovation by embodying it, the chapters in this final section are more explicitly evaluative of the new forms of scholarship and pedagogy that they describe. In the course of describing a large ethnographic project of their own, Brito, Gordon, and Pate propose and evaluate what they claim to be a productive new research methodology for studying urban core issues. In the course of describing a clinic project focused on "training up" generations of public interest municipal lawyers, Morris explores such a curricular innovation as an important space for urban core development. Finally, by describing a social-justice lawyering curriculum for first-year law students, Enrich explores and evaluates the efficacy of such a pedagogical approach in training lawyers better positioned to make change in the urban cores.

In the concluding chapter of this volume, we extrapolate some of the important lessons that these contributions might teach in lighting a path forward for those seeking to make meaningful and lasting progress in American urban cores. We also discuss core features – and commonalities – among these contributions that may suggest productive ways forward in legal scholarship as well.

PART I

Change on the Ground

Case Studies of Law Reform in Action

2

The Drive for Economic Justice at America's Port

*Scott Cummings**

INTRODUCTION

This chapter is about the struggle over the future of work on the edge of the global economy. It traces the history of conflict in an industry that is not widely known, but sits at the epicenter of the global supply chain: short-haul trucking responsible for moving the mass of imports from enormous cargo ships to warehouses and retailers around the country. The chapter's specific focus is on the nation's largest and most important port complex – America's port – which straddles the border of Los Angeles and Long Beach, California, and includes the ports in both cities. Here, for nearly two decades, labor and environmental groups – bound together in a pivotal "blue–green" alliance – carried forward a monumental campaign to transform working conditions for drivers and environmental conditions for communities.

This chapter evaluates this campaign, which began in the mid-2000s and continues to this day, focusing on the role of local movements mobilizing to reshape the nature of work in the urban core. It traces the campaign's first key phase, in which the alliance organized around passing a new local policy that would jointly address the economic and environmental harms of port trucking by attacking the independent contractor relationship at the heart of the industry (called the "Campaign for Clean Trucks"). The labor movement viewed this campaign as a chance to reclaim employee status for thousands of port drivers who were misclassified as independent contractors and thus forced into lives of low-wage work without the legal right to organize for a better future. The campaign itself rested on an innovative legal hook: the ports, as publicly owned and operated entities, had the power to define the terms of entry for trucking companies through concession agreements – private contracts permitting trucks onto port property. Success therefore hinged on how these agreements treated drivers and what types of

* Robert Henigson Professor of Legal Ethics and Professor of Law, UCLA School of Law.
Portions of this chapter were originally published in Scott L. Cummings, *Preemptive Strike: Law in the Campaign for Clean Trucks*, 4 U.C. Irvine L. Rev. 939 (2014).

standards the agreements set. As the chapter recounts, labor and environmental activists formed a coalition with residents of low-income communities adjacent to the ports. Together, they sought to pass a local law, the Clean Truck Program, which would convert truck drivers into employees of their companies (thus enabling unionization), while requiring the gradual upgrading of trucks to reduce pollution. Lawyers working with the coalition crafted that law to minimize ex ante legal risk and ultimately defended – with mixed results – the law against a federal preemption challenge. The chapter uses the campaign, and its mixed results, to examine the power and limits of local mobilization targeting municipal governments as sites of labor law innovation.

LOCAL IMPACT: COMMUNITY, LABOR, AND THE ENVIRONMENT

The problem targeted in the Campaign for Clean Trucks had its origins in the conservative push for trade liberalization and industry deregulation decades before. Beginning in the 1970s, legal rules promoting free trade transformed the ports from engines of regional growth to conduits of globalization, imposing negative externalities on surrounding communities in the form of pollution and incompatible development. Deregulation facilitated the explosion of trade by reducing the cost of transport, while also producing the specific problem of fragmentation in the drayage trucking industry and the shift toward independent contractor drivers. Since that fragmentation occurred, starting in the 1980s, the independent contractor relation has been the crucial legal barrier to unionization, since independent-contractors receive no labor protection and are legally proscribed from organizing under antitrust law. Therefore, from the perspective of organized labor looking at port trucking at century's end, weak federal labor law interacted with federal deregulation and antitrust law to put port drivers in a legal box: economically marginalized, but unable to organize to improve their dismal working conditions.

As a result, the conditions of port truckers deteriorated sharply. In Los Angeles and Long Beach, the independent contractor form came to predominate in the drayage trucking sector, with nearly 90 percent of truckers so designated. For these drivers, the average annual salary, after expenses, was $28,000.[1] In part because of delays, drivers worked on average fifty-six hours per week, thereby earning an effective wage rate of less than $10 per hour.[2] Because they were designated independent contractors, they received no health insurance or pension contributions from their companies. The drayage labor force also came to be defined by workers of color. By

[1] David Bensman, *Port Trucking Down the Low Road: A Sad Story of Deregulation*, DĒMOS 3 (2009), www.demos.org/sites/default/files/publications/Port%20Trucking%20Down%20the%20Low%20Road.pdf.

[2] Some studies of the overall industry, not just Los Angeles/Long Beach, put the wage rate much lower. *See* Ted Prince, *Endangered Species*, J. COM. 12, 13 (2005); *see also* Edna Bonacich, *Pulling the Plug: Labor and the Global Supply Chain*, 12 NEW LAB. F. 41, 46 (2003).

2000, in Los Angeles and Long Beach, port truckers were almost entirely Latino and nearly half were immigrants.[3]

At the start of the new millennium, there were roughly sixteen thousand drayage trucks servicing the Los Angeles and Long Beach ports each day. Because drivers could not generally afford to upgrade, this fleet was aging – the ports were the place where "old trucks went to die" – and ran on diesel fuel, a known carcinogen. Truck emissions, combined with those from ocean vessels and dock transport equipment, caused significant air pollution, which threatened trucker and broader community health. A 2007 NRDC report showed that the black carbon inside truck cabs increased "health risks by up to 2,600 excess cancers per million drivers."[4] Overall, the California Air Resources Board found that diesel particulate matter emissions from all port-related activities constituted roughly one-fifth of all such emissions in the Los Angeles basin.[5] Communities near the ports had cancer risk levels that "exceeded 500 in a million"; further from the port, the risk was less but still significant.[6] From the perspective of community and labor groups, law had contributed to these harmful effects – by disempowering local communities and truck drivers relative to the port. Their response would be to try to reshape local government law to fix the problems that deregulation had produced.

LABOR'S MUNICIPAL STRATEGY: CONTRACTING AROUND THE INDEPENDENT CONTRACTOR PROBLEM

As the labor and environmental movements converged around a common analysis of the problem to be addressed – a dysfunctional drayage trucking market producing economic precarity and air pollution – their formulation of a solution necessarily came to be shaped by the legal possibilities for local redress. The ports of Los Angeles and Long Beach were targeted together by the coalition as a strategic site because they were city entities with authority to enact a city policy to address truck emissions and driver status. Local government law would be the lever to transform a drayage trucking industry ravaged by deregulation and promote union organizing among drivers prevented from doing so under federal law. To achieve this result, the

3 Kristen Monaco, Incentivizing Truck Retrofitting in Port Drayage: A Study of Drivers at the Ports of Los Angeles and Long Beach 18–19 (2008), www.metrans.org/research/final/0602%20Final%20Report.pdf (finding that 91.24 percent of port truck drivers were Hispanic and 44 percent were noncitizens).

4 *See, e.g.*, Diane Bailey et al., *Driving on Fumes: Truck Drivers Face Elevated Health Risks from Diesel Pollution* 4, Nat. Resources Def. Council, www.nrdc.org/health/effects/driving/driving.pdf.

5 Pingkuan Di, Diesel Particulate Matter Exposure Assessment Study for the Ports of Los Angeles and Long Beach: Final Report 2 (2006), www.arb.ca.gov/ports/marinevess/documents/portstudy0406.pdf (report for the California Environmental Protection Agency, Air Resources Board).

6 *Id.*

policy had to be crafted to take advantage of local government law power while avoiding federal preemption under the Federal Aviation Administration Authorization Act (the FAAAA), which prohibited localities from enacting any law "related to a price, route, or service of any motor carrier ... "[7]

The challenge of promoting local labor reform for port drivers within the contested boundaries of federal preemption fell to the Teamsters union. In 2000, the Teamsters, through its Port Division, announced a nationwide port trucker campaign, run by assistant director Ron Carver. Although many inside the union believed that independent contractors were misclassified as such, the barriers to individual enforcement were too high to justify a case-by-case litigation strategy and, as earlier cases highlighted, even success in court did not ensure change in industry practice. As Teamsters attorney Mike Manley reflected, the union's view was that "you really can't [address the industry] through a campaign of [NLRB] elections and slugging it out in representation cases. The industry is too vast ... you'd be doing it forever." In Los Angeles, there were some unionized firms, like Horizon, and others that still hired truckers as employees, like Toll, but without addressing the independent contractor problem, the industry would remain low wage. The key was to "transform the market."

Despite significant challenges, port trucker unionization remained one of the major prizes of Teamsters organizing in the new millennium. In raw numbers, the scale of port trucking was modest, with approximately 40,000 port truckers operating as independent contractors out of an overall trucking industry of almost four million. However, port trucking was an area of historic strength, and there were practical and strategic reasons to pursue unionization in that sector. As a practical matter, there was a potential legal hook for organizing: The legal status of ports (like Los Angeles and Long Beach) as proprietary departments under the umbrella of local government meant that the ports could potentially influence the nature of trucking through their contracting power. Discussions of how to make this happen were underway in 2004 when Manley was hired in the Teamsters' DC-based office of general counsel.

As Manley quickly learned, the plan was to change port drivers' independent contractor status by focusing on the ports' role as market participants. In his conversations with Ron Carver, Manley said the question was: "Is there a way to ... leverage the port to declare [truckers] to be employees?" Figuring out an affirmative answer to that question was not only important on its own terms but also had broader strategic implications. The ports were key nodes in the larger supply chain that led from manufacturing exporters to regional warehouses, and ultimately to large retail chains, such as Walmart. Some labor leaders believed that if unions could gain a stronger foothold in the ports, it would contribute to a longer-term campaign to organize retail giants. This was something that the Teamsters had

[7] 49 U.S.C. § 14501(c)(1).

argued for, but "didn't get necessarily a lot of traction . . . in terms of resources" from union leadership at the AFL-CIO.

That changed with the formation of Change to Win – an alliance of progressive unions that broke away from the AFL-CIO in September 2005. Change to Win – established to focus on organizing – set up the Strategic Organizing Center, which was built around different industry sectors, with the goal of identifying "how the pool of existing resources at Change to Win could expand the pace [of] organizing."[8] The center was "like a startup" that put "together experienced organizers and campaigners [to take] a fresh look at industries that were basically nonunion."[9] By bringing together organizers and researchers from different unions, the goal was to innovate according to best practices. It divided up the economy into different industry sectors: transportation, retail, home construction, and food processing.

Within the Strategic Organizing Center, John Canham-Clyne and Nick Weiner set out to research the trucking industry, becoming the bridge between Change to Win and the existing Teamsters leadership. Through their research, Canham-Clyne and Weiner identified the ports as a potential target of opportunity for organizing. As one of the few publicly owned pieces of freight infrastructure, ports offered "potential hooks" for organizing: Many were in friendly political jurisdictions and drayage was a relatively sticky industry because of the massive infrastructure investment at the ports.[10] On the basis of this research, Change to Win launched a national ports campaign, directed by Canham-Clyne, to build upon the Teamsters' existing organizing efforts and "move [that] work forward faster."[11] The larger goal, in line with that articulated by the Teamsters, was to "organize the supply chain."[12] The ports were the first link in this chain because they were a "chokepoint" that could be used to produce other wins.

An early question focused on the legality of different possible options for organizing port truckers specifically and low-wage workers in contingent work arrangements more broadly. In 2006, there was a meeting of the "legal tribes" in Washington, DC, where prominent labor lawyers gathered to discuss new strategies.[13] This meeting included the Teamsters' Manley, as well as Pat Szymanski, who had left the Teamsters to become general counsel to Change to Win; Brad Raymond, the new general counsel of the Teamsters; Judy Scott, general counsel to the Service Employees International Union; and long-time outside union counsel Stephen Berzon of Altshuler Berzon, and Richard McCracken of Davis, Cowell & Bowe.

8 Telephone Interview with John Canham-Clyne, Campaign Dir., Change to Win (May 20, 2013).

9 Telephone Interview with Nick Weiner, Nat'l Campaigns Organizer, Change to Win (Apr. 17, 2013).

10 *Id.*

11 Telephone Interview with Canham-Clyne.

12 *Id.*

13 Telephone Interview with Michael Manley, Staff Att'y, Int'l Bhd. of Teamsters (Feb. 20, 2013).

One of the issues discussed was the legal feasibility of using the port's status as a city entity to convert truck drivers into employees. It was a familiar idea to those present, discussed in various forms for some time. But at that point, with Change to Win backing, the time had finally come to advance the strategy. The question was: "Is this doable?"[14]

The concession model held appeal for a number of reasons. For one, it had been tested in other forms and had proven an effective tool for organizing. In particular, lawyers associated with the unions had done work on airport organizing in which the airport authorities, as public agencies, had used concession agreements, or franchises, to require food and beverage vendors to remain neutral in union organizing campaigns. Thus, from a mechanical point of view, union lawyers were familiar with the technical aspects of city contracting and how it potentially related to labor issues. Perhaps most crucially, the concession model was viewed as legally defensible against federal preemption. The union lawyers involved had experience with city contracting models to create living wage laws and job training programs, and believed that the same concept could be adapted to the ports under a market participant theory. For this analysis to work, there had to be a justification for the ports' market participation itself. That justification turned out to rest less on port trucking's effect on labor relations than its impact on the environment.

REFORMING THE PORT: THE CAMPAIGN FOR CLEAN TRUCKS

The opportunity to advance a serious local campaign to achieve employee status for drivers came in an unforeseen package: an environmental legal challenge to port expansion that laid the groundwork for a sweeping environmental overhaul at the ports. This challenge itself was created by sustained community push-back against port expansion, amplified by the Los Angeles port's 2001 announcement that it was expanding into adjacent communities to accommodate a massive new China Shipping terminal. In response, NRDC sued on behalf of resident groups under the California Environmental Quality Act (CEQA), winning a 2002 state court ruling that the port had not complied with its duty to identify and mitigate environmental harm resulting from the China Shipping project. As a result, the port was ordered to conduct a new Environmental Impact Report (EIR) and was enjoined from completing an expansion that was already 90 percent finished.

The legal challenge to the China Shipping project – strengthened by the simultaneous effort by San Pedro to secede from the city of Los Angeles – extracted political concessions from local politicians: James Hahn's election as Los Angeles mayor, accompanied by his sister Janice Hahn's election to city council, were built on promises to community groups to mitigate the port's impact. At the height of the China Shipping dispute, Mayor Hahn committed his administration to a policy of

[14] *Id.*

"no net increase" – promising to cap port emissions at 2001 levels – which sparked a policy dialogue that led to the 2004 creation of a No Net Increase Task Force. Members included the NRDC lawyer who had brought the China Shipping suit, Gail Ruderman Feuer, along with labor and community representatives who would become central to the Campaign for Clean Trucks. The work of this Task Force laid the groundwork for the next Los Angeles mayor, Antonio Villaraigosa, to initiate discussions in 2005 between the Los Angeles and Long Beach ports around a comprehensive policy, the Clean Air Action Plan (CAAP). It was CAAP, which introduced standards for reducing emissions by diesel trucks, that provided the policy framework and political leverage for the labor movement to finally translate employee conversion from theoretical concept to concrete reform – embedded in a local policy designed to promote environmental remediation.

By highlighting the need to clean up 16,000 dirty diesel trucks, CAAP made a potential link between environmentalism and unionism – which the labor movement was eager to strengthen through coalition building. In July 2005, the Sierra Club's Carl Pope met with top officials at Change to Win to discuss potential collaborations. At that time, although Change to Win had begun to move forward with its five-port concession strategy, the ports team did not have a strong grasp of the local situation in Los Angeles. The Sierra Club, in contrast, had just completed a video about the China Shipping case – called "Terminal Impact" – and, through the local chapter, was deeply engaged in ongoing efforts to stem port pollution. In discussing Change to Win's ports campaign, Pope, who was closely connected to local Sierra Club activists, mentioned the CAAP process. Change to Win's Nick Weiner, who was at the July meeting, remembered that Pope's mention of Los Angeles, although "just happenstance," allowed the port team to key in on Los Angeles as an auspicious site and to "connect the dots" between the concession model and the environmental piece. As Weiner recalled, "We discovered that, oh right, these are old polluting trucks and they contribute to the pollution in L.A. in particular. [The Pope meeting] kind of just happened ... around the same time so that we were able to then further develop [the concession] theory." From there, Weiner and his colleagues were asked to "figure out L.A." – a task they undertook with speed and intensity.[15]

Weiner and John Canham-Clyne immediately reached out to Maria Elena Durazo, head of the powerful Los Angeles County Federation of Labor, and Madeline Janis, director of the Los Angeles Alliance for a New Economy (LAANE), which was known for spearheading passage of Los Angeles's Living Wage Ordinance in 1997. LAANE's mission, creating a "new economy that works for everyone," was advanced by "championing the role that local government can play in nudging either individual industries or the broader regional economy." With LAANE's

[15] Telephone Interview with Nick Weiner.

support, the local campaign "took off" toward the goal of passing a concession policy at the ports of Los Angeles and Long Beach. Although Change to Win launched its campaign nationwide, there was optimism about Los Angeles because "the politicians and politics lined up ... [and] our ability to build a coalition lined up" because the "infrastructure was already there."[16]

Weiner and Canham-Clyne advanced the concession model against the backdrop of careful legal analysis, which had been conducted by the Teamsters' Mike Manley and Andrew Kahn of the Teamsters' outside law firm Davis, Cowell & Bowe in San Francisco. The Teamsters retained Kahn because they needed California counsel and because Kahn and Richard McCracken, another partner at Davis, Cowell & Bowe, had been involved in the early conversations about port organizing – and were among the nation's leading labor lawyers on strategic campaign work. The legal question to Manley and Kahn was: "politically if we could pull this off, would it withstand challenge?"[17] Their analysis looked at the possibility of a lawsuit based on federal preemption. The lawyers were sure that the American Trucking Associations (ATA) would sue the ports if the Clean Truck Program passed, but they believed that the ports would ultimately prevail. With Manley's analysis of the program as a valid exercise of port authority, the campaign was given legal clearance. As Weiner recalled, "the attorneys thought we had a pretty good case in the Ninth Circuit" and the "likelihood was remote" that the Supreme Court would ultimately take the case.

With legal clearance in hand, Teamsters and Change to Win leaders developed a campaign plan, reached out to LAANE to host the local campaign staff, and hired the LAANE port team (Jon Zerolnick and Patricia Castellanos), who then undertook extensive outreach to local union leaders, NRDC lawyers and representatives from other key environmental justice groups, like East Yard Communities for Environmental Justice, as well as public health groups, like the Long Beach Alliance for Children with Asthma. Some of these environmental and public health organizations were already involved in bottom-up advocacy – led by the Sierra Club, East Yard Communities, and the Coalition for a Safe Environment – which had sought a larger voice in harbor commission governance and came together in formal networks, like the Green LA Port Working Group, created after Mayor Villaraigosa's election to develop plans for port environmental clean-up and CAAP development.

In this way, the Coalition for Clean and Safe Ports brought together national labor leaders focused on the independent contractor problem with local organizations fighting against the environmental and community impact of port expansion. As it formally convened in 2006, the coalition operated as a group of representatives from these diverse organizations. The coalition did not formally include drivers themselves, whose interests were represented by the Teamsters. Decision-making

[16] *Id.*

[17] Telephone Interview with Michael Manley.

processes were established in democratic fashion: major decisions required a supermajority of all coalition members (though were typically by consensus); policy development on issues like truck routes and parking was assigned to subcommittees staffed by members with relevant expertise; time-sensitive strategic issues were delegated to an elected steering committee, whose members thought of themselves as representing the campaign, even as they also worked to ensure that their particular group interests were heard.

THE OUTSIDE GAME: DEVELOPING THE PROGRAM, EXERTING PRESSURE

The campaign's ultimate goal was to persuade the cities of Los Angeles and Long Beach to enact a Clean Truck Program to modify the ports' concession agreement to require a *double conversion*: of *trucks* from dirty diesel to clean fuel and of *drivers* from independent contractors to employees. Under the program, the environmental movement would achieve one of its long-standing goals – emission reductions in the drayage trucking fleet as a step toward "greening" the port – while the Teamsters could win employee status for drivers that enabled potential unionization.

Beginning in the spring of 2007, negotiations over the terms of the Clean Truck Program began in earnest. During this period, coalition pressure was applied in open spaces and behind closed doors. The coalition staged a number of public actions, including a caravan of 100 big rigs down the 110 freeway to the Port of Long Beach. Coalition members also met privately with harbor commissioners, mayor's office staff, and city council staff in both cities – though the approach increasingly diverged between Los Angeles and Long Beach. In Los Angeles, the coalition had allies in key elected politicians and harbor commissioners, and thus the outreach was designed to give them the materials and arguments necessary to hold the line against industry lobbying. The big push was convincing "people to understand that the employee provision was an environmental provision."[18] This was true at the commission level and in the mayor's office, where there were some divisions among the mayor's staff about whether the program should just focus on the green elements or should also include the blue focus on employee drivers. As a result, the coalition had to "fend off repeated attempts by ... forces within the mayor's office who wanted to jettison the labor components of the Clean Truck Program."[19] In Los Angeles, the coalition also had a powerful champion in City Council Member Janice Hahn, with whom members met regularly to work out strategy and policy

[18] Telephone Interview with Candice Kim, Senior Campaign Assoc., Coal. for Clean Air (Apr. 26, 2013).

[19] Telephone Interview with Nick Weiner, Nat'l Campaigns Organizer, Change to Win (Apr. 25, 2013).

details. In Castellanos's view, Hahn "genuinely was supportive of workers and workers' issues. I think this was in her district and she cared about it."

In Long Beach, the approach was different given the perceived skepticism of recently elected Mayor Bob Foster to the employee provision of the program. Foster, a Democrat who had headed Southern California Edison, won the Long Beach mayor's race in a run-off election in June 2006. He took office that next month, just as CAAP was moving toward approval and the battle for clean trucks was taking shape. Los Angeles Harbor Commissioner Jerilyn López Mendoza recalled having lunch with Foster early in his term to discuss the prospects for port coordination around CAAP. After the lunch, she called LAANE organizer William Smart to ask: "Have you guys talked to Bob Foster yet? ... I don't think he's on board with an employee mandate ... I think you all have some work to do."

Coalition members played different roles in exerting outside pressure over the course of the two-year campaign. In private meetings and public hearings, LAANE and Change to Win made the case for industry restructuring, while NRDC emphasized the environmental benefits (and held out the implicit litigation threat). LAANE's Castellanos, Change to Win's Weiner and Canham-Clyne, and NRDC's Martinez, Perrella, and Pettit met regularly with port staff, both mayors' offices, and both city councils, though the emphasis was on the Long Beach City Council because of Janice Hahn's support in Los Angeles. The goal of these meetings was to make the case for sustainability, while also demonstrating the power of the blue–green alliance. In this regard, Castellanos recalled the coalition's first meeting with the Los Angeles mayor's office and port staff: When NRDC showed up with the Teamsters, port director Geraldine Knatz was "a little confused" and there was a lot of "brow raising."[20] To complement these efforts, environmental justice organizers mobilized their base. Marquez and Logan would turn out community members to attend commission meetings and meet with elected officials. Other groups similarly engaged in turn out efforts, and everyone attended periodic public rallies.

Although all the groups played their roles, some also acknowledged that LAANE was in charge. While each coalition member spent considerable time and resources advancing the campaign, in the end, LAANE "had staff dedicated to this campaign" and was "really in the driver's seat."[21] Some members expressed concerns about being tokenized but generally praised LAANE's ability to "really listen" to coalition members and bring everyone on board.[22] With the coalition thus united, members worked to hold officials accountable as they attempted to move the program through internal political channels.

[20] Interview with Patricia Castellanos, Director of Clean and Safe Ports Project (Feb. 23, 2012).

[21] Telephone Interview with Colleen Callahan, Deputy Dir., UCLA Luskin Ctr. for Innovation & Former Manager of Air Quality Policy, Am. Lung Ass'n (Apr. 15, 2013).

[22] *Id.*

THE INSIDE GAME: MOBILIZING LEGAL EXPERTISE, MOVING POLICY

In Los Angeles, as the Campaign for Clean Trucks heated up in 2007, internal policy development proceeded along parallel, though deeply interconnected, paths. It started at the very top, with an effort by the Teamsters to obtain a commitment by the Los Angeles mayor, Antonio Villaraigosa, and port officials to support some version of the Clean Truck Program. In November 2006, in a meeting brokered by the L.A. County Federation of Labor chief, Villaraigosa met with Teamsters President James Hoffa and agreed to a working framework for advancing employee conversion at the ports.

Accordingly, inside the Los Angeles mayor's office, staff understood that a clean truck policy was a priority and worked to advance it. In Deputy Mayor Larry Frank's terms: "The work was outrageously difficult ... the biggest lift I was involved in during my eight years." A key challenge was advancing the program in the face of increasingly intense industry opposition – and, partly as a consequence, some opposition within the mayor's office itself and at the port, where LA port director Geraldine Knatz and board of harbor commission chair David Freeman were uncertain about the viability of the Teamsters' proposal and concerned about the political fallout. The employee provision remained on the table – and remained controversial. To effectively engage the opposition – and to assess whether it was worth spending political capital to do so – Mayor Villaraigosa's staff and the Port of Los Angeles staff needed to be comfortable with the legal foundation for the program.

In early 2007, the coalition's legal analysis was presented to the mayor's staff members, who wanted assurance that it had been done. Once it became apparent the program was really moving forward, port lawyers began "leading the charge" to make sure they had their "ducks in line" on the legal issues.[23] As a result, there were several meetings attended by the port's general counsel, city attorney Thomas Russell; other city attorney lawyers assigned to the port, particularly Joy Crose; the Teamsters' Mike Manley; and lawyers from NRDC. These meetings focused on solidifying the legal argument for the concession approach. Manley circulated versions of the memos he had drafted for the Teamsters to the city attorneys, came out to meet with them, and responded to questions and concerns. In these discussions – also attended by LAANE and Change to Win organizers – Manley viewed his role as "trying to convince [port lawyers] not to recommend to the port commission to reject" the program. Manley's analysis when he talked to port counsel was "that the ATA is going to sue you," but "if you're sued you can win." He argued for the program as a "unified whole": "We had these allies and the thing about labor and environmental groups is we always accuse each other of ditching ... for our

[23] Telephone Interview with Sean Arian, President, Eos Consulting (Apr. 26, 2013).

own interests . . . And so I was careful not to come across as if I were saying, 'Well, this 2007 truck stuff doesn't matter as long as they're employees.'"

Labor and environmentalists converged around legal theory as well as political interests. NRDC was present at the meetings with port lawyers as the legal "hammer," but also to help make the case for local authority.[24] As Pettit remembered, NRDC and other environmental groups were independently "pushing using this market participant exception and at the same time, labor had been eyeing it as a potential approach to resolve several issues. And so it kind of came together where we were both saying" the same thing. NRDC, like the labor lawyers, understood the legal risk of the concession plan and believed that there was "a unified view of how strong the arguments were."

Ultimately, it was port counsel who had the last word on the legal analysis. Much of this work fell to city attorney Joy Crose, who was lead counsel to the Port of Los Angeles on the Clean Truck Program. Her role was to conduct a "legal review of the program" and prepare all "program implementing documents, including contracts, tariffs, ordinances and resolutions."[25] To do this, Crose worked with her counterpart in Long Beach, and also engaged outside counsel, Steven Rosenthal, chair of litigation in the Washington, DC office of Kaye Scholer. After interviewing a number of law firms toward the end of 2006, the city attorney's office hired Rosenthal and his team to advise the port. Rosenthal had deep expertise on "the commerce clause, federal preemption, and federal statutes relating to the regulation of commerce," gained in representing airports and ports over the course of his thirty-year career.[26] Together with the city attorneys, Rosenthal advised the port on the legal issues related to enacting the Clean Truck Program. Reflecting on his general approach to city policy, Rosenthal noted that when it came to reviewing "new, complex programs, you can identify risks" and suggest "this is why we think this approach is a better idea" – but always in a context in which the client understood that "there is no certainty."

The policy makers and their staff were not seeking certainty, just credible assessment. Weiner felt that the campaign's legal groundwork helped to get the port attorneys to "buy into our analysis," which was basically: "yeah, there's a risk. But it's good policy . . . [W]e've got a good legal case." NRDC's Martinez described the value of the legal analysis in similar terms. He believed that the legal analysis empowered the city and port to take a stronger position on the bottom-line policy details: If the ATA was going to sue on whatever policy passed, he argued, it freed

24 Telephone Interview with Nick Weiner, Nat'l Campaigns Organizer, Change to Win (Apr. 25, 2013).

25 Email from Joy Crose, Assistant Gen. Counsel, Office of the City Att'y, to Scott Cummings, Professor, UCLA School of Law (May 7, 2013) (on file with author).

26 Telephone Interview with Steven S. Rosenthal, Partner, Complex Commercial Litig. Dep't, Kaye Scholer (Dec. 16, 2013).

the port to develop the most effective policy on its own terms and then to "go to court with the best program we have."

Similarly, the initial legal analysis provided a ready response to the industry's legal pushback that would occur during policy formulation. Martinez recalled that industry groups had "a lot of legal power, so whenever the port or somebody would propose something, they'd give this very long, threatening legal letter that said you can't do this, you can't do this, you can't do this, you can't do this and here's the legal reasons why." But the coalition had "lawyers on the other side . . . firing back comment letters: oh, but look at this case, look at this case, and making these similar sophisticated arguments on why you can do it. And I think that was the big difference." David Libatique, who worked on port issues for Mayor Villaraigosa, believed that for the mayor's office staff tasked with advancing the program, this legal analysis was critical as a predicate to moving forward: "the legal analysis that was provided by the attorneys basically told us if . . . we're going to have an effect on port trade . . . we would have to act as a market participant and the way we would do that would be through a concession-based model." The mayor's general counsel, Tom Saenz – who had joined Villaraigosa in 2005 after serving as director of litigation at the Mexican American Legal Defense and Education Fund – also reviewed the program and provided a legal opinion to his client.

The context of mayoral decision-making was also shaped by politics. Mayor Villaraigosa's first major policy initiative – a controversial attempt to take over the Los Angeles Unified School District board through the enactment of a state law – was held unconstitutional by a superior court judge in late 2006, giving the mayor a stinging defeat. The mayor needed a policy win and a strong pro-environment position at the port promised to deliver political dividends, while also solving a critical regional problem. While Villaraigosa supported employee conversion, he understood its legal and political vulnerabilities – and could not risk a signature policy going down in the courts twice in a row. In this context, Villaraigosa and his team discussed what would happen if a court struck down employee conversion while leaving clean truck conversion in place, although Deputy Mayor Frank made clear: "that was not what we were planning on." Although the mayor's team knew the plan could fail and truckers could be left bearing the cost of clean truck conversion without the benefit of employee status, Frank remembered feeling a sense of cautious optimism: "We really were hopeful based on our analysis and what we were told."

The ports had to calibrate their response to increasing industry resistance to the Clean Truck Program, which focused on concerns about cost. After the ports released their joint proposal in April 2007, "the real fight began. Once that was public . . . industry came out strong and . . . the ports, the mayors, the electeds reacted to that."[27] A report by the Los Angeles Economic Development Corporation

[27] Interview with Patricia Castellanos.

in May warned that the cargo fee proposed to fund clean trucks might divert cargo to other ports. In June, agricultural exporters complained that the program could make US agriculture "uncompetitive."[28]

The ports' response was to conduct their own economic analysis of the proposed program, which was contracted to outside consultants at Economics & Politics, Inc. Completed in September 2007, the report (called the Husing Report after its main author, economist John Husing) rested on extensive interviews with industry actors, as well as a statistical analysis of a variety of economic data. The report compared the cost of converting the estimated 16,800 trucks regularly serving the ports to clean trucks through the existing structure of independent contractor drivers to the cost of a plan based on employee conversion. It estimated that trucking firms would raise their prices by an average of 80 percent to offset the cost of implementing the Clean Truck Program. Although emphasizing that this would be a "relatively insignificant" increase in overall shipping costs, it was notable that the price increase under a fleet conversion plan that continued to use independent contractors was significantly lower (at less than 50 percent).[29]

Predictably, industry reaction focused on the Husing Report's cost analysis, which strengthened opposition to employee conversion. The Pacific Merchant Shipping Association and National Industrial Transportation League – jointly representing Walmart, Exxon, General Motors, and other major importers – formally asked the Federal Maritime Commission to intervene to stop the Clean Truck Program. Some trucking company owners threatened dire consequences. One family-run business owner said in response to the Husing Report: "Do the math. They want just a handful of companies to do business with ... I am not interested in having 500 truck drivers as employees. If I have to remodel my business, I will probably walk away. I won't want to go through it."[30] Industry groups pressed their position and ratcheted up the litigation threat. In a letter sent to both harbor commissions and mayors, a coalition of business groups urged that the ban on dirty trucks be scrapped in favor of emission standards, and warned that the proposal was "anti-competitive," was outside the ports' "legal authority under state law," and thus "will result in litigation."[31] Against this backdrop, staff members within the Los Angeles mayor's office and port were legitimately concerned and a key question became why employee conversion was essential to a program that purported to advance environmental goals. Even Los Angeles Harbor Commission President David Freeman, a

[28] Ronald D. White, *Exporters Making Waves over Ports' Clean-Air Plan*, L.A. Times, June 1, 2007, at C3.

[29] John E. Husing et al., San Pedro Bay Ports Clean Air Action Plan, Economic Analysis: Proposed Clean Truck Program (2007), www.cleanairactionplan.org/civica/filebank/blobdload.asp?BlobID=2260.

[30] Ronald D. White & Janet Wilson, *Opposition Grows to Ports' Clean-Air Plan*, L.A. Times, Sept. 29, 2007, at C1.

[31] Ronald D. White, *Changes Urged in Proposal for Ports*, L.A. Times, Oct. 10, 2007, at C2.

staunch program supporter, appeared to equivocate: "We all, of course, want to get the truck program up and running ... But quite frankly, when we do the economic analysis it raises some questions." In response, coalition members expressed frustration that the ports were mishandling program implementation and had lost valuable momentum. As NRDC's David Pettit put it: "The ports of Los Angeles and Long Beach get a failing grade for slipping behind in the implementation of their landmark Clean Air Action Plan." It was fall 2007 and the program was at a crossroads.

Two decisions changed the program's course – at least in Los Angeles. First, staffer Sean Arian, a former McKinsey analyst, and others within the Los Angeles mayor's office recognized that for the program to succeed, staff at the port had to buy in. To achieve this, Arian – working closely with Castellanos and Weiner – was able to convince the mayor to "put somebody high ranking" in charge of developing the program at the Los Angeles port. That person turned out to be John Holmes, who held what was arguably the second most important job in the port after the director: overseeing day-to-day operations as the port's deputy executive director. Holmes had spent nearly thirty years in the Coast Guard, the last three directing operations in Southern California – making him a "known quantity" at the port.[32] In Holmes's view, he was charged with designing the Clean Truck Program because figuring out how to get clean trucks in and out of the terminals was ultimately an "operational issue." When he was assigned to the program by Knatz in late 2007, the "two things" he knew were that the program was "going to have a rolling ban ... to culminate in five years in having all the trucks ... be EPA 2007 or newer" and there was going to be employee conversion. As Holmes recalled: "My role was to basically figure it all out." Holmes accepted the main thrust of the coalition's argument: that if the maintenance costs were not shifted onto the trucking companies, the maintenance could not be sustained over the long term since the drivers could not shoulder the expense. From there, Holmes began to work on the program details. Given concerns about cost, a key issue was determining the appropriate level of financial incentives, which trucking companies had advocated for as necessary to make the conversion "happen as soon as possible."[33] For the incentive piece, Holmes brought in the port's director of finance. But they were working off the basis of the Husing Report, which did not provide a strong framework for advancing the entire clean truck package.

This led to the second crucial decision. After Holmes was on board, Arian received the mayor's permission to bring in another consulting firm to reevaluate the economics of the Clean Truck Program. After reviewing the Husing Report, Arian believed that there was an insufficient "fact base" to convince stakeholders of the need for industry transformation and thus argued for what amounted to a more

[32] Telephone Interview with John Holmes, Deputy Exec. Dir., Port of L.A. (Apr. 29, 2013).
[33] *Id.*

sophisticated cut at the economics done by "one of the top consulting firms." Using his connections, Arian was able to bring in Boston Consulting Group (BCG) (his former firm's chief rival), which agreed to send in its "A Team" on a pro bono basis to analyze the economic impact of converting to clean trucks. To justify this, Arian dissected the Husing Report in a way that conveyed to port staff that: "Your analysis didn't go far enough to give us the information we need to evaluate our options." From Weiner's perspective, Arian was able to "basically rip apart" the analysis of John Husing – setting the stage for the entry of BCG.

As Holmes and BCG carried out their analysis, the harbor commissioners were also working to iron out the policy details. Commissioner Mendoza recalled that her starting point was at odds with Freeman's, who thought that the Los Angeles port should simply "mandate the purchase of 500 [Liquid Natural Gas] trucks" and thus become the direct owner of a portion of the port trucking fleet. However, as the program developed around employee conversion within the mayor's office, Freeman embraced the concept and fought for it like a "momma bear."[34] Together, Mendoza and Freeman took the lead in moving the entire program forward. Mendoza described her approach to dealing with the city attorneys assigned to the program:

> [W]e didn't ask them, we would tell them, "This is what we're going to do. You guys have to figure out how to make it work." And although we got a lot of push-back and a lot of "you know, we've never done that before," or "we have outside consultants who have done the analysis and they think that we don't have a really good chance." Our response was, "Okay, do we know for certain that this would not be successful in court? No. Well, if we don't try, we won't know."

THE END GAME: PASSING THE CLEAN TRUCK PROGRAM

As BCG worked on its analysis, the Los Angeles and Long Beach ports initiated a sequential approach to program implementation. Based on a political calculus that it was best to lock in elements of the program in stages – ranging from least to most controversial – the ports began moving forward specific elements of the Clean Truck Program: from clean truck conversion to industry incentives to employee conversion. This order tracked the key elements of the program debated from the outset and set an agenda for phased implementation: first, the progressive ban on dirty trucks; second, the Clean Truck Fee; and third (and most controversially), the concession plan with employee conversion. In the first two steps, the ports of Los Angeles and Long Beach moved in sync, but in the third, they diverged. Throughout the process, industry pressure mounted to split off the environmental standards

[34] Telephone Interview with Sean Arian.

from the employee conversion piece – and to sever the environmentalists from organized labor in the coalition.

The first step was, in relative terms, the easiest. On November 1, 2007 – as the BCG team was just getting under way – the Port of Los Angeles Board of Harbor Commissioners unanimously approved a progressive dirty truck ban.[35] Legally, the order amended port Tariff No. 4, which was originally adopted in 1989 to govern the rates and terms of terminal operations.[36] As amended, Tariff No. 4 imposed a prohibition on the *terminal operators* – not the trucking companies or the truck drivers. Specifically, the ban stated that "no Terminal Operator shall permit access to any Terminal in the Port of Los Angeles" to nonconforming trucks.[37]

With the dirty truck ban legally and logistically in place, the battle immediately turned to the issues of new truck financing and employee conversion. On the financing side, the issue from the outset had been at what price to set the Clean Truck Fee (a charge on containers carried by drayage trucks to be imposed on shippers) in order to create a fund for clean truck conversion. Long Beach made the first move, approving a cargo fee of $35 per loaded twenty-foot container on December 17, 2007. The Clean Truck Fee would be "assessed on containerized merchandise entering or leaving the Ports by Drayage Truck," to be paid by the "Beneficial Cargo Owner," and collected by the terminal operator.[38] The fee was expected to raise $1.6 billion for a Clean Truck Fund, to be used by the port "exclusively for replacement and retrofit of Drayage Trucks serving the Ports of Los Angeles and Long Beach."[39] Still marching in lockstep, the Los Angeles harbor commissioners approved an identical fee four days later.

Finally, the stage was set for the showdown over employee conversion. To increase pressure, the coalition sought to make clear that the legal consequences of inaction would be further logjam. In Los Angeles, a proposed expansion of the TraPac Terminal became the legal flashpoint. On December 6, 2007, the Los Angeles harbor commission, in a statement of overriding considerations, unanimously approved the EIR for a $1.5 billion upgrade projected to create 6,000 jobs and $200 million annually in taxes. Four individuals and sixteen groups – including the Coalition for Clean and Safe Ports, NRDC, the Coalition for Clean Air, the American Lung Association, Sierra Club, and LAANE – appealed the approval to the Los Angeles City Council on the ground that it did not adequately address the air pollution impact. One of the individual appellants was Kathleen Woodfield, president of the San Pedro and Peninsula Homeowners Association, which had

35 Louis Sahagun, *L.A. Panel OKs Plan to Cut Port Truck Soot*, L.A. TIMES, Nov. 2, 2007, at B1.

36 L.A., Cal., Ordinance 165789 (Apr. 10, 1990) (adopting L.A. Bd. of Harbor Comm'rs, Order No. 5837 [July 12, 1989] [adopting Port of L.A. Tariff No. 4]).

37 L.A. Bd. of Harbor Comm'rs, Order 6935, Items 2010, 2015, 2020.

38 Long Beach Bd. of Harbor Comm'rs, Clean Truck Tariff Amendment and Fee, Item 1030 (Dec. 11, 2007), www.polb.com/civica/filebank/blobdload.asp?BlobID=4708.

39 Long Beach Bd. of Harbor Comm'rs, Clean Truck Tariff Amendment and Fee, Item 1035.

been a lead plaintiff in the China Shipping litigation. As she recalled, the appellants were not represented by legal counsel: "NRDC was clear that they were not representing us." Yet NRDC did flex its own legal muscle, indicating its intent to file a CEQA lawsuit if the council appeal was unsuccessful. In response, City Council Member Hahn blocked the EIR from getting out of a key council committee and began negotiating with environmental and neighborhood groups.

Two months later, in Long Beach, NRDC and the Coalition for a Safe Environment filed an intent-to-sue letter with the port, asserting an innovative legal theory: that the port was an entity subject to federal oversight as a hazardous waste site under the federal Resource Conservation and Recovery Act.[40] If the NRDC letter was meant to put pressure on the Port of Long Beach as the clock ticked down toward a resolution on employee conversion, it did not have that effect. To the contrary, on February 16, 2008, the Port of Long Beach officially broke ranks with its Los Angeles counterpart, announcing a meeting to approve the final element of its Clean Truck Program – a concession plan – without the employee provision. "Their announcement caught us all by surprise," said LAANE's Castellanos. It was, as Frank recalled, "one of the earliest signs there was trouble." In its concession plan, trucks would be granted a "right of access to port property" in exchange for Licensed Motor Carriers (LMCs) entering into contracts that ensured compliance with existing laws (including the preexisting elements of the Clean Truck Program), as well as "local truck route and parking restrictions."[41] The ordinance also modified the Clean Truck Fee for cargo moved on trucks not purchased with port subsidies, waiving the fee for containers transported on alternative fuel trucks and halving it for clean diesel trucks.

All eyes therefore turned back to Los Angeles. Industry opponents of employee conversion sought to cast it as a union ploy. NRDC's Martinez perceived that opponents were "freaked out" by the unified front maintained by NRDC and the Teamsters and recalled a lot of "fearmongering." The *Los Angeles Times*, in reporting on the ongoing battle, emphasized the unionization angle: "Critics of the employee provision of the clean truck program ... are concerned that it could be used by the Teamsters as a springboard to launch unionization efforts at ports nationwide."[42] It also noted that that Change to Win had donated $500,000 to Mayor Villaraigosa's local telephone tax initiative, Proposition S, insinuating that the unions expected a quid pro quo. A month later, an editorial began: "Pollution, death and economic stagnation. These catastrophes are being brought to you by the Natural Resources Defense Council and the International Brotherhood of Teamsters." It argued that the clean trucks deal was being jeopardized over a "dispute that has nothing to do with pollution and everything to do with an unholy alliance

[40] Louis Sahagun, *Long Beach Port Faces Suit Threat*, L.A. Times, Feb. 7, 2008, at B3.
[41] Long Beach, Cal., Ordinance No. HD-2011, ¶ 14 (Mar. 17, 2008).
[42] Louis Sahagun, *Officials of Area Ports Split Over Truck Issue*, L.A. Times, Feb. 19, 2008, at B1.

between environmentalists and organized labor." Noting that Long Beach had already passed its plan without employee conversion and that Los Angeles seemed on the verge of doing the opposite, the editorial board suggested that the Clean Truck Program of both ports would be tied up for years in litigation – in Long Beach by NRDC and in Los Angeles by the ATA. The editorial argued that it did not have to be so, since "[u]nder a lease-to-own program, a nonprofit or other organization could buy new trucks and lease them to the truckers, charging low fees that would be subsidized by the ports."[43]

By March 2008, on the brink of the Los Angeles port's final decision on employee conversion, the political back-and-forth reached a fever pitch. The coalition had taken out five full-page color advertisements in the *Long Beach Press-Telegram* denouncing Mayor Foster, while Los Angeles City Council Member Janice Hahn was privately urging him to reconsider. For their part, the Teamsters were seeking to use their political clout to block state funding for Long Beach to complete renovation of the Gerald Desmond Bridge. LAANE sent Foster a public records request seeking all his communications with industry representatives. Yet Foster remained defiant: "So the end result is, if this happens to be the only office I ever hold and the only term I ever serve, I'm comfortable with that." Industry groups also struck a strident tone in advance of the Los Angeles decision. Curtis Whalen, executive director of the ATA, stated that Villaraigosa's "biggest problem is he has good intentions, but they are not legal."

It was at the height of this debate, on March 7, 2008, that BCG released its long-awaited report – which had been delayed in the wake of the Long Beach decision. At its heart was an analysis of the economics of employee conversion – the sole remaining piece of the Los Angeles Clean Truck Program. In clinical terms, far removed from the supercharged rhetoric of campaign adversaries, the report evaluated three program options: The first would permit the continued operation of independent contractors and give them a share of the incentive financing to acquire clean trucks; the second would also permit continued operation of independent contractors, but limit incentive financing to LMCs; and the third would require LMCs to make what it called an "employee commitment." The report's key move – and what made it different than the Husing Report – was that it compared short-term (one to five year) and long-term (more than five year) outcomes in relation to stated environmental, port operations, and safety and security goals. The report's bottom line was that the employee model provided "the best path to long term sustainability," although it posed some "near term risks." Specifically, the report concluded that the employee model would "maximize the likelihood of creating a market in which the reciprocal obligations between the Port (granting a commission) and LMCs (providing drayage services) create a sustainable reliable supply of truckers attracted to stable and relatively well paying jobs in an operationally efficient and

[43] Editorial, *A Storm in Every Port*, L.A. Times, Feb. 24, 2008, at M2.

orderly drayage market." It went on to recommend that a "100% employee driver requirement, phased in over five years" was the best option: "transparent, aligning incentives and easiest to administer." Financing support for clean truck conversion was set at 80 percent for new diesel trucks and up to 80 percent for Liquid Natural Gas trucks, with $5,000 given to scrap pre-1989 trucks.[44]

The report was not all rosy. It predicted that under the "employee commitment" scenario, there would be more cargo diversion – approximately 3 percent – than under the other options, but that this cost would likely be outweighed by overall benefits. The "key risk" was that shippers would divert cargo over and above this 3 percent threshold based on factors other than increased price, such as fear of "future disruption or instability."[45] This risk would be exacerbated, the report stated, if the Port of Los Angeles and the Port of Long Beach adopted different programs – which, of course, had already happened, though the report seemed to hold out hope that there was still a possibility that Long Beach might reverse course. In reporting on the plan, the *Los Angeles Times* highlighted the cargo risk, beginning its article by emphasizing its conclusion "that 'substantial diversions' of the Los Angeles port's business probably would shift to the neighboring port of Long Beach or to other harbors."[46] On March 12, 2008, a staff report authored by the port's Deputy Executive Director Holmes and Deputy Director of Finance Molly Campbell recommended approval of the concession and incentive plans analyzed in the BCG report. At the board level, Arian recalled that the report was the "key study" that persuaded skeptical commissioners to move toward approval.

On the day that the Los Angeles board was set to meet on the concession plan, the *Los Angeles Times* took one last opportunity to hammer home the litigation threat. In an editorial titled "Harbor No Illusions: L.A.'s Plan to Clean Up Port Pollution Is Sure to Wind Up in Court," the editorial board argued that "[i]n the real world of lawsuits and endless court proceedings, [the truck plan] would stall progress on cleaning the air indefinitely."[47] Yet at this stage in the game, the early legal work on the port's authority to pass the program seemed to fortify city staff. As mayor's office staff member Libatique recalled, staff did not shy away from the concession model: Because of "the amount of work and time we put into the legal underpinnings of the program ... I think there was a level of confidence here that we had a strong legal case." If litigation came – which it would – the city was prepared to defend its program then, rather than back off it now. The program that the board did adopt on March 20, 2008 contained the signature element of what the coalition had spent almost two years working toward: the concession plan. Resisting industry pressure, the board in Order 6956 (again drafted by Crose) further amended Tariff No. 4 to

[44] The Bos. Consulting Grp., San Pedro Bay Ports Clean Truck Program: CTP Options Analysis 68 (2008).

[45] *Id.* at 9.

[46] Ronald D. White & Louis Sahagun, *Risk Seen in Port Plan*, L.A. Times, Mar. 8, 2008, at C1.

[47] Editorial, *Harbor No Illusions*, L.A. Times, Mar. 20, 2008, at A20.

"require parties who access Port land and terminals for purposes of providing drayage services to the Port of Los Angeles to have a Concession Agreement" with the port.[48] Following the same format used in the earlier order banning dirty trucks, the amendment placed enforcement responsibility on the terminal operators, stating that "no Terminal Operator shall permit access into any Terminal in the Port of Los Angeles to any Drayage Truck unless such Drayage Truck is registered under a Concession."[49] Terminal operators that violated the order were subject to criminal sanction under the tariff's general penalties provision, which made any violation of the tariff a misdemeanor punishable by a fine of up to $500 and imprisonment of up to six months.

The order set forth the legal justification for the concession plan. Expressing concern about the "environmental, operational, and safety and security objectives of the Port" (language adapted from the BCG report), the findings emphasized the goal of encouraging "evolution of the Port drayage market towards an asset-based market in which Licensed Motor Carriers that hold the motor carrier concessions also own the truck assets used to perform under the concession." After noting that the port "currently has no business relationship with the thousands of trucks, drivers or licensed motor carriers" hauling cargo, the order mandated a concession program "that specifies conditions that must be met in order to provide drayage services" at the port. It stated that a drayage company "must enter into" an agreement, which would last for a term of five years, "in order to access" the port. Although the order itself did not explicitly discuss employee conversion, a separate transmittal by staff (circulated to the full board) proposed a "non-exhaustive list of the main Concession requirements," which included that LMCs "[t]ransition to 100% employee drivers for Port of Los Angeles drayage in five years, according to a schedule specified by the port." The list also included the concessionaire's commitment to create an "off street parking plan"; to affix "placards on all Concession controlled trucks referring to a 1–800 phone number to report concerns regarding truck emissions, safety and operations"; and to pay a concession fee of "$2500 plus an annual fee of $100 per truck."[50]

In what appeared as recognition of the legal vulnerability of at least some elements of the concession plan, a severability provision was also added. It stated: "If any provision of Port of Los Angeles Tariff No. 4 shall be determined by court or agency of competent jurisdiction to be unenforceable, unlawful or subject to an order of temporary or permanent injunction from enforcement, such determination shall only apply to the specific provision and the remainder of the provisions … shall continue in full force and effect."

48 L.A. Bd. of Harbor Comm'rs, Order No. 6956 ¶ 3 (Mar. 20, 2008).
49 L.A. Bd. of Harbor Comm'rs, Port of L.A., Tariff No. 4, Item No. 2040 (Mar. 20, 2008).
50 Transmittal 1, Port of Los Angeles Drayage Truck Concession Requirements ¶¶ (f), (m), (o).

The purpose of the severability provision was to reduce legal and political risk to the overall Clean Truck Program. Legally, the severability provision would permit a court to excise some provisions, while keeping intact the broader plan. Commissioner Freeman recalled "the meeting in the mayor's office where we decided, well, we want a severability clause ... so that if we lose that one, it doesn't contaminate the rest of the case. And we all went ahead with that." For the mayor, there were also political implications. Severability maximized the possibility of sustaining some aspects of the Clean Truck Program – and thus being able to declare political victory while also addressing an important policy concern. Perhaps most crucially, if the employee provision was ultimately struck down, progress could still be made toward greening the port, and organized labor would be no worse off than if the effort had not been made at all.

In connection with the board order establishing the concession plan, a separate resolution drafted by Crose and approved by the board laid out the market participation rationale, while also adding in the core financial incentives. The resolution noted that the objective of the plan was to "create and sustain an efficient, reliable supply of drayage services to the port," which "as land owner of the Harbor District land and assets has the right and the obligation to manage and control the access to its land by tenants and invitees to ensure that operations thereon maintain safety and security of Port operations on a sustainable basis." The resolution went on to stress that the "air quality, port security, and safety goals" of the plan were "more likely to be achieved and sustained over the long term" through concessions. It also pointed to the "[s]erious and long-standing problems" produced by "inadequate maintenance" and "unsafe, negligent or reckless driving of trucks" at the port, and asserted that the concession model was the "most efficient," "greenest," "safest," "most community friendly," "most responsive and flexible," and "easiest model to administer." In addition, the resolution – following the staff report and BCG analysis – authorized a Truck Funding Program, to "provide funding of up to 80% of the value" of clean trucks (in the form of either a lease-to-own agreement or up-front grant to purchase or retrofit) "in order to make the transition ... more affordable." Other incentives included a Truck Procurement Assistance Program to "provide volume discounted pricing" to concessionaires and a Scrap Truck Buyback Program providing $5,000 to owners of pre-1989 trucks who turned them in. With that, the centerpiece of the Clean Truck Program was approved.[51] The following day, the ATA's Whalen called it a "scheme to unionize port drivers" and vowed that: "We're going to go after Los Angeles with everything we've got so their plan goes to hell in a handbasket. We will win and we will win handily."

Yet a few steps still remained. The Los Angeles port wanted resolution of the dispute over the TraPac expansion – which had served as the coalition's final

[51] L.A. Bd. of Harbor Comm'rs, Resolution 6522 (Mar. 20, 2008).

"bargaining chip."[52] As homeowner activist Kathleen Woodfield recalled, the port "wanted to move forward with the TraPac project. For as long as it was appealed it was in limbo." To move this along, Woodfield, Martinez, and other coalition members met with City Council Member Hahn, Mayor Villaraigosa, port director Knatz, and Commissioner Freeman to hammer out a deal. Working closely with Hahn – whose support coalition members thought was "strong and pretty much unequivocal" – the coalition negotiated a settlement in early April.[53] Under its terms – negotiated primarily by Martinez and port general counsel Tom Russell – the port agreed to create a Mitigation Trust Fund with an immediate $12 million contribution toward community improvements and an air filtration system for local schools. The agreement also provided – as a means of avoiding future litigation – that more funds would be contributed for mitigation in conjunction with future expansion projects at the port: $1.50 for each additional cruise ship passenger and $2 for each additional container. The funds were to go to a nonprofit group, the Harbor Community Benefit Foundation, created for the purposes of disbursing the money. The agreement also committed the port to continue working to support the Clean Truck Program. It was the first EIR approved at the port since China Shipping, and Commissioner Freeman touted the agreement as a model for pending expansion plans. "The entire environmental community is giving its blessing to Mayor Villaraigosa's green growth program ... We will work together on all future [projects] and not resort to litigation." The NRDC's Pettit, though pleased with the outcome, did not go quite that far, emphasizing that: "The agreement does not give up our right to sue on any project other than TraPac."

The accord did, however, clear the way for the concession agreement itself to be approved. The draft agreement, circulated in early May, spelled out the mechanics of "driver hiring" in detail, setting forth a phased implementation in which a concessionaire "shall be granted a transition period ... by which to transition its Concession drivers to 100% Employee Concession drivers by no later than December 31, 2013." Under the transition plan, 20 percent of drivers had to be converted by the end of 2009, 66 percent by the end of 2010, 85 percent by the end of 2011, and 100 percent by the end of 2013. The agreement also required concessionaires to "submit for approval ... an off-street parking plan," "post placards" on their trucks, agree to regular maintenance, attest to financial capability, and pay the concession fees. The agreement further specified enforcement procedures, identifying (though not defining) minor and major defaults, and imposing sanctions, which included revoking the concession agreement itself. The final loose ends were quickly tied. The board approved the concession agreement on May 15. Then, at a meeting on

[52] Telephone Interview with Tom Politeo, Volunteer, Sierra Club Harbor Vision Task Force (Mar. 26, 2013).

[53] *See* Press Release, Port of Los Angeles, Mayor Villaraigosa, Councilwoman Hahn Announce Historic Agreement That Will Allow TraPac Terminal Renovations to Go Forward at Port of L.A. (Apr. 3, 2008).

June 17, the city council approved the final concession plan. With the mayor's signature, the Clean Truck Program was city law.

In the end, after nearly two years of struggle, the coalition had won a program in Los Angeles that included the twin goals of fleet and employee conversion. Both were achieved through a legal structure that linked the port's contractual and police powers: Trucking companies were required to sign concession agreements to enter the port and terminal operators were required to bar entry to any trucking companies that did not comply with port rules – or incur criminal sanctions. The program was to be financed primarily through the imposition of cargo fees, which would shift the costs of clean truck acquisition to shippers while providing incentives for trucking companies to upgrade their fleets. Looking at the final program as a whole, there were some details with which the coalition could quibble. At the outset, the coalition had set its sights on full conversion to alternative fuel trucks, a higher fee, and immediate employee conversion. What it got was partial alternative fuel conversion, a lower fee with significant exceptions, and a five-year phase-in for employee conversion. However, these were minor sacrifices to achieve the ultimate program, which closely tracked the outlines proposed in the coalition a year earlier.

IMPLICATIONS FOR THE URBAN CORE

The Divided Impact of Local Reform

The Los Angeles Clean Truck Program was a policy solution to port trucking nested in local government law that provided the crucial legal fix to the independent contractor and pollution problems – but also built in legal vulnerabilities. The fix, enacted in the Los Angeles Clean Truck Program in 2008, was a win-win solution: By taking maintenance out of the drivers' hands and making the companies internalize the costs, the program promised to create a sustainable foundation for clean trucking and driver prosperity over time. The legal foundation of the Clean Truck Program was the doctrine of market participation, which justified a local government's proprietary action to enact labor-enhancing regulation without running afoul of federal preemption under the FAAAA.

The Clean Truck Program required trucking firm compliance with operational standards such as off-street parking and placard posting, and mandated truck and employee conversion as a way to solve the port's essential proprietary problem: its inability to achieve necessary growth due to legal fights over environmental pollution caused by diesel trucks. This problem was laid bare by the China Shipping litigation, which effectively halted growth at both ports. The market participant argument for the Clean Truck Program, therefore, was that it was necessary to reduce air pollution, which would in turn eliminate the potential for future environmental legal challenges that would stymie port growth and competitiveness. Converting drivers to employees was an essential part of that goal, since their precarious status as independent contractors prevented them from maintaining trucks – so any one-time fleet conversion would be unsustainable over time. Failure to comply with the Clean Truck Program on the part of trucking firms subjected them to penalties – including contract termination and port disbarment. The program hinged on enforcement by terminal operators, which were prohibited from admitting non-compliant trucks on the threat of port-imposed criminal sanctions.

These features of the policy solution succeeded in leveraging local government power to address the structural legal problems at the heart of port trucking, but in so doing also provided the basis for the program's legal demise in the American Trucking Associations (ATA) preemption lawsuit that immediately followed. In that suit, which bounced back and forth between the district court and Ninth Circuit before resulting in a Supreme Court victory for industry, the program's legal assets – welding together truck and employee conversion, and enforcing concession agreements through the port's police power – became legal liabilities. The Ninth Circuit ruled that employee conversion was too tenuously connected to environmental remediation to qualify as permissible market participation (a ruling not appealed by the port),[54] while the Supreme Court invalidated off-street parking and placard provisions on the ground that their enforcement via criminal sanctions constituted a regulatory, not proprietary, act.[55]

In terms of policy impact and industry reform, one can trace distinct blue and green trajectories through the Campaign for Clean Trucks. The seminal policy achievement of the Campaign for Clean Trucks produced mixed results for its labor and environmental coalition partners – a function of its initial legal architecture. The Clean Truck Programs in Los Angeles and Long Beach contained two essential components. The first, adopted in identical form by both ports, required trucking companies to convert their fleets to clean emission vehicles through a progressive ban on old model-year trucks. The financial impact of that ban was lessened by a set of incentives passed shortly thereafter. Each port imposed a $35 per container Clean Truck Fee on shippers and used the revenue generated to subsidize the "replacement and retrofit" of noncompliant trucks. From this point, the ports diverged on the second essential Clean Truck Program component, with the Port of Los Angeles passing a concession plan in 2008 that mandated employee status for drivers, while the Port of Long Beach's concession plan rejected employee conversion in favor of simply requiring trucking firms to ensure compliance with existing law. Thus, as enacted, the ports' Clean Truck Programs contained different results for the coalition's environmental and labor partners: Environmentalists won publicly subsidized clean truck conversion at both ports as organized labor secured employee conversion only in Los Angeles.

[54] *Am. Trucking Ass'ns, Inc.* v. *City of L.A.*, 660 F.3d 384, 408 (9th Cir. 2011).

[55] *Am. Trucking Ass'ns, Inc.* v. *City of L.A.*, 133 S. Ct. 2096 (2013).

Yet even that more limited victory by labor was short-lived, as employee conversion was struck down in the Ninth Circuit and other features of the Los Angeles concession plan were held to be preempted by the Supreme Court. The one silver lining of the Court's decision was that it did not erode the underlying doctrinal basis for local government authority to address port trucking through the market participant exception to federal preemption – leaving the door cracked open for a new concession policy on more solid legal grounds. But that was cold comfort to the campaign lawyers and activists, particularly those on the labor side, who had worked so hard to get the Clean Truck Program passed in the first instance. It was also a blow to officials at the Los Angeles port, who viewed themselves as caught in a bind: accountable for pollution and other negative externalities, but without complete authority to redress them. Most profoundly, the litigation outcome was a serious setback for port drivers, who found themselves additionally burdened: obliged to acquire (mostly through leasing) and maintain new, more expensive low-emission trucks, yet still in the degraded economic position of independent contractors without the financial means to do so.

How one judges these disparate outcomes for the labor and environmental movements at the ports is a function of their relation to each movement's legal endowments. Because of the exclusion of independent contractors from the protections of federal labor law, the labor movement from the outset of the campaign was cast in the difficult position of having to use alternative legal regimes as proxies to leverage stronger labor rights. The Campaign for Clean Trucks, in particular, was an instance in which the Teamsters, lacking legal power because of independent contractor rules, sought to build on the power that NRDC litigation created to change the union's structural bargaining position – using environmental law as a springboard to surmount the legal barrier to organizing posed by drivers' independent contractor status. However, once organized labor decided to take advantage of the opportunity that environmental law afforded, it simultaneously became bound by its legal constraints: tethering labor goals to environmental policy in ways that affected their legal viability within the contested confines of federal preemption.

For the environmental coalition partners, in contrast, litigation was a strong tool in the port context to advance emission reduction objectives. The NRDC challenge to China Shipping changed the power dynamic of port growth by demanding greater accountability in port expansion plans. Environmental review, while affecting process not outcomes, could prove costly if the ports had to redo EIRs for failing to consider and mitigate significant impacts. In the ports campaign, environmental litigation had the power to force environmental reform in a context in which two factors were present: the polluting industry was fixed in place based on massive up-front infrastructure investment and there was intense interregional competition for the industry's service. Because the ports were geographically tethered, but could potentially lose business to other regional competitors, delay and uncertainty were potent bargaining chips. Since litigation could impede port expansion plans and shippers could reroute cargo to other West Coast ports (or even through the Panama Canal), the Los Angeles and Long Beach ports had a strong incentive to mitigate uncertainty to maintain profitability. This incentive gave NRDC negotiating power through lawsuits to enforce environmental compliance. In addition, because environmental review of port development ultimately had to be approved by city council, it provided a means for exerting political influence in that body.

It was political influence that organized labor brought to bear in passing the Clean Truck Program, though on terms that could not ultimately overcome its structural legal deficits. To win the concession plan, labor's argument for driver employee status was firmly connected to the idea of environmental sustainability: Without employee drivers, a short-term incentive program might produce clean truck conversion, but over time drivers would be unable to maintain truck quality, thus necessitating another round of public funding. That argument proved compelling as a way of advancing the Clean Truck Program through political channels. However, it was legally insufficient to survive preemption, with the Ninth Circuit characterizing employee conversion as an effort to "impact third party behavior unrelated to the performance of the concessionaire's obligations to the Port"[56] – in other words, an attempt to change trucking company labor practices to enable unionization. The court thus did not buy the argument that employee conversion was about environmental sustainability first and unionization second (if at all). As a result, the environmental components of the Los Angeles Clean Truck Program were left standing, while the labor and community provisions were gutted.

This outcome correlated to ex ante legal strength: because environmental law was the most potent weapon in thwarting port growth, mitigating environmental concerns was ultimately viewed by the court as most central to the ports' role as market actors. Conversely, requiring employee conversion (and thereby strengthening labor law) was not seen as market participation, despite the arguments connecting conversion to long-term environmental sustainability. The policy outcome in the Campaign for Clean Trucks was a product of the deeply uneven playing field on which organized labor sought to advance. The campaign itself spotlighted the high threshold barrier to effective local labor activism in low-wage sectors defined by contracting: Specifically, the legal predicate for unionization – employee status – had to be in place before local government-based legal strategies to facilitate it could work. As labor scholars have pointed out, in industries in which statutory employees already exist, local governments may bargain with employers for labor neutrality agreements in exchange for public benefits in order to facilitate union organizing without running afoul of labor preemption.[57] However, the Campaign for Clean

[56] *Am. Trucking Ass'ns, Inc.*, 660 F.3d at 408.

[57] *See* Benjamin I. Sachs, *Despite Preemption: Making Labor Law in Cities and States*, 124 HARV. L. REV. 1153 (2011).

Trucks underscored the challenge of getting to this step in low-wage industries characterized by pervasive independent contracting and thus outside the formal purview of labor law. In such industries, where baseline employment conditions are not established, federal preemption on nonlabor law grounds (i.e., deregulatory transportation rules codified in the FAAAA) can preclude local legal reforms to create employment relationships and thus get to a locally mediated bargaining process in the first instance.

As this suggests, the structure of low-wage industries defined by independent contracting creates a formidable double barrier to labor organizing since unions must *first* overcome the legal challenge of transforming the employment status of workers in the industry in order to even create the *possibility* for unionization – which still has to be fought for and won. Because this weak starting position is a product of federal law – and organized labor is too politically disfavored to change that law outright – the labor movement has sought to anchor reform efforts in receptive local government law processes. But doing so subjects labor efforts to the risk of nonlabor-law preemption – underscoring the movement's deeply disadvantaged position in pursuing unionization. Thus, it is *both* the weakness of labor law *and* the strength of nonlabor law (antitrust and deregulation) that converge to erect substantial challenges to organizing industries – like port trucking – in which workers are assigned the label of "owner-operators" but live a reality indistinguishable from that of low-wage employees. In such industries, even if (against the odds) efforts to change local policy to reclassify workers as employees manage to succeed, they do so merely by restoring workers back to the baseline of being *organizable* – aligning their legal label with their lived reality – and thus removing extant legal barriers that now preclude even the possibility of demanding better conditions.

In the wake of the failure of employee conversion in the Campaign for Clean Trucks, the labor movement has rebooted and retooled, launching a new Justice for Port Drivers' misclassification campaign, which has endeavored to get out of the independent contractor box by bypassing the need to establish employee status *before* initiating collective action. To do so, it has advanced a strategy of "suing and striking": challenging independent contractor firms for unpaid wages and unlawful business expenses on behalf of misclassified drivers at the California Department of Labor Standards Enforcement (DLSE) and in court; using the precedent from successful cases in those venues to pursue federal labor protection for misclassified drivers at the National Labor Relations Board (NLRB); leveraging that federal protection to launch driver strikes against targeted trucking firms, which (along with litigation liability) is designed to pressure firms to negotiate union contracts; and building political power from this suing-and-striking model to bring port and city officials back to the negotiating table. This strategy has hinged on defining the problem in terms of misclassification in order to draw crucial legal enforcement resources from sympathetic labor agencies – the state DLSE and federal Department of Labor (DOL) – while building a pipeline of cases against campaign targets in the venues where the campaign believed it had the best chance of success. Redefining the port trucking problem more explicitly around misclassification facilitated the campaign's pivot away from the local policy arena toward state and federal administrative agencies, where they sought to develop facts on the ground that could reestablish the political capital needed to eventually return to the ports to make the case for a new policy solution to the fundamental independent contractor problem.

Thus far, this strategy has proven legally potent, resulting in $35 million in DLSE awards against port trucking firms and extending protection for misclassified drivers within NLRB Region 21 – with important cases still pending. This legal success has resulted in tangible and unprecedented union advances: three collective bargaining agreements in an industry without any for forty years (at Toll (2012), Eco Flow (2016), and Shippers Transport (2015)); and labor peace agreements at three others: Green Fleet (2015), Pac 9 (2016), and Gold Point (2016).

In addition to tangible organizing outcomes, the campaign's misclassification strategy, by combining suing and striking to disrupt port options, also builds a legal foundation for a potential labor peace policy at the ports that responds to the legal deficits that undermined the Clean Truck Program. It does so by seeking to convert the legal vulnerability of employee conversion as a mechanism to address *environmental harm*, and thereby reduce costly environmental litigation, into a legal asset as a way to avoid costly *labor strife*. In this sense, the misclassification strategy is geared toward surmounting the preemption hurdle by repositioning employee status for drivers within the space for market participation that the Ninth Circuit and Supreme Court left open in the ATA case. By firmly linking driver misclassification to the problem of labor unrest, any new concession policy would thus seek to avoid the legal weakness at the heart of the campaign's loss of employee conversion in the Clean Truck Program litigation: that it was disconnected from the port's interest as a market participant in environmental protection. Whether this strategy can withstand a Trump administration now making antilabor appointments to the NLRB and a newly fortified conservative majority on the Supreme Court is the critical question now confronting the campaign – one that underscores the ongoing vulnerability of organized labor in American politics.

The Role of Countermobilization in Local Economic Justice Movements

For port trucking firms in Los Angeles and Long Beach, conditions at the outset of the Campaign for Clean Trucks were the mirror image of those confronted by organized labor – and thus placed industry in a favorable starting position. The legal playing field that disadvantaged labor mobilization empowered industry countermobilization. Just as the structure of local government law and its relation to preemption placed limits on coalition efforts to reform port trucking, it facilitated industry resistance and, ultimately, industry success in overturning the Los Angeles concession plan. Industry began from a position of strength – seeking to protect the legal and economic status quo against change. Its strategy from the outset was to defend against structural market reform and thus keep labor in the posture of litigating individual misclassification suits, which the industry could defend in a war of attrition.

Politically and legally, industry sought to sow division in the Campaign for Clean Trucks where the coalition attempted to build unity. When industry could not stop the Clean Truck Program in Los Angeles, it ramped up lobbying pressure on Long Beach and succeeded in defeating employee conversion there. The Los Angeles–Long Beach split paid political and legal dividends. Politically, it heightened inter-union division, further undercutting the support of already unionized longshoremen by increasing the risk that the Los Angeles program would divert cargo to neighboring Long Beach – or other West Coast ports. The split also posed a challenge to Los Angeles officials who confronted the prospect of lost economic benefit to the city and the real chance of political failure. This concerned Los Angeles city officials, who feared an outcome in which the blue–green goals of the Clean Truck Program would be only partly realized: If employee conversion ultimately failed in court, there could be environmental victory and labor failure. Although the administration fought against this outcome, the possibility was embedded in the structure of the policy, which contained legally severable provisions allowing the overall plan to remain in effect even if individual provisions were invalidated in court. In the end, the ATA exploited this structure to focus its attack on employee conversion while professing support for clean trucks. The split between the two ports therefore produced legal benefits for the ATA: sharpening the legal focus on employee conversion (and its connection to unionization), facilitating the ultimate legal settlement with Long Beach (thus allowing the ATA to direct its full resources to defeating the Los Angeles plan), and adding weight to the ATA's preemption claim (by revealing the danger of inconsistent port regulation).

In similar fashion, industry also aimed to weaken the ties binding the labor and environmental coalition partners – using litigation to promote the breach it could not achieve during the policy campaign. This divide-and-conquer strategy was enabled by the industry's favorable legal starting point. Labor and environmental partners had to overcome substantial legal uncertainty weighing against their core argument that local government had authority to enact joint clean truck and employee conversion as a coherent – and intrinsically connected – market participation strategy. Recognizing this vulnerability, industry pushed against the weakest part of the coalition's argument: that employee conversion was central to the port's proprietary interests in mitigating environmental harm. And industry skillfully pitted the coalition partners' ultimate interests against each other. Although the labor and environmental movements stood firm in their commitment to the integrity of the Los Angeles Clean Truck Program as an integrated package of reforms, their constituencies ultimately had distinct aims: environmentalists wanted emission reductions, while organized labor sought unionization. The industry plan was to drive a wedge by effectively conceding on emissions in order to thwart unionization. This plan was advanced through the industry's litigation decision not to challenge the progressive dirty truck ban and its public relations strategy repeatedly linking the concession plan to the Teamsters. Although NRDC lawyers steadfastly defended the environmental–labor linkage, they could not convince courts to agree on the connection between employee conversion and long-term environmental sustainability. In the end, whereas NRDC litigation brought the coalition together, ATA litigation succeeded in splitting the coalition's achievement apart.

Accountability in Local Reform Coalitions

The problem, from labor's perspective, was how to evaluate the legal viability of the Clean Truck Program in relation to the ambiguous and contested boundaries of preemption – and how to pursue the program in a way that served the interests of port drivers while also advancing the labor movement's broader ambitions for organizing supply chain workers and rebuilding its national power to promote workers' rights. That decision, although resting upon legal analysis, was ultimately one made by top campaign leadership, which included key non-lawyer members of the campaign team from the Teamsters, Change to Win, and LAANE. The crucial legal prediction centered on the risk of litigation failure – specifically, the risk that the program in general and the employee conversion piece in particular would be struck down. Movement lawyers from the Teamsters and NRDC believed that the ports would win a FAAAA challenge at the Ninth Circuit and that the Supreme Court would not grant certiorari. This prediction turned out to be wrong: Only the concession plan was challenged, the Ninth Circuit struck down the critical employee conversion provision, and the Supreme Court decided to consider, and reject, remaining concession provisions.

At one level, this outcome, while disappointing for the campaign, is analytically mundane. Legal predictions turn out to be wrong all the time, in part because law is indeterminate and judges have significant discretion, and in part because lawyers and their clients are fallible. However, the nature and process of legal analysis in relation to the Clean Truck Program was itself not mundane. The dynamics of crafting legal opinions may shape their content and accuracy. Legal opinions generated by movement lawyers may be influenced by lawyers' bias in favor of their reform position. However, in policy campaigns, movement-side legal analysis must be accepted by lawyers on the inside of the political decision-making process. In Los Angeles, the coalition's preemption analysis in support of the Clean Truck Program was also vetted by inside and outside port counsel, as well as the mayor's general counsel – which enhanced opportunity for independent review. All converged around the same ultimate conclusion: that the Clean Truck Program was a legally defensible exercise of local government power under the market participant exception to preemption. All of the legal reviews acknowledged the risk of litigation failure, but ultimately concluded that it was a risk worth taking.

As part of a social movement-led, local policy-making campaign, the movement lawyers drafting the preemption analysis were not representing drivers directly, but rather were representing their own organizational interests. And the stakes were high: The legal judgment about preemption affected passage of a significant social policy reform affecting a critical national industry. Although legal judgments from government lawyers routinely precede the enactment of significant policies, a unique feature of the legal decision making in relation to the Clean Truck Program was the extent to which movement-generated doctrinal interpretation informed internal government legal analysis and political decision making. Understanding the contours of that decision-making process and how it misjudged the legal outcome, then, presents the accountability question most directly: Given the risk of error, was analysis and decision making sufficiently accountable to the group on whom error would fall most heavily?

Coalition leaders knew that there was a small, but nontrivial, risk that if clean truck conversion passed without employee conversion, drivers could be left worse off: remaining independent contractors forced to bear the cost of acquiring and maintaining more expensive clean trucks. In a context in which the prize was so big (trucking industry transformation with the possibility of organizing the entire logistics supply chain) and the legal analysis suggested that the risk of losing was so small, coalition leaders decided to pursue the policy in the face of risk. Because drivers were not members of the coalition, there was no formal mechanism for them to formally weigh in on the risk, though it is reasonable to believe that those who were active in the campaign would have agreed with the coalition's analysis and thus supported the policy. On the ground, organizers promoted the promised benefits of the Clean Truck Program to drivers without engaging in deep analysis of potential costs. This was, undoubtedly, because the campaign was so invested in playing to win – and believed winning was likely – that it did not want to dwell on the complexities of what it would mean to lose.

Yet, even with activist driver support of the plan, the accountability problem in the Campaign for Clean Trucks was a thorny one. The activist drivers were only a fraction of the total port trucker population and could not claim representative status (and, indeed, there were challenger groups, like the National Port Drivers Association, which purported to represent thousands of owner-operators who wanted to maintain that status). Without organizing and polling all drivers, coalition leaders had to rely on the support of those drivers most committed to the clean truck project.

Moreover, the nature of the coalition itself – while strengthening its claims to broad stakeholder representation – complicated its members' representative roles. Environmentalists were committed to emission reduction and not in a position of direct accountability to the drivers. Although the Teamsters' constituency, broadly defined, included port truck drivers, the drivers were not union members – only potential ones. The Teamsters and their allies at Change to Win thus had to consider the impact of a successful Clean Truck Program not just on port truck drivers but on the union movement more generally. And this was a judgment ultimately made by labor movement leaders, *not* the movement lawyers, who were in a more conventional position of general counsel to the unions – thus shifting the crucial representational choices to the client level. In the end, labor movement leaders decided that the campaign was strategically important enough (with significant potential benefits to a much wider universe of workers), and the downside limited enough, that it was worth the risk – that to change the equation for organized labor in the United States, it was necessary to seize the once-in-a-generation chance to go big at the ports. Once the political decision was made to pursue this chance in tandem with clean truck conversion, the potential conflict with driver interests was unavoidable: if the total package succeeded, drivers would benefit, but if employee status failed, the largest cost would fall on the constituency members with the most to lose and the weakest voice in movement decision making. That it ended precisely so underscores the unequally distributed risks of movement ambition and the challenge of ever neatly resolving the dilemma of "serving two masters" in complex and high-stakes campaigns for transformative social change.

The Contested Nature of Localism

The ports campaign illustrates the broader trend of "local labor activism," in which labor–community alliances leverage local government law powers to achieve labor regulation – like minimum wage and big-box ordinances – around the country.[58] Academic interest in this form of labor localism has intersected with recent legal scholarship focused on "law making from below," in which social movements organize outside of formal legal institutions to create new meanings of justice – for example, around ideals of women's and civil rights – that shape the content of formal law as it becomes codified by legislatures or issued by courts.[59] Arguments in favor of a bottom-up approach to lawmaking in general and labor regulation in particular stress that localism gives affected communities more direct say in and control over regulatory processes, and builds public support by shifting culture before changing law. However, the ports campaign reveals a more complicated and dynamic process in which the fight for control over the content and meaning of law is always influenced by contending local and national legal forces.

In this critical sense, the port struggle teaches a basic but important lesson: Localism is never entirely local. To the contrary, a key takeaway from this study is

58 Katherine V. W. Stone & Scott L. Cummings, Labor Activism in Local Politics: From CBAs to "CBAs," *in The Idea of Labour Law* 273 (Guy Davidov & Brian Langille eds., 2011).

59 *See, e.g.*, Lani Guinier & Gerald Torres, *Changing the Wind: Notes toward a Demosprudence of Law and Social Movements*, 123 YALE L.J. 2740 (2014).

that political control of the federal system – particularly the courts and the administrative state – profoundly affects the power of social movement-driven local regulatory action. Local efforts are significantly influenced by federal law and legal processes, playing out on multiple levels, with proponents of labor reform selecting a hospitable arena for policy reform – the progressive city – while opponents try to pull the struggle into venues where they have legal advantages: in the case of the Clean Truck Program, the federal court.

In this battle over work regulation at the ports, one thus hears echoes of Progressive Era legal struggle in which the labor movement sought to mobilize its significant state and local power to pass pro-worker legislation, like minimum wage ordinances and workday limits. The difference now is that the barrier to local labor regulation is not a constitutional vision of substantive due process, as in the famous 1905 Supreme Court case of *Lochner* v. *New York*,[60] but a legal laissez faire advanced under a deregulatory doctrine of FAAAA preemption. In this struggle over local labor regulation, courts are placed in the role of policing city policy making, which in the Clean Truck Campaign was invalidated not on the basis of a higher affirmative law, but a claimed commitment to the *absence* of law: a prohibition against local trucking law mandated by federal deregulation used as the basis for preemption. And this is not preemption because an affirmative regulatory scheme, like labor or environmental or immigration law, occupies the space, but rather because of the *withdrawal* of legal regulation mandated by the FAAAA.

This focus on federal–local interaction has important implications. One is that the current version of labor law localism, at least as it has been expressed in Los Angeles campaigns challenging low-wage work in the trucking and other service industries, is fundamentally *strategic* – in the sense that labor localism is a product of political calculation by labor leaders that progressive local reform is the best that can be achieved in an era of national political polarization. From this perspective, labor law localism has advanced less as a first-order political priority of the labor movement than as a second-best strategic necessity. A key element of strategic calculation is determining on which institutional level to fight – fundamentally a calculation about institutional advantages and power. The Campaign for Clean Trucks targeted policy change at the port as a city entity precisely because of the campaign's local political leverage. When that was undercut in court, the campaign turned to other favorable venues: first, Congress to change law, and when that failed, to the DLSE and DOL to enforce law.

This is not to suggest that labor and other progressive social movements should abandon progressive city-building as a central goal, or that such bottom-up investments in organizing strength and regulatory success cannot over time feed into larger national currents of reform. But it is to express caution about risks: one of which may be that social movement efforts to build progressive cities may create

[60] 198 U.S. 45 (1905).

islands of greater equality amid a larger sea of inequality and that the gap between the politics of progressive big cities and the politics of everywhere else may grow wider, reinforcing polarization, and making it more difficult for progressivism to gain a wider audience and political traction. In this sense, progressive city making may deepen the blue–red division across city boundaries even as it reduces the blue–green division within them. Another risk is that the pull of local activism and responsive regulation will obscure the extent of national-level problems in need of national-level solutions. In this regard, although proponents of localism might extol the benefits of local regulatory flexibility, such flexibility is most useful when local conditions are significantly different; yet with respect to many of the core problems facing American workers, such as the inadequacy of the basic wage and enforcement, local variation is not the key issue.

The experience of Los Angeles, often held out as a paragon of the progressive city, in many ways validates what Schragger calls "the possibility of an urban democracy that promotes individuals' participation in economic and political life on terms of equality."[61] Indeed, one of the important aspects of the port struggle is that bringing together two of the most powerful progressive movements in America today around one goal strengthens the potential for an enduring collaboration that fuses interests to achieve over time changes impossible when groups work in isolation. In this sense, the port struggle is not just about clean trucks and better conditions for drivers, but about showing political decision makers that a blue–green alliance can deliver on its promise to deepen democratic participation and expand equality over the long term.

In doing so, progressive movement-led local law making necessarily asserts greater space for local power, pushing back against the boundaries of federalism even as it may reinscribe other types of inter-jurisdictional borders. Understanding how to harness the dynamic relationship between the federal and local spheres is one of the most critical legacies of the ports campaign: one that underscores how local politics is enervated without an energized national counterpart, while also showing how federal law making is itself challenged and transformed by robust social movement activism that claims the power to make local law. The legal history of port struggle illuminates how the social movement pursuit of local regulation necessarily reconstitutes relations with the federal government. By creating new facts on the ground that challenge federal authority, local mobilization is always a legal act that advances a program of national reform: revising the scope of federal law, even as it seeks to escape its reach.

[61] Richard Schragger, *City Power: Urban Governance in a Global Age* 16 (2016).

3

Making Good on the "Primacy of Labor"

A Case Study of Democratic Participation in a Pioneering American Cooperative

*Rashmi Dyal-Chand**

The worker cooperative presents a conundrum for community economic development. In theory, it is a business form that seems to match perfectly the ideals and goals of CED. It is one in which workers are the owners – the shareholders – of the business.[1] By placing workers at the top of the hierarchical structure of a business, the worker cooperative ought to serve as a powerful vehicle for empowering individuals in the urban core to control their own access to market participation.[2] Moreover, by reserving for worker-owners the surplus profit of a business, the cooperative

* Professor, Northeastern University School of Law. I am grateful to Tonya Brito and Peter Enrich for comments to this chapter, and to Peter Enrich for sharing the experience of editing this book with me. My research assistants, Andrew Farrington, Brianna Paton, and Jacob Steinmann, provided excellent research assistance, and Elliott Hibbler of the Northeastern Law School Library was once again indispensable to the completion of this project. Finally, I thank my interviewees at HCA and CHCA, and the contributors to this volume, for your time and engagement. I continue to be inspired by your work.

1 Scott L. Cummings, *Community Economic Development as Progressive Politics: Toward a Grassroots Movement for Economic Justice*, 54 STAN. L. REV. 399, 474 (2001); Priya Baskaran, *Introduction to Worker Cooperatives and Their Role in the Changing Economy*, 24 J. AFFORDABLE HOUSING AND COMMUNITY DEV. L. 355 (2015); Sara Tonnesen, *Stronger Together: Worker Cooperatives as a Community Economic Development Strategy*, 20 GEO. J. POVERTY L. & POL'Y 187, 194 (2012); Gowri J. Krishna, *Worker Cooperative Creation as Progressive Lawyering? Moving Beyond the One-Person, One-Vote Floor*, 34 BERKELEY J. EMP. & LAB. L. 65, 84 (2013) ("The democratic foundation of a cooperative enables members to exercise democratic control and engage in democratic decision-making, leading to greater confidence in one's self and, in turn, to a greater potential for action at the collective level.").

2 Carmen Huertas-Noble, *Promoting Worker-Owned Cooperatives as a CED Empowerment Strategy: A Case Study of Colors and Lawyering in Support of Participatory Decision-Making and Meaningful Social Change*, 17 CLINICAL L. REV. 255, 267 (2010) (Empowerment is defined as "a collective, participatory process that redistributes power and wealth and enables communities and their individual members to gain more control over the forces that affect their lives." However, the meaning of empowerment has been "diminished by depoliticizing and reducing its meaning to individual efficiency."); Peter Molk, *The Puzzling Lack of Cooperatives*, 88 TUL. L. REV. 899, 918 (2014) (Worker ownership offers "improved employee productivity, avoidance of opportunism associated with employee lock-in, less strategic behavior in bargaining

should be an efficient mechanism for poverty alleviation.[3] The key to accomplishing these goals is democratic participation by the workers in the business: The workers own and control the business and consequently their economic destiny. However, the sheer paucity of worker cooperatives in the urban cores signals the difficulty of converting theory to practice.[4] For reasons that remain under-analyzed, and thus elusive, worker cooperatives are relatively uncommon in American urban cores. Those that do exist typically are small and undercapitalized. Repeated attempts to grow and replicate them have generally foundered.[5]

This state of affairs is particularly puzzling given the proliferation in the United States of consumer cooperatives, such as local food coops, where the ultimate buyers of the products or services are the owners of the business.[6] The relative success of consumer cooperatives suggests that there is no categorical reason why cooperatives should not be able to succeed in American markets. Indeed, in the last two decades, there have been indicia of successful experimentation in the development of robust American worker cooperatives as well. Thus, it is particularly useful today to return to a meticulous examination of worker cooperatives as a model for future efforts at poverty alleviation and economic development in the urban core.

This chapter examines a pioneering example of a worker cooperative in Philadelphia for just this purpose. In particular, my study seeks a deeper understanding of a threshold assumption that is often made about worker cooperatives. Both in the theory and the practice of cooperative formation and development, it is regularly assumed that worker cooperatives must be managed by the workers themselves in order to achieve the eminent goal of democratic participation within the cooperative. As a result, worker cooperatives are often by default formed as worker-managed cooperatives in which workers are both the owners of the business and the exclusive decision makers about the strategic direction – and the day-to-day operation – of the business. The purpose of my case study is to question this assumption. I examine a cooperative that is described in the literature as "professionally managed," rather

[between management and employees], better communication of employee preferences and reduction in worker alienation.").

3 Carmen Huertas-Noble, *Worker-Owned and Unionized Worker-Owned Cooperatives: Two Tools to Address Income Inequality*, 22 Clinical L. Rev. 325, 342 (2016) (Worker cooperatives are a way to address income inequality because the structure is based on the principle of "payment solidarity which means 'sufficient and fair pay for work as a basic principle of its management'"); Baskaran, *supra*, Note 1, at 365 (Worker cooperatives offer low-income populations "an opportunity for stable employment, wealth retention and better working conditions").

4 Elaine W. Wilson, *Cooperatives: The First Social Enterprise*, 66 DePaul L. Rev. 1013, 1020 (2017) (noting that success in United States cooperatives has been mostly in the field of agriculture).

5 Ariana R. Levinson, *Founding Worker Cooperatives: Social Movement Theory and the Law*, 14 Nev. L.J. 322, 354 (2014).

6 The largest consumer coop in the US is REI. Eric H. Franklin, A *Rational Approach to Business Entity Choice*, 64 Kan. L. Rev. 573, 622–62 (2016).

than worker managed, in order to ascertain whether, to what extent, and in what forms democratic participation exists in such a cooperative.

In the first section, I examine the issue of democratic participation as described in the literature on cooperatives, and I explain my choice of case. In the second section, I provide a report about my case. I begin with a methodological discussion and then continue with a description of the forms of democratic participation apparent in this cooperative, the issues that were most saliently the subject of such participation, and the value of democratic participation to the workers and to the business. In the final section of this chapter, I analyze what could be learned from this case study about democratic participation in and through a worker cooperative.

WORKER COOPERATIVES: WHAT QUESTIONS DO WE STILL NEED ANSWERED?

As David Ellerman describes in his Harvard Business School case study of the venerable Mondragon network of cooperatives in Spain:

> A worker cooperative could be theoretically defined as a firm where the membership rights are personal rights attached to the functional role of working in the firm. Then the firm is an industrial democracy in analogy with a political democracy where the voting and other citizenship rights are personal rights attached to the functional role of residing in the community. The assignment of the membership rights to labor follows from the primacy of labor among the factors of production. The primacy of labor implies that labor shall not have the role of a hired factor; labor shall hire capital. Workers should always be the members of the firm, not the employees of the firm, and the net return (after a payment for the other factors) should be a return to labor.[7]

In summarizing the scholarship and practice of the community economic development movement, James Rowan and I have claimed that the twin goals of CED are poverty alleviation and local economic development. We have also claimed that the CED movement has sought to achieve these goals for several decades by prioritizing (and investing vast financial and other resources in) small business development by low-income, urban core individuals.[8] If we take these two claims as our starting point, then it is patently obvious why the worker cooperative structure should be such a powerful tool for CED.[9] As Ellerman describes, the worker cooperative

7 David P. Ellerman, *The Mondragon Cooperative Movement* at 10, Harvard Business School Case Study, www.ellerman.org/wp-content/uploads/2012/12/Mondragon-HBS-Case.CV.pdf.

8 Rashmi Dyal-Chand & James V. Rowan, *Developing Capabilities, Not Entrepreneurs: A New Theory for Community Economic Development*, 42 Hofstra L. Rev. 839 (2013).

9 Scott L. Cummings, *Developing Cooperatives as a Job Creation Strategy for Low-Income Workers*, 25 N.Y.U. Rev. L. & Soc. Change 181, 185 (1999); Huertas-Noble, *supra* Note 2, at 266 ("Worker-owned cooperatives can foster two essential goals of empowerment-centered CED: 1) promoting individual efficiency through meaningful job creation and 2) promoting

embeds in its structure the "primacy" of the workers' success and well-being. In a context emerging from the brutalities of white flight, disinvestment in the urban cores, and reallocation of resources to the suburbs, this form of entity should serve to prioritize the retention of resources, opportunity, and wealth in the urban cores. It should be a means for workers to control the development of businesses in such a way as to be responsive to local market needs and also to provide a steady source of income to the workers. Because they can control all the important decisions about business development and growth, worker-owners in coops should be able to learn all they need to control their economic circumstances.[10]

But these theoretical arguments remain relatively untested. This is not for lack of trying. Many CED organizations have attempted to develop and sustain worker cooperatives in a broad range of business sectors in urban cores across the United States.[11] But in the end, many of these businesses fail. In other cases, the proprietors of these businesses default to more traditional forms of business, where ownership is separated from employment. In many cases, it appears that they do so because they perceive the risk of failure to be greater for a cooperative than for these other business forms. For some untested set of reasons, the assumption appears to be that the employees of a business cannot or do not make the best decisions for its ongoing sustainability and success.[12] Thus, the failure of many worker cooperatives – and

collective empowerment by keeping jobs, income and profits within the community and serving as a space for community organizing that enables cooperative members to participate in the larger economic justice movement."); Alicia Alvarez, *Lawyers, Organizers, and Workers: Collaboration and Conflict in Worker Cooperative Development*, 24 GEO. J. POVERTY L. & POL'Y 353, 353 (2017) ("Worker cooperatives fit into a vision of community economic development that looks to create stable and quality jobs, foster opportunities for personal advancement, establish grounded and credible institutions, and drive change in distressed areas and economic sectors.").

[10] Huertas-Noble, *supra* Note 2, at 266 (The participatory process of worker owned cooperatives "redistributes power and wealth and enables communities and their individual members to gain more control over the forces that affect their lives.").

[11] Attempts at worker-owned cooperatives can be found as early as the mid-nineteenth century. Steve Leikin, *The Cooperative Coopers of Minneapolis*, 57 MINNESOTA HISTORY 386, 366–405 (Winter, 2001/2002). The pressures of the depression caused several groups to turn to cooperative structures in an attempt to alleviate some of the economic difficulties experienced in both urban and rural environments. *See* Thomas J. Kriger, *A Very Unusual Partnership: The Consumer-Farmer Milk Cooperative in New York City*, 1938–1971, 80 NEW YORK HISTORY, 305, 305–32 (July 1999). *See also* Laura Renata Martin, *"California's Unemployed Feed Themselves": Conservative Intervention in the Los Angeles Cooperative Movement*, 1931–1934, 82 PACIFIC HISTORICAL REVIEW, 33, 33–62 (Feb. 1, 2013). Many of these attempts were met with resistance from established business structures, government actors, or both.

[12] G. Mitu Gulati et al, *Critical Race Studies: When a Workers' Cooperative Works: The Case of Kerala Dinesh Beedi*, 49 UCLA L. REV. 1417, 1422–27 (2002) (listing some of the reasons why cooperatives are considered unworkable: "workers are inadequately diversified," "workers are bad bosses," "workers will be locked in and there will be no share-market discipline," "workers will vote for inefficient compensation systems," "workers will have heterogeneous goals, which will lead to inefficient decisionmaking," "workers face higher barriers to raising financial capital," and "workers are likely to shirk and will not provide adequate monitoring"). Sauser

equally, their lack of proliferation as a business form – suggests that in American urban cores, the theoretical virtues of worker cooperatives are more aspirational than pragmatic. It is not clear exactly what aspects of the theory are supported by practice. It also appears from the many and varied attempts that each of the assumptions about the virtues of worker cooperatives is quite broad, and that the devil of successful cooperative development may well be in the details.

Consequently, both theoretical and pragmatic questions about the benefits and achievability of worker cooperatives still abound. For example, are some business sectors more conducive to the development of successful worker cooperatives? If so, what are the features of those sectors that contribute to success? Do cooperatives consistently fall prey to certain identifiable risks in business development, such as the failure to reinvest profits in the business? How, if at all, do different management structures contribute to ongoing success or failure for cooperatives? These are important questions to address, and empirical examinations ought to go a long way in answering them and in bridging the gap between theory and practice.

In this chapter, I examine a small subset of these questions. The focus of my analysis is on the particular set of questions pertaining to the claimed virtue of democratic participation that worker cooperatives embody. If, as Ellerman claims, worker cooperatives are "an industrial democracy in analogy with a political democracy," then what value does such democratic participation add, and for whom? Does it benefit the workers, and if so how? Does it benefit the business, and if so how? Perhaps most basically, what exactly does democratic participation mean in a cooperative business setting? Are there some issues that are more appropriately or fruitfully the subject of democratic decision-making, and if so, what might those be? Finally, how might the forms of democratic participation that are achieved in successful worker cooperatives in American urban cores contribute to the goals and ideals of CED? In particular, might there be a connection between the successful practice of democratic participation in American worker cooperatives and the ultimate challenge of supporting the proliferation of urban American worker cooperatives?

These, then, are the research questions that I analyze in this chapter. My goal is to begin to develop some answers by looking at a single, pioneering case. In the next section of this chapter, I will detail my reasons for choosing this particular case. But at the outset here, it is important to describe one foundational choice that I made in

suggests seven patterns or problems that often lead to the demise or decline of worker cooperatives. William I. Sauser, Jr., *Sustaining Employee Owned Companies: Seven Recommendations*, 84 J. Business Ethics, 151–64 (Jan. 2009); *see also* Molk, *supra* Note 2, at 905. The Burley design cooperative provides a paradigmatic example of this sort of decline. Joel Schoening, *The Rise and Fall of Burley Design Cooperative*, 111 Oregon Historical Q., 312, 312–41 (Fall 2010).

selecting the case because it fundamentally narrows and shapes my research questions. As I will describe in more detail, the cooperative that I study here has since its inception been "professionally managed," as distinguished from "worker-managed." This means that the workers who are responsible for producing the goods or providing the services to the business's consumers do not make the major operational and strategic decisions for the business. Instead, such decisions are made by so-called "professional managers," who bring either educational background, management experience, or both to their work as managers of the cooperative. As is true in my case study, such managers regularly also have ownership shares in the cooperative, and they are hired by – and answerable to – a board of directors or similar entity that is at least equally composed of "non-management" workers. But their jobs at the cooperative are to serve as "managers," rather than as "laborers" whose primary job is to make the products or services sold by the business.

This distinguishes my choice of case study from many, probably the majority, of American urban worker cooperatives, which are "worker-managed," meaning that workers in the cooperative have the *dual role* both of providing the labor for producing the goods or services *and* the management required to run the cooperative.

If, however, we were to review a list of the largest American urban worker cooperatives, defined by number of employees, my choice of a professionally managed cooperative as a case would be quite representative of that list.[13] Filtering American urban cooperatives by size reveals that professionally managed cooperatives appear to be more likely to grow, survive, and succeed over the long term in American urban cores than their worker-managed counterparts. Despite this reality, it appears that many legal experts and scholars supporting the development of cooperatives conflate the ideal of worker *ownership* with the imperative of worker *management*. Indeed, this conflation may well result from their assumption that

[13] Although there is a paucity of statistical data available on urban worker cooperatives, my research assistants and I cross-checked a number of lists of the largest cooperatives, as measured by the number of employees. We found the list maintained by the Democracy at Work Institute, available at http://becomingemployeeowned.org/learn/, to be most useful for our purposes. We then made phone calls to each of the largest fifteen cooperatives on that list to ask them whether their top managers also participated in making or providing the goods or services sold by their businesses. The largest cooperative on the list is Cooperative Home Care Associates, with 1,900 employees. The second and third largest, The Green Taxi Cooperative in Denver and the Taxi Drivers Association of Austin, have 800 and 500 employees, respectively. The next 5 largest cooperatives on the list have between 220 and 260 employees. The remaining cooperatives on the list of the twenty largest cooperatives have between 44 and 76 employees. According to our research, eight of the ten largest cooperatives are professionally managed. We do not have definitive enough information to be able to say whether the remaining two on the list of top ten largest coops are professionally managed. Interestingly, all but one of the remaining cooperatives that we researched (namely the tenth through fifteenth largest), are worker managed. Of this latter group, only one cooperative has more than 100 employees.

worker management is the ideal form of democratic participation that derives from the cooperative form.[14]

My case study is designed to question this narrow, but crucial, assumption. By examining forms of democratic participation in a highly successful, professionally managed cooperative, I seek to ascertain the value of democratic participation within a worker cooperative that is not managed by its workers. Thus, the important narrower questions that this study begins to answer are these. What is the nature and value of democratic participation in professionally managed worker cooperatives? Moreover, assuming that professionally managed cooperatives have a better chance of growth and success than worker-managed cooperatives, what can this case study teach us about how best to develop democratic participation in such settings?

At the same time, it is clear that my choice of a professionally managed cooperative has limited my ability to gather information about certain forms of democratic participation. The most obvious form that I cannot study via this case is participation by worker-owners in decision making relating to the process of starting up a cooperative. In the case described here, even though the very first group of workers had the opportunity to become owners, the cooperative was operational by the time they received that opportunity. It had acquired financing, a business location, a business plan, and the other critical pieces of starting up, thanks to the work of professional managers. More broadly, this case study does not provide details about the particular nature of democratic participation by worker-owners who are the exclusive day-to-day managers of a cooperative. As a result of this choice, this case study cannot claim to answer the question of what *all* the possible forms of democratic participation in worker cooperatives might be. Nor can it provide information about the nature, advantages, and disadvantages of some of those forms. We cannot learn much from this study about forms of democratic participation that are unique to *worker-managed* cooperatives.

WORKER DEMOCRACY AT HOME CARE ASSOCIATES: FORMS, SUBSTANCE, AND VALUES

Methodology and Features of the Case

As I have described, there is an odd disconnect between the theoretical allure of worker cooperatives and their practical implementation. Ellerman and others have

14 Thus, it is fairly typical to see statements in the literature such as the following: "[C]ooperatives provide domestic workers with opportunities to acquire and advance their job skills. In taking on the responsibility of owning and running a business, the workers necessarily commit themselves to continuing self-education," which encourages development of skills such as "accounting, marketing, sales, computer literacy, legal skills, negotiation, and management." Reyna R. Hayashi, *Empowering Domestic Workers through Law and Organizing Initiatives*, 9 Seattle J. Soc. Just. 487, 521 (2010).

performed sophisticated economic modeling for American cooperatives.[15] Worker cooperatives have also been the subject of theoretical analyses grounded in political economy and social theory.[16] What is needed is an examination of how, and how much of, the theory of worker cooperatives is put into practice. For such a purpose, a qualitative methodology seems ideal.

Moreover, from the range of qualitative methodological options, a case study is an appropriate beginning point. By interviewing participants in a worker cooperative, it should be possible to gain a more intimate understanding of what democratic participation looks like in an urban American cooperative, how it is valued, and by whom. A case study also has the virtue of grounding the answers to these questions in the perspectives of the participants. The participants define the basic terms of the inquiry, such as "participation," "decision-making," and "control." They articulate, and thus define, the value of such participation. They articulate its connection, if any, to their understanding of business success. Such a methodological approach also may be useful in refuting, or at least questioning, some of the assumptions that are made in purely theoretical analyses of worker cooperatives. If democratic participation, at least in some forms, simply has no effect in empowering individual workers, then that is an important challenge to a key theoretical claim about worker cooperatives.

The drawbacks of this methodological approach are in many respects the flip side of the benefits. The most significant questions raised by this approach are those of representativeness. Here it is important simply to acknowledge that a single case can only teach so much about the ubiquity of the lessons learned from it. In size, business sector, and even business structure, my chosen case does share similarities to most of the ten largest worker cooperatives. For example, seven of the ten largest cooperatives are service-providing cooperatives that require little upfront investment in heavy equipment or capital. However, it will be important to use other empirical methods to test representativeness. For example, it ought to be fruitful to use my analysis of an ideal or pioneer case to further analyze issues of democratic participation by means of comparative case study analysis, ethnographic research, and ultimately perhaps also quantitative research. Comparing cases can allow researchers to begin to identify the range of forms of democratic participation and values that flow therefrom. Ethnographic study can supplement the perspectives of participant workers with in-depth observations by the researchers, thereby providing additional lenses on the definitions used and the answers obtained. Finally, quantitative

[15] *See, e.g.*, David Ellerman, *Worker Cooperatives as Based on First Principles*, 5 J. Entrepreneurial and Organizational Diversity 20 (2016); *Handbook of Economic Organization: Integrating Economic and Organization Theory* (Anna Grandori ed. 2013).

[16] *See e.g.*, Michael Bull & Rory Ridley-Duff, *Social Enterprise as a Socially Rational Business*, 14 Int'l J. Entrepreneurial Behavior & Research 291 (2008); Samuel Bowles & Herbert Gintis, *A Political and Economic Case for the Democratic Enterprise*, 9 Economics & Philosophy 75 (1993).

analysis layered on these qualitative inquiries can begin to provide information about the ubiquity of the observed forms of democratic participation.

Home Care Associates in Philadelphia, Pennsylvania (HCA) is a worker cooperative with over 200 employees, the majority of whom are women of color. Founded in 1993, HCA is one of the largest worker cooperatives in the United States. Approximately 30 percent of its employees are owners.[17] It is the third-largest women-owned business in Philadelphia.[18] HCA's business is to provide home health care and other long-term health services to individuals in the Philadelphia metropolitan area. Many of the consumers whom it serves are low-income individuals. HCA in fact has a dual mission: in addition to providing quality home health care to those in need, HCA also has the mission of providing long-term and livable jobs to local, low-income residents.

HCA is part of a larger network of organizations that includes Cooperative Home Care Associates (CHCA) in the Bronx, which is the largest worker cooperative in the United States with more than 2,000 employees, most of whom are owners. The network also includes Paraprofessional Healthcare Institute (PHI), a nonprofit that provides training for home health care workers, consulting services to the home health care industry, and research and policy development in the areas of eldercare and disability services.

I chose HCA as the subject of my analysis of democratic participation in worker cooperatives for several reasons, including its affiliation with CHCA and PHI. This affiliation provides a natural research platform for comparing the experiences of workers at HCA and its sister cooperative, CHCA. For example, while both HCA and CHCA have high percentages of worker-owners, CHCA's workers are also unionized. HCA's are not. Thus, although I am focusing on a single case, my interviews of workers in both of these affiliated cooperatives allow for some level of comparison between the two.

HCA has been in existence for twenty-five years, and it has weathered both ordinary and extraordinary changes in the marketplace for health care services. During that time, HCA has grown to be one of the largest worker cooperatives in the United States, though it has not grown as astonishingly large as its affiliate CHCA. This history allows for a meaningful level of analysis of the relationship between democratic participation by employees and business survival and growth. HCA appears to have a fairly typical trajectory for a successful business in its field. Finally, HCA is located in a fairly typical urban area, and the vast majority of its workers are people of color from urban cores with relatively low incomes compared to the area median. These are exactly the characteristics of

[17] Interview with Jerilyn Dressler, Controller, Your Part-Time Controller LLC (Mar. 23, 2017).

[18] Sharon Oliver, *The Largest Women-Owned Businesses, Ranked by Total Local Employment*, Philadelphia Bus. J., June 19, 2013.

the individuals and communities that the community economic development movement seeks to support.

The primary data source for my analysis is a set of twenty-three semi-structured interviews of individuals who participate in the collaborative business network of which HCA is a part. Within this network, I interviewed individuals employed at different levels, including both "management" and "workers." I interviewed individuals involved in what I describe as "intermediary" organizations that facilitate sharing within this network as well as those who work in the for-profit businesses in the network. The focus of my analysis in this chapter is a set of eleven interviews of both workers and managers at HCA. In addition to the interviews, I relied on secondary sources, including books, newspaper and academic articles, and documents internal to HCA and the broader network in which it functions. My original purpose in conducting interviews at HCA and its affiliates was for a book-length comparative examination of three cases exemplifying what I describe as "collaborative capitalism."[19] In the course of conducting and coding those interviews, I began to discern a robust commentary on the theme of democratic participation. For the purpose of this chapter, I recoded the interviews with HCA and its affiliates in order to explore this theme more fully.[20]

Democratic Participation at HCA

The purpose of this section is to describe the forms of democratic participation that exist at HCA. It is to examine the issues that are most frequently or saliently the subject of democratic decision-making. Finally, it is to examine the value of such participation, both for the workers at HCA and for the business enterprise as a whole. The main focus of this report is on the subjective perspectives of my interviewees. In the latter part of my interview questionnaire, I included a set of questions about the interviewees' knowledge of and participation in the cooperative aspects of the business. Because my interviews were semi-structured, however, I was able to reorganize the interviews in response to the flow of the conversation with my interviewees. In a number of my interviews, the interviewees raised the subject earlier. Often, they did so in response to my early and open-ended questions about whether they liked their jobs. In addition to commenting on the value of being in a cooperative business, interviewees answered questions about job satisfaction with comments about having a voice, knowing more about the business than in other jobs they had had, running and controlling more aspects of the business, and being more connected to the business.

[19] Rashmi Dyal-Chand, *Collaborative Capitalism in American Cities: Reforming Urban Market Regulations* (2018).

[20] For a description of my methodology for the book, *see id.* in the appendix.

Forms of Democratic Participation

As is exemplified by Ellerman's analysis of worker cooperatives, the literature identifies the most salient form of democratic participation in such businesses as being the very institution of worker-ownership.[21] By replacing equity investors (i.e., the providers of "capital") with workers (i.e., "labor") in the hierarchy of decision making and control, the worker cooperative reserves the most momentous business decisions for worker-owners. My interviews certainly confirmed the subjective relevance of worker-ownership as a key form of democratic participation. But as I will describe in this section, when they answered questions about whether they liked their jobs and why, both workers and managers at HCA and its affiliate CHCA identified at least two other organizational practices that they articulated as important means of giving workers control and decision-making power at work.

Beginning with the most traditional form, that of worker-ownership, while the institution of ownership appears to have some value as an abstract idea, its real power for worker-owners at HCA lies in the formality of annual and regular meetings of the worker-owners and in the equal representation of workers and management at the board level. As Ronnette Perkins, who began at HCA as a home health aide and now is the human resources director, described:

> If the company makes money . . . you know, we did well this year, and then we have an excess of x amount of dollars, we actually vote on how we're going to use that money. If it's to have better health insurance, if we take it out in a dividend . . . so I just really love it about the company. As well as whenever there's . . . any major hiring going on, we had a say in who was being hired into our company. So that person would be approved by the Board of Directors, then they would have a committee of Home Care Associates employees who they had to also impress . . . [The board is] always an even ratio of office staff and home health aides.[22]

HCA's part-time controller, Jerilyn Dressler, provided a similar picture:

> About half of the board members are worker-owners. Many of them have had a good deal of longevity with the company, so they've seen ups and downs, and they understand decisions that are being made. I think that the board meetings are very productive, because they're honest, transparent, and the worker-owners ask great questions. Part of my job in talking about the finances is making it understandable to the worker-owners. I use data visualizations such as charts and graphs to present the results. I can then explain to them why the results happened, what we propose to do, and obtain their input regarding the plan of action.[23]

[21] Linda D. Phillips, *Worker Cooperatives: Their Time Has Arrived*, 40 Colo. Law. 33, 34 (2011); Baskaran, *supra* Note 1.

[22] Interview with Ronnette Perkins, Human Resources Director, Home Care Associates (Mar. 23, 2017).

[23] Dressler Interview. Dressler is HCA's part-time controller, who is a consultant to HCA and an employee of an agency that provides part-time controllers mostly to nonprofit organizations in the area. These views are clearly shared by workers at HCA's sister cooperative in New York.

Participation and representation on the board of HCA clearly has more than symbolic importance for HCA workers, but it is not the only form of democratic participation that they identified. My interviewees also identified participation in committees as an equally – perhaps even more – important form of democratic participation. Consider this description by Ronnette Perkins:

> [There] was a political activation group that . . . would march down on D.C. and try to get laws passed in regards to home health aides, and home health care, and the pay rate. There was what we call the happiness committee that was in charge of company morale. So what we did was through mostly birthday parties, to acknowledge everyone's birthdays, we would send out birthday cards, and letters of acknowledgment, and kudos, and help with the newsletter . . . We would do these summer events maybe at an amusement park, or a recreational park, and just have a huge picnic, and everybody comes together and has a good time. And we also do a winter event, and, and it's done around the holidays, where we would have a holiday party, and if there was a dividend to be received, we would pass that out at that party.
>
> And then there was another committee: if there were any changes that you felt needed to be made within the company in regards to your benefits, we've always had an open forum, with a drop box for . . . your concerns, because people don't always want to come forth with those things. So you can just put it in the box, and we would address it. So say for instance I pulled something out of the [drop] box, and it stated something as simple as they're concerned about the safety in the bathroom, because the bathroom is entered with a key. But people would leave the key hanging in the door. Then, we would just put it in the newsletter, that we did receive this complaint, and it was a concern of some of our employees, and if you wouldn't mind just, when you enter the bathroom, to not leave the key in the door because it was a safety hazard.
>
> We have the safety committee, where we go around, and we make sure the office is safe, and in order, you know, as to not cause workers' compensation issues while you're in here. We have peer mentors . . . senior home health aides, who've been around for a long time, and they had the position of going out and helping the [newer] ones in the home.[24]

Both at HCA and CHCA (its sister cooperative in New York), workers emphasized the value of committees and committee participation. They commented on the significance of a business structure that allows them to flexibly create and participate in committees that directly respond to the issues they raise and about which they are

According to one long-time worker-owner: "I'm a board member and I'm on the finance committee also. Lot of things I didn't know about the finances I know. I know when we're making money, when we're not making money, and everything." Interview with Deborah O'Bryant, Home Health Aide, CHCA (June 23, 2017).

[24] Perkins Interview.

most concerned.[25] They described a process of self-growth through committee participation.[26] And they emphasized the value of committees as a means of engaging with the larger enterprise and business mission.[27]

Finally, workers at both HCA and CHCA described a third form of participation that has both formal and informal manifestations. It is the ability regularly to see and talk face-to-face with the senior leadership of the business. This access is not just reserved for workers who are board or committee members. Rather, as home health aide Angelique Montgomery's comments suggest, it is baked into the company culture and everyday practices:

> [F]rom the jobs I've had and now – the other jobs, you never got to see the higher-up person. You're only seeing like the shift manager, who actually ran the shift … Here, it's like I see the president, you know. When I'm in the office, she asks how it's going … how's it out there, [as] opposed to working for a company where you don't really know who actually the president is, or the CEO of the company. So I think [it's] better, yeah. It's definitely a difference working with this company.[28]

Home health attendant Stephanie Whitehead commented: "[Karen Kulp, the CEO of HCA] actually did my interview. I don't know if she remembered. Well, she actually did my interview."[29] HCA's Jane Dixon connected this kind of interaction with a broader set of opportunities for workers to represent the business:

> Karen [Kulp] goes somewhere, like she went to Hong Kong, she took Terrell, and she took Tatia. And … when she went … to meet President Barak [Obama], she took some of the aides with her. So, that was awesome. … Most companies don't do that.[30]

CHCA (HCA's affiliate in New York) supplements this informal structure with a formal open-door policy for all managers:

> The other thing … and I think it's probably one of the most effective mechanisms that we have in terms of involvement, is what we call our open-door policy. Any worker can come at any time during the day to see anybody that they want, about anything that they want. They don't need an appointment, and they'll be able, maybe not ten minutes after they walk in, it may take twenty minutes. But they'll

25 Perkins Interview; O'Bryant Interview; Interview with Michelle Smith, Home Health Aide, CHCA (May 5, 2016) (I have used a pseudonym for this interviewee).

26 O'Bryant Interview; Smith Interview.

27 O'Bryant Interview; Smith Interview; Perkins Interview.

28 Interview with Angelique Montgomery, Home Care Aide, Home Care Associates (Mar. 23, 2017). Workers at CHCA described similar experiences. O'Bryant Interview; Smith Interview.

29 Interview with Stephanie Whitehead, Home Care Attendant, Home Care Associates (Mar. 23, 2017).

30 Interview with Jane Dixon, Training Coordinator, Home Care Associates (Mar. 23, 2017).

> have the opportunity to voice their concern. Does everybody do that? Absolutely not. Do ten people every week do it? Yeah.[31]

As home health aide Michelle Smith described, this kind of accessibility makes an enormous difference to workers: "To know that [the President] is accessible like that, yeah, that knocks me out. Matter of fact, it's not just him. It's a lot of the staff here. A lot of the administrators."[32]

Substance: What Do Workers Wish to Control?

As these comments about forms of democratic participation reveal, worker-owners at HCA have knowledge and decision-making voice over a relatively broad range of issues. At the board level, of course, they vote on the most significant business decisions. But the committee structure and open-door company culture allows workers to be involved in many other aspects of business operations. The variety of participatory forms appears to achieve a breadth of involvement that covers many issues, large and small. Nevertheless, it is telling to note which issues are the most frequently described by interviewees as important topics of democratic decision making and participation – and also which issues are not described as critical areas of democratic control.

Easily, the three most prioritized areas of democratic control as expressed by both workers and managers at HCA (and also CHCA) are decisions about the distribution of dividends, the choice and allocation of health and other employment benefits, and work conditions and worker safety. On the subject of dividends, home health attendant Stephanie Whitehead summarized the feelings of many of my interviewees when she commented on the value of cooperative ownership:

> I think it's a good investment. I really think it's a good investment. Like at the end of the year they get incentives. So that might be just at the time when you need that money ... You know, from the profits and stuff like that. So how many of us out here nowadays can actually say, "My job did this," you know, "My job helped me do this. My job helped me do that." So I think it's cool. I think it's real cool.[33]

In addition to emphasizing the importance of dividends, interviewees across the board also commented extensively about the excellent benefits they receive, as well as the opportunity to decide what benefits should be available to employees and how to ensure access to those benefits. Both workers and managers at HCA and CHCA articulated a connection between quality employment, employee support, democratic control, and employment benefits. At the top of the list of important benefits at HCA are health benefits and the monthly pass for riding on public transportation. In addition, workers value the banking access to a local credit union (by means of

[31] Interview with Eric Jensen (May 4, 2016). I have used a pseudonym for this interviewee.

[32] Smith Interview.

[33] Whitehead Interview.

direct deposit and other services), the 401K, and a range of workshops and trainings that have been provided over the years for such things as budgeting, buying a home, and continuing education.[34] This praise also came from workers who have thus far chosen not to become owners:

> Best thing about this job is the benefits that come with it. That's the best thing about this job. It does have benefits, and the fact that it has free training. Not every company has free training. You have to pay. And transportation . . . we get monthly trans passes every month, to make sure we get to work. That's a lot . . . a lot of companies [are] not offering that. So, yes . . . that's it right there.[35]

Finally, as Ronnette Perkins's description of the committees at HCA made clear, interviewees value the ability to control work conditions. Through both formal and informal means, worker-owners participate extensively in increasing and ensuring safety, flexibility, autonomy, and support at work. A number of interviewees talked about the simple but striking value of a workplace that provides iced water and snacks to employees when they go to HCA's office to drop off their time sheets.[36] Many appreciated the flexibility shown by the manager who schedules their shifts. Home health aide Angelique Montgomery commented: "Home Care [Associates] has worked with me a lot . . . I had knee surgery three years ago, where I was out for three months. You know, they say you have a certain amount of time out, but I needed one extra week off to complete my physical therapy and they extended that week."[37] Several interviewees also commented on the importance of being able to talk to any member of the leadership about safety and other conditions at work.[38]

Relatedly, across the board, workers connected the high quality of the training they received with the high quality of their work conditions, and even to their personal development: "[T]he one part of the training that sticks out for me the most . . . is what they call the four Ps [paraphrasing and repeating, pulling back, presenting options, and passing it on]. . . I use them in my everyday life, with coping with people and decisions."[39] "I became a changed person. . . [T]his job keeps me positive. . . I never, ever wanted to buy a house in my life . . . [Now] I'm about to go through a first-time buyer's program . . . I matured . . . I'm saving money now."[40] "It helps you to have patience. It helps you with just how to deal with people in general."[41] "It made me more sensitive, and I teach my kids to be like that."[42]

[34] Montgomery Interview; Whitehead Interview; Interview with Recanell Carroll, Home Care Aide, Home Care Associates (Mar. 23, 2017).
[35] Carroll Interview.
[36] Dixon Interview.
[37] Montgomery Interview.
[38] Whitehead Interview; O'Bryant Interview; Smith Interview.
[39] Montgomery Interview.
[40] Whitehead Interview.
[41] Carroll Interview.
[42] Interview with Clara Calvo, Home Health Aide, CHCA (June 23, 2017).

The Importance of Democratic Participation to Individual Workers

When describing the value of working in a cooperative, my interviewees often expressed an abstract, though still very real, sense that worker-ownership somehow sets the job apart and makes it "better." Perkins's comments are an excellent example:

> I became a worker owner as soon as I was eligible. So that was many moons ago ... after my probation period, so it was in 1995, probably in December of 1995, I became a worker owner. I felt like that was one of the things that this job offered that was really appealing to me, that helped to draw me in ... That was one of the selling factors, the fact that you could own part of this company while you were here, and had a say in the way that the company was developed and shaped. I thought that was just totally awesome.[43]

Often, either as a result of my probing or of their own initiative, interviewees supplemented these more abstract comments with a very specific set of benefits they perceive from such participation. Most of those who discussed the value of ownership emphasized the financial investment.[44] As Dixon described, "You know there's a lot of home health agencies out there. And we have this cushion ... we bought up a share ... [I]t can be distributed [to] the workers-owners [as] dividends."[45] Even though dividends are typically small (and indeed they have been unavailable at CHCA for the last few years), workers clearly expressed both the financial advantage of ownership – and also the symbolic value and connection that dividends provide.

Most interviewees also emphasized the personal significance to them of participating in decision making for the company.[46] Indeed, Dixon concluded her commentary about the benefit of dividends by saying that even though the workers could have received dividends last year, they "chose to put it back into the company, so we can [have] jobs."[47] Dixon also described a board decision to provide pay for hours that might qualify as "overtime."[48] Similarly, Perkins commented that workers-owners have voted to improve employment benefits rather than taking dividends.[49] Interviewees regularly made these comments in the context of discussing job

43 Perkins Interview.

44 Montgomery Interview; Perkins Interview.

45 Dixon Interview.

46 Montgomery Interview; Smith Interview; Perkins Interview. Interview with Margarita Pillot, Home Health Aide, CHCA (June 23, 2017) (Pillot is an interesting example of a worker at CHCA who chose to be a union representative rather than joining the board of CHCA. For her, these two options provided many of the same advantages.).

47 Dixon Interview.

48 Dixon Interview.

49 Perkins Interview.

satisfaction and a feeling of connection to the business's mission, and to the collective well-being of the business and its workers.

Many also articulated the more abstract – but as they described, extraordinary – value of having a voice in making the company a better business and a better workplace. For example, home health attendant Stephanie Whitehead commented:

> You get to make the different decisions . . . to better the company. . . I think it's cool because a lot of women work here . . . and [typically] people don't listen to us too much.[50]

Clara Calvo, who has served on CHCA's board for a number of years, stated:

> You get a voice in the agency . . . I was next to the president, next to all the people . . . [A]nd when they ask some question, when I have some question, I can say, "OK." I can raise my hand, and I can say, "no, I [don't] agree with that, and yes, I agree with that." That's the best part . . . I can raise my hand, and they listen, and they respect my idea.[51]

Finally, virtually all of my interviewees at HCA emphasized the personal value of working as part of HCA's family. "[T]hey really make you feel like family, you know . . . They make you feel good, they make you feel like you're part of something. And that's what I like about it . . . [T]hey really pay you some attention, and they really show you a lot of love, and it's kind of needed."[52] "[T]his is home, this is how Home Care Associates is. You come in . . . nobody is on your back . . . Other companies I worked for, they stop you at the door. You couldn't even get a glass of water. Here we got water, food, and we [are] like a family."[53] "[When a relative] passed away, they called, they were asking me, 'How you doing? How you pulling through?' That's . . . love."[54] "[I]t's like a family here . . . When the aides come in, it's like they're coming home, you know. They're embraced, we love to see them. Our whole temperament here is different."[55]

Only a few of my interviewees expressly connected the warm family atmosphere with the cooperative form of the business. This connection was perhaps most poignantly articulated by CHCA's Margarita Pillot: "When you are part of the owners, you feel like you belong to something."[56] Given the small number of comments on this point, it would be premature to draw any definitive correlation. However, it is worth at least raising the question whether this more abstract sense of

[50] Whitehead Interview.
[51] Calvo Interview.
[52] Carroll Interview.
[53] Dixon Interview.
[54] Interview with Nana Nemeiar, Home Care Aide, Home Care Associates (Mar. 23, 2017).
[55] Perkins Interview.
[56] Pillot Interview.

family and belonging flows from the feeling of being represented, and of having a voice in the business's decisions.

The Importance of Democratic Participation to the Business

Both workers and managers at HCA and CHCA also articulated a powerful set of benefits to their companies that they view as flowing at least partly from the cooperative structure. Perhaps the two most important are the related benefits of high quality services and job longevity and stability. As HCA's President, Karen Kulp, stated, "every decision that I make, everything I think about really is around that ... focus ... [W]ithout a quality job, is it going to be quality care?"[57] This mission makes it imperative for HCA to develop an ethic of the highest possible quality of services as compared to the industry standard. This ethic, in turn, prioritizes job longevity, for without it, the turnover of employees could not justify the high investment in training. The result is a very long-term and multifaceted investment in employees.

From the workers' perspective, Ronnette Perkins exemplifies a noteworthy, though not atypical, career path. She described a journey that began with the position of home health aide to continuing her education in the area of human services to becoming the human resources director. Perkins drew a direct connection between the company's cooperative structure and its desire to "look internally" for talent, an approach that ensured continuity in prioritizing the company's mission of "quality care and quality jobs."[58] Jane Dixon described a similar path for herself and her colleague in the training department Terrell Cannon.[59] The result is an astonishingly high level of worker investment in HCA. For example, in the course of describing her intended career path of becoming a registered nurse, which she developed through her work for sixteen years as a home health aide at HCA, Angelique Montgomery stated:

> [B]efore, my other jobs, I worked maybe eight months, not for a long period of time. And then I didn't like the job, and then I would leave ... [B]ut I don't think I would ever leave Home Care Associates completely. I somehow would still find a spot at Home Care, whether it would be dropping down to part time, working on a weekend.[60]

57 Interview with Karen Kulp, President/CEO, Home Care Associates (Mar. 23, 2017).

58 Perkins Interview.

59 Dixon Interview.

60 Montgomery Interview. Denise Clark, who began as a home health aide at CHCA and now holds a supervisory role, commented: "It's the environment that encourages the growth, that opens the door to the opportunities. I think that makes us different from other organizations. I've known people who have left Cooperative seeking other opportunities. But when they went to those other organizations, it was nothing like here. They didn't get the support. They didn't get the additional training. So ultimately they're back at Cooperative." Interview with Denise Clark, Service Delivery Supervisor, Cooperative Home Care Associates (June 23, 2017).

WORKERS, MANAGEMENT, AND DEMOCRACY: HOW DO THEY CONNECT?

My interviews with members of HCA and its affiliate organizations provide a clear – though narrow – picture about the nature and value of democratic participation in an American, urban, professionally managed cooperative. In this section, I analyze the main themes that emerged from the descriptions of democracy as experienced by workers at HCA and its sister cooperative CHCA. As I describe in the first subsection in this section, the key themes that both workers and managers articulated in different ways revolve around the values of control, voice, and power in the workplace. After analyzing the manifestation of these values in my case study, I turn in the remaining sections to the lessons about democracy in the workplace that researchers and practitioners could learn from this case.

Control, Voice, Power – and Scale

If we were to pick a few key words to describe the nature of democratic participation at HCA, it is likely that the list would include a more diffuse set of terms than the literature on worker cooperatives might provide. Words such as "voice," "family," "love," and "belonging" were equally prominent in my interviewees' descriptions as terms such as "control," "decisions," and "success." While my interviewees across the board demonstrated a high level of investment in their workplace and in their work, they did not exclusively – or even often – connect that investment to control of the business or its economic future. Workers clearly value equal representation on the board. At the same time, their expressions of connection and investment are much more multi-faceted in nature.

Perhaps as a result, so are their descriptions of the processes through which those feelings of investment developed. As I recoded the transcripts of my interviews with employees at HCA and CHCA, one of the most surprising connections that emerged was the strong correlation between democratic participation and committee participation. It seems that the committee structure at HCA and CHCA allows for a unique combination of advantages. First, the committees have developed flexibly to respond to the variety of concerns raised *by workers*, and they also have developed as a means of prioritizing those issues. Second, the flexible committee structure allows workers to participate directly in addressing those issues. Flexibility is a critical attribute, because it promotes the institutional reliance on committees as a place for sorting out priorities and assigning individuals who first articulated those priorities a voice in addressing them. At times, workers articulate concerns by means of an anonymous suggestions box located in the common area of HCA. At times, these priorities might first be raised at a board meeting. At times, they might arise during a face-to-face meeting between a worker and a manager meeting in the kitchen or hallway. The committees provide a structure for receiving and addressing these priorities, and, importantly, one that is heavily staffed by the workers.

Third, the committee structure allows the cooperative to address issues in smaller, "bite-sized" pieces. This in turn allows different workers to participate in the committees working on issues that most interest or concern them, or about which they feel they have expertise or wish to develop expertise. No individual worker has to assume – in addition to her own full-time job of home health care – the job of understanding all aspects of the business sufficiently to make important decisions about business operations and direction. Instead, that job is divided and shared both by professional managers and by a board composed equally of workers and managers. As a result of the division of committee work into bite-sized pieces, more workers are able to participate in shared decision-making on issues they have prioritized as important in the first place.

Fourth, the committee structure engenders a great deal of access, allowing workers to reach out to their peers on committees for help with issues. This access is further enhanced by structures such as the anonymous suggestions box. Fifth, the committee structure democratizes transparency. Workers are able to raise issues easily and learn at the most "local" of levels whether and how those issues are being addressed. This function also has been enhanced by such mechanisms as newsletters, and by more traditional cooperative structures such as annual meetings.

The committee structure at HCA teaches us a great deal about some of the assumptions most frequently made in the literature about the value of democratic participation in worker cooperatives. This case study suggests that a committee structure may be one relatively ideal forum for such participation. It gives workers meaningful voice – and meaningful control – over the issues they themselves determine are important for them to control. It allows for collective action and decision-making without imposing an overwhelming level of responsibility and business (and personal) risk-taking. By delegating control over key decisions to the committee level, this structure achieves many of the advantages envisioned by scholars in theorizing about worker-managed cooperatives. It allows for participants to engage in a "direct democracy" at the committee level. But by reserving major decisions about business strategy, direction, and operations to professional managers, and to a board comprised of workers and managers, such a structure removes the risk of making "wrong" or "uninformed" managerial decisions for the business as a whole. In this way, the committee structure may contribute to business growth beyond a size that is manageable for a worker-managed cooperative using a direct democracy model.[61]

[61] *Cf.* Peter Pitegoff, *Worker Ownership in Enron's Wake – Revisiting a Community Development Tactic*, 8 J. SMALL & EMERGING BUS. L. 239, 250 (2004) ("A worker-owned business faces the pressures of any competitive market enterprise, with added risk to worker-owners and with stress to any underlying democratic values.").

The committee structure is also connected to mission investment and job longevity. For example, in the admittedly small set of individual examples I have, it seems strikingly connected to the development of personalized career ladders. Ronnette Perkins, who began as a home health aide and grew into the position of human resources director for HCA, developed her career path partly through her participation in the "happiness committee." Similarly, it appears that Jane Dixon and Terrell Cannon, who are both educators at HCA, were involved in the committee that worked to establish the peer mentorship program at HCA.

Relatedly, the committee structure allows for individual training and growth about the nuts and bolts of business management, while limiting the business risks that flow from such a process. Take the example of Deborah O'Bryant at CHCA, who expressed a strong desire to understand the "financial side" of the business. O'Bryant had not had training or experience with business finance or development. By joining the finance committee at CHCA, she was able to learn about business financing from her peers, in the safety of a structure with more experienced workers and managers, by means of democratic participation, but without the burden of making important business decisions while lacking adequate knowledge or training.

I do not want to suggest here that this case study is one in which democratic participation is defined just as individual "empowerment" or personal development. It is clearly not. These committees have done real work, on real issues, requiring meaningful expertise, and with meaningful results in the lives of their peers. Many of those who participated in committees expressed feelings of being empowered and having a "voice" in the process, but these benefits were by no means claimed as the ultimate or only benefits or outcomes of committee work. However, it also appears to be the case that the committees encapsulate a balance of voice, control over meaningful resources, and the power to make real change on a manageable scale within the business.

Finally, it is important to recognize the connection between the committee structure and the cooperative structure within which it is housed. One lesson that may be tempting to take from this study is that it may be possible to achieve many of the benefits of democratic participation simply by housing a robust committee structure such as HCA's within a traditionally organized (non-cooperative) business. This may or may not be true. My own interpretation of the data from these interviews is that there is an important connection between HCA's committee structure and the institution of worker-ownership. Most obviously, the representation of workers at the highest levels of HCA's governance seems to have contributed to the development of committees so focused on the support of HCA's workers.

"Labor shall not have the role of a hired factor; labor shall hire capital."

But how does all of this implicate Ellerman's claims about the basic economic virtue of a worker cooperative, namely the ability of labor to control the business and thereby also its economic destiny? It seems almost a trope in the literature to say that the great value of worker-ownership is the control over profit. (Consequently, one corresponding negative trope about cooperatives is that workers misuse, or unwisely use, the business's profit.)[62] To what extent is the picture of democratic participation at HCA a picture about "labor hir[ing] capital"? How much value do worker-owners themselves place in the ability to control the business as an economic entity? While the data from my case study are skewed on this topic by my focus on a professionally managed cooperative, they nonetheless provide some fascinating clues.

As I have described, overwhelmingly, the three focal points of democratic control that were prioritized by both workers and managers in my case study were decisions about the distribution of dividends, employment benefits, and work conditions. Dividends come from profits; so at least formally speaking, there is a direct connection between workers' own expressions about the value of democratic control and control over profits. But if we dig deeper into these expressions, it becomes apparent that the comments fall into two categories, neither of which clearly supports the claim that worker-owners most value the right to control the economic destiny of their business. The first category of comments consists primarily of expressions of the *personal* value to the interviewees of receiving the typically small financial infusions when the business does well.[63]

In the second category are relatively abstract comments about the symbolic value to the interviewees of having the right to vote on the business's use of profits.[64] Tellingly, the majority of comments in this category were followed by favorable commentary about the cooperative's decision to spend profits on employment benefits and other forms of investments in the workers. Taken together, these comments suggest that the interviewees who discussed profits and dividends clearly valued the opportunity to participate for many of the same reasons they valued the committees: participation gave them a voice, access, and the right to share their opinions. It allowed for greater transparency about the business's operations and contributed to a feeling that the business was ultimately accountable to its workers. But these comments did not suggest that workers necessarily valued the right to exclusively make or control the highest-level strategic decisions about the business's future direction and operations.

The comments about the use of profits to improve employment benefits and work conditions take on additional significance when considered in light of the other two areas that interviewees highlighted as important subjects of democratic control, namely employment benefits and work conditions. Overall, the comments from

[62] *See*, Gregory K. Dow, *Governing the Firm: Workers' Control in Theory and Practice* (2003); Gregory Dow & Louis Putterman, Why Capital (Usually) Hires Labor: An Assessment of Proposed Explanations, *in Employees and Corporate Governance* 17 (Margaret Blair & Mark J. Roe, eds., 1999).

[63] Dixon Interview; Montgomery Interview; Perkins Interview.

[64] Montgomery Interview; Smith Interview; Perkins Interview. Pillot Interview.

these interviews about voting rights and democratic control present a strikingly consistent picture about the matters that worker-owners most wished to control. Not surprisingly, my interviewees wanted the right to shape their own experiences on the job and to determine the nature and scope of employment-related benefits. While some also valued learning about the financial and operational sides of the business, and many valued the transparency about these matters, none said that they valued or wanted exclusive worker control of these matters.

Importantly, many of the comments suggested that the desire to control work conditions and benefits was by no means just about individual rights or benefits. Several of my interviewees discussed the importance of making decisions that would allow more equitable distribution of work hours, employment benefits, training, and other job-related advantages among all the workers in the business. This was one of many indicia of widespread investment in the business's mission, across all levels of employment. Many of my interviewees stressed that these are exactly the things that differentiate this job from jobs they had previously held.

Making Democracy Work for Urban Worker Cooperatives

The most important conclusion that is appropriate to take from this case study is that democratic participation is not a magic powder or secret sauce that can be tossed into a worker cooperative with the assumption that it will somehow elevate the cooperative above other business forms that might be available to low-income workers. The values, principles, and mechanics of democratic participation in worker cooperatives are more varied and nuanced than much of the literature assumes. It is thus vital to study this issue using a range of empirical methods. That said, even this initial case study on democratic participation in an urban American worker cooperative provides a foundation for a few tentative conclusions, which also ought to be guiding questions for future study.

First, the experiences of workers at HCA and CHCA strongly suggest that Ellerman's ideal of labor hiring capital, though powerful, may not alone be an adequate guiding principle for successful cooperative development in American urban cores. Specifically, democratic participation need not automatically or necessarily equate to control of the business as a going concern or economic entity. Given the rich sense of voice, control, power, and connection expressed by workers in these two cooperatives, it seems too simplistic to assume that the only – or best – way to achieve democratic participation is by giving workers the exclusive right to control the high-level decisions of the business.

This insight is important because it challenges the modus operandi for many CED practitioners who have worked hard to develop worker cooperatives. The information from this study ought to break the impulse to start up a cooperative by means of a process in which workers exclusively are responsible for making the key startup decisions. As is the case for any small business, these decisions are difficult to make, requiring experience, time, connections, and (perhaps most importantly) the ability to take financial and other risks.[65] The typical response by CED practitioners has been to provide extensive technical assistance to the workers in order to support them in developing the knowledge to do this well. This has taken a great deal of resources and time, thereby also delaying the startup process.[66] Most importantly, it is reasonable to ask whether imposing such decision-making burdens on a startup cooperative significantly increases its risk of failure in the startup stages.

It is equally important to recognize that *not* imposing such decisions on a startup cooperative is not tantamount to abandoning a commitment to democratic participation. As this case study shows, there may be equally and perhaps more robust ways to achieve significant levels of democratic participation about key aspects of business operation. In this regard, the evidence from my case study is compelling. When they first began operations, HCA and CHCA were able to train unskilled, low-income workers to be home health aides without imposing on them the responsibilities of also learning the complexity of Medicaid and Medicare reimbursements that were the basis for financing the businesses. As the cooperatives grew, they developed a range of strategies for providing training to workers interested in career paths that included business management, human resources, and nursing education. Without this initial division of responsibility between "workers" and "managers," however, it is hard to imagine a cooperative succeeding in a market reliant on such a complex financing structure. This lesson is more broadly applicable than may at first be evident. While only a few industries are financed through Medicaid and Medicare reimbursements, many American industries have equally complicated financing structures. This simple fact may go a long way in explaining why so many American worker cooperatives are under-financed and struggling.

These two insights about democratic participation in turn provide the basis for two recommendations that may inform the development of new worker cooperatives. First, while it may not be sensible in some industrial sectors or markets to give workers the responsibility of deciding *everything* at the startup phase, it is important at the startup phase to develop a process for determining the issues that matter most to workers. I think of this as a limited needs assessment about workers' priorities. In the case of HCA and CHCA, workers clearly and consistently articulated the desire to exercise control on issues of employment benefits and work conditions. These may or may not be relatively common areas of importance to workers, a question

65 Dyal-Chand & Rowan, *supra* Note 8.

66 Pitegoff adds to this list the importance of political education. Peter Pitegoff, *Organizing Worker Cooperatives*, 7 L. & POL'Y 45, 46 (2018) (The creation of worker cooperatives depends on employees having "years of patient political education and organizing" because "[t]hat context is essential to developing the cooperative values and political strength necessary to organize a successful worker cooperative").

that ought to be the subject of further study.[67] But my interviews do suggest that it will be difficult to institutionalize a sense of voice, participation, and meaningful control without asking workers very early in the life of a business what issues they wish to have more power to decide or control.

Second, it will be necessary to develop the institutions within a worker cooperative that will achieve meaningful democratic participation on the substantive matters about which workers wish to have more control. At HCA and CHCA, it seems that the combination of equal board representation and a robust committee structure is ideal for achieving a balance between business success and democratic participation. This may or may not be true for other cooperatives, and again this ought to be the subject of more extensive inquiry.

Indeed, the experiences of more recent cooperative efforts, such as the Evergreen Cooperatives in Cleveland, provide important information on this subject. The impetus for creating the Evergreen Cooperatives came from the powerful "anchor institutions" – local hospitals and universities – in the so-called Greater University Circle in which the businesses are located. The first three cooperatives that were started were a laundry company, a construction company, and an urban greenhouse. As the literature on these cooperatives describes, it took some time for these businesses to find their footing, stabilize, and begin to grow. While there were doubtless many factors contributing to the turnaround these businesses began to experience, one of the transitions that occurred in the process was the hiring of professional managers, a step that seemed essential given the complexity of the three industrial sectors in which the cooperatives operate. It is interesting in that context to see the development of a different balance between management and democratic participation than that originally envisioned by the cooperatives' founders.

The Evergreen example is also useful because it supports a final tentative conclusion from this case study. If a range of robust forms of democratic participation is available within worker cooperatives, then it should be possible for the next generation of CED practitioners to develop worker cooperatives in a broader range of business sectors, not just those about which it is easy to teach business management, financing, and control. This too is an important insight for future efforts at cooperative development because it opens up essential space for taking advantage of market opportunities and developing market niches in more complex sectors that require prior experience or more extensive resources. And this in turn ought to result in cooperatives that have the potential to be better capitalized, better poised to capture new market opportunities, and better able to grow quickly. In the first generation of worker cooperatives, the paradigm cooperative has been service-oriented, such as a

[67] Indeed, other research has identified these as common priorities among cooperatives. *See, e.g.*, Elizabeth A. Hoffmann, *Law in the Workplace: Dispute Resolution in a Worker Cooperative: Formal Procedures and Procedural Justice*, 39 LAW & SOC'Y REC. 51, 55 (2005) (discussing use of democratic process to "create their grievance procedures and to hire their managers").

house cleaning or childcare cooperative. It has been difficult for such enterprises to develop large enough markets, with expansive enough financing, to grow or even to remain sustainable over the long term. By reexamining the connection between democratic participation and worker management, CED practitioners ought to be able to explore a broader range of markets and financing platforms that may be appropriate for cooperative development.

While the operationalization of both these recommendations may well be led by workers and managers in a cooperative, it is important to note that these recommendations can also be the subject of legal support. In other words, the lessons from this case study are lessons relating to law, law reform, and lawyering as well as to institutional design and development. Decisions about forms of entity, governing documents, and other legal infrastructure can – and should – be used to support the development of rich forms of democratic participation in the workplace.

Although it makes our understanding of the imperative of democratic participation in worker cooperatives more complex, this case study also provides fresh and promising information about how democracy in the workplace can be achieved. The range of mechanisms used to engender meaningful participation – and the resulting high levels of worker investment and voice – provide good reasons for remaining optimistic about the future of worker cooperatives in American urban cores. Importantly, the economic success of both HCA and CHCA (and thus the job stability and success of their workers) is a core part of this story. The challenge now is to dig deeper into such examples with the goal of creating a new generation of more economically resilient cooperatives that remain committed to the success of their worker-owners.

PART II

Reimagining Law for the Urban Core

4

Community Development Finance and Economic Justice

*Peter Pitegoff**

INTRODUCTION

On the rugged coast of Maine in 1978, an emerging community development organization called Coastal Enterprises, Inc. (CEI) helped secure financing to successfully rebuild a fish storage and processing plant that had been destroyed by fire.[1] Founded a year earlier, the organization began as a modest effort to create and preserve jobs in Maine's natural resources industry and rural small business sector. It was modeled on the community development corporation (CDC), a form of non-profit entity that emerged in the civil rights era of the 1960s and proliferated primarily in disadvantaged urban neighborhoods in the years to follow. In contrast to the dominant *urban* CDC model, CEI worked in the rural setting of Maine and focused its housing and job-creation efforts in small towns and in the state's natural resources sectors of fish, farms, and forests.

In the four decades since its inception, CEI has grown from a CDC into a sophisticated community development financial institution, consisting of several

* Professor and former Dean, University of Maine School of Law. My sincere thanks to Alex Harriman for her excellent work as my research assistant, and to Ron Phillips, Ellen Seidman, Steven Dawson, Elizabeth Rogers, Keith Bisson, Carla Dickstein, Charlie Spies, Peter Enrich, and Rashmi Dyal-Chand for their review and insightful comments on successive drafts of this chapter.

[1] Sophie Nelson, *The Visionary Practitioner: Behind Coastal Enterprises, Inc.*, ME. MAGAZINE (Sept. 2015), https://themainemag.com/people/2807-the-visionary-practitioner-behind-coastal-enterprises-inc/ (featuring Ron Phillips, founder of CEI, who stepped down as CEO in 2016 after thirty-eight years). Throughout this chapter, references to CEI include its subsidiary for-profit entities, including CEI Capital Management LLC, Bright Community Capital, and CEI Ventures Inc. Accounts here of CEI are drawn in part from my conversations with senior staff and directors and from my engagement on the CEI board of directors from 2006 to 2017.

corporate entities and driving multi-million dollar transactions in distressed rural regions in Maine and nationally. With a half a billion dollars now under its management, CEI's total investment activity has exceeded $1.3 billion and has leveraged over twice that amount in capital from banks, foundations, and other sources. CEI presents a microcosm of the evolution of community economic development over forty years and its robust use of complex legal and financial tools in urban and rural America today.

This chapter reflects on the history of community economic development, community development financial institutions, and their relationship with law and legal scholarship. Part II places CEI in the wider context and history of community development finance and of the dramatic expansion in tax credit financing. Part III explores the implications of this trend for sustainability and local accountability, underscoring the distinction between community organizing and community development and some distancing of community development from its activist origins. Part IV mines connections between community development practice and the legal academy, from the proliferation of law school transactional clinics to an emergent body of applied scholarship that impacts policy and strategy in community economic development.

EVOLUTION OF COMMUNITY ECONOMIC DEVELOPMENT

Recent History

The Coastal Enterprises Inc. story is a window into the recent history of community-based economic development and finance and suggests a rural complement to this volume's theme of revitalizing the urban core. A local, Maine-based community development corporation born in the 1970s is a complex institution today. CEI has expanded and diversified its portfolio, assembling capital from numerous sources to provide and leverage financing for small and medium-sized businesses, affordable housing, and community facilities such as child care or health care centers. It has financed roughly 2,700 businesses, creating or preserving thousands of jobs and affordable housing units. In dozens of larger projects in Maine and throughout the nation, CEI has structured multi-million dollar financing packages for industrial development, manufacturing facilities and equipment, renewable energy, sustainable forestry and agriculture, and construction of research, cultural, and commercial facilities. Its business-advising programs have counseled over 50,000 aspiring entrepreneurs and enterprises, and the organization has developed expertise in particular industries and sectors. It is active in policy research and development and collaborates with kindred institutions to advocate for state and federal policies to increase opportunity for underserved populations. CEI's 2017 strategic plan emphasizes outcomes, not simply in volume of activity but in the quality of jobs created or improved, environmental sustainability of the enterprises it advises and finances, and measurable prosperity shared by residents of low-income communities.[2]

At its core, CEI remains a nonprofit community development corporation that provides technical assistance and financing, not otherwise available, to small and emerging businesses. It works with community partners, banks, religious and philanthropic institutions, industry and trade associations, advocacy groups, and state and federal government agencies for capital investment and supportive policies. It runs programs tailored for particular constituencies, populations at risk, and entrepreneurs, including business planning and start-up assistance for women business owners and Maine's growing immigrant population. Underlying all of these efforts is CEI's touchstone of a "triple bottom line" – economic benefit to communities in need, equitable social impact, and environmental sustainability.

Traditional economic development, historically and today, encompasses a wide range of public policy and government programs, urban and regional planning, infrastructure development, industry incentives, support for small businesses, and housing development. *Community* economic development (CED) adds elements of accountability to and participation by a wider range of local stakeholders, especially those ordinarily excluded from centers of wealth and power, and implicates an advocacy role in public policy. It reflects an ethic of social entrepreneurship, using the tools of business and finance to develop affordable housing, jobs, and business opportunities for low- and moderate-income people. It taps market forces and capital for goals beyond profit, such as creating stable quality jobs, driving change in distressed regions, providing opportunities for education and advancement, and building capacity for sustainable institutions.[3] Community development *finance* is one aspect of community economic development, a transactional subset that has grown in scale and complexity since the 1980s.

Legal scholar William Simon discusses several core themes of CED in his 2001 book, *The Community Economic Development Movement*.[4] First is the principle of the "community as beneficiary of economic development" – positing community members as "residual claimants" on the proceeds of development.[5] Second is the principle of "community as agent" of economic development, implicating an entrepreneurial role for local institutions and evidenced by a profusion of legal entities and their various combinations.[6] Another theme is constraint on property

2 *See* CEI, www.ceimaine.org/ (last visited June 21, 2018); *see also* Coastal Enterprises, Inc., *From Civil Rights to Sustainable Solutions* (2003); Note 52 (citing additional resources on workforce development and job quality).

3 *See* William H. Simon, *The Community Economic Development Movement* (2001); *see also* Peter Pitegoff, *Child Care Enterprise, Community Development, and Work*, 81 Geo. L.J. 1897 (1993). *See generally* Robert O. Zdenek & Dee Walsh, *Navigating Community Development: Harnessing Comparative Advantages to Create Strategic Partnerships* (2017).

4 Simon, *supra* Note 3.

5 *Id.* at 76–78.

6 *Id.* at 113.

rights – in some cases arising from the charitable purposes and non-distribution constraint of nonprofit organization actors, in other cases a product of conditions attached to socially targeted financing, or sometimes based upon internal charter restrictions as in limited equity housing cooperatives or worker cooperatives. Finally, there is the imperative of local participation or "induced mobilization" – a condition for certain public and philanthropic support, in some cases a community organizing complement to development, and, arguably, a key part of the "community" in CED.[7]

Economic development and, indeed, community economic development have long been a part of the American social and economic fabric and the subject of research, scholarship, and public policy. We can trace this history to a time well before the start-up of CEI and at least back to a period of widespread social activism and political reform in the 1890s and early twentieth century. Workplaces were the site of ferment and creativity, from labor organizing to union engagement in worker cooperative development and in banking.[8] Many efforts at that time aimed at addressing the downside of industrialization and challenges of urbanization, including the settlement house movement and assimilation of new Americans in densely populated cities, and intentional strategies among African American leaders to increase minority business participation.[9] Without recounting the full panoply of twentieth-century community development policies and practices, this section provides some historical context for the thread of community development finance, leading eventually to today's proliferation of tax credits, expanded bank engagement, and increased scale. While a signature attribute of community economic development is local initiative and control, it is also intertwined with serial federal and state policies that have provided government funding and have increasingly leveraged private sector capital.

In the 1930s, in the aftermath of the Great Depression, President Franklin D. Roosevelt's "New Deal" policies signaled a sea change in federal policy and an array of economic development programs both urban and rural. From the Tennessee Valley Authority building dams and bringing electric power to rural areas, to public housing projects and massive public employment initiatives, the New Deal harnessed the resources of the federal government and created new agencies to

7 *Id.* at 143, 168.

8 *See* John Curl, *For All the People: Uncovering the Hidden History of Cooperation, Cooperative Movements, and Communalism in America* 86–110 (2009); *see also* Peter Pitegoff, Unions, Finance, and Labor's Capital, *in Unions and Public Policy: The New Economy, Law, and Democratic Politics* 65, 67 (Lawrence G. Flood ed., 1995).

9 *See* Roger A. Clay, Jr. & Susan R. Jones, What is Community Economic Development?, *in Building Healthy Communities: A Guide to Community Economic Development for Advocates, Lawyers, and Policymakers* 3–12 (Roger A. Clay, Jr. & Susan R. Jones eds., 2009) (presenting a concise history of community economic development, including reference to the turn-of-the-century dialogue and debate between Booker T. Washington and W. E. B Du Bois over strategies for African American economic and political advancement).

address multiple social problems. Underlying these initiatives was a federal government taking at least a modicum of responsibility for the welfare of its citizens, allocating federal funds to economic development, and foreshadowing subsequent growth in community development finance. The New Deal, though, was an essentially top-down administrative structure.[10] Unprecedented in its historic impact and its establishment of the modern administrative state, and with material effect on the lives of people in need, the New Deal had a mixed record of local accountability and engagement of local constituents in decision-making – key elements in *community* economic development.

Such a top-down approach to federal economic development policies continued in the 1950s on the heels of World War II. The National Housing Act of 1949 gave rise to a period of "redevelopment" that has been widely criticized for destructive effects on the ground and insensitivity to local residents. With a putative goal of supporting local revitalization efforts in distressed inner-city neighborhoods, this redevelopment or "urban renewal" often saw wide areas (blighted or not) taken by eminent domain, existing structures demolished, and low-income neighborhoods giving way to private development or to construction of the new US Interstate Highway system.[11] Racial inequities, apparent earlier in the New Deal, persisted in the postwar era as development of public housing projects, for instance, tended further to perpetuate racial segregation in urban areas.[12]

The 1960s and 1970s witnessed a surge of anti-poverty measures, in both public policy and grassroots activity that influenced such policy.[13] The "War on Poverty" of President Lyndon Johnson's administration included the Economic Opportunity Act of 1964, the Model Cities program, and a wide range of community action agencies subsidized in part by the federal government, while the Ford Foundation's Gray Areas program in selected cities promoted community development. Although successful in generating local activity in pre-school learning, job training, health counseling, housing, and other neighborhood improvement, this period arguably

[10] Alexander von Hoffman, The Past, Present, and Future of Community Development in the United States, *in Investing in What Works for America's Communities* 10, 12–13 (N. Andrews et al, eds., 2012).

[11] *Id.* at 14–15.

[12] The Federal Housing Authority, created in 1934 to regulate a mortgage insurance system and stabilize the housing market following the Great Depression, expressly identified and red-lined poor and minority neighborhoods as too risky for lenders. *See* Richard Rothstein, *The Color of Law: A Forgotten History of How Our Government Segregated America* (2017); *cf.* John Eligon et al., *Program to Spur Low-Income Housing Is Keeping Cities Segregated*, N.Y. Times, July 3, 2017 (describing how the contemporary Low-Income Housing Tax Credit program disproportionately locates affordable housing development in minority urban communities, thus continuing to reinforce racial segregation).

[13] The civil rights movement, welfare rights advocacy, and direct-action community organizing were important drivers in the War on Poverty and in subsequent policy initiatives, and in the evolution of community economic development. *See* Notes 58–61 and accompanying text.

suffered from atomization and a lack of coordination.[14] Community action agencies that sought to maximize participation, a stated objective of federal policy, were perceived by some local leaders as a threat to the political status quo. This generated pushback, imposition of greater control by local government officials, and pressure on many community action agencies to emphasize social services rather than activism.

In the mid-1960s, racial tensions spiked in many large cities with violent confrontations and urban unrest. A National Advisory Commission on Civil Disorders (the "Kerner Commission") shone a light onto the destructive impact of racial segregation and concentrated poverty and triggered federal policy changes. With leadership from then New York Senator Robert Kennedy, the Economic Opportunity Act was amended in 1966, adding a "Special Impact Program" to fund community development ventures. Two years later, the Fair Housing Act – Title VIII of the Civil Rights Act of 1968 – sought to correct longstanding housing policies that perpetuated racial segregation and to prevent red-lining, then a widespread banking practice that deprived predominantly minority neighborhoods of needed access to loans.[15] These policy initiatives were accompanied by an explicit turn to the private sector – national corporations, banks, and developers – to finance housing and job development in distressed neighborhoods. Large philanthropic institutions, too, joined in this nascent community development financial push, with nine foundations collaborating in the creation of the Cooperative Assistance Fund in 1967 to invest in minority enterprises and the Ford Foundation taking a lead in targeted grants and loans ("program related investments") for social enterprise.[16]

The Housing and Community Development Act of 1974 signaled a shift in federal funding for local development to more diffuse revenue sharing and the Community Development Block Grant (CDBG) program. It combined more than a half-dozen housing and neighborhood improvement programs, each with particular dictates on local use of funding, into a single grant program administered by the US Department of Housing and Urban Development. The Act concentrated federal funding in discretionary block grants to local governments. Within broad parameters, including a nominal requirement of public participation, local authorities had wide discretion in use of the funds, a portion of which were and continue to be applied to community development activities. Despite inefficiencies and a lack of consistent focus, and threatened with elimination by the Trump administration, the

14 Von Hoffman, *supra* Note 10 at 16–20. The Small Business Administration (SBA), created by Congress in 1953 to support development of small business with direct loans and loan guarantees, a decade later launched an Equal Opportunity Loan Program to assist applicants living below the poverty line. U.S. Small Business Administration, www.sba.gov/about-sba/what-we-do/history (last visited June 21, 2018).

15 *See The Fight for Fair Housing: Causes, Consequences and Future Implications of the 1968 Federal Fair housing Act* (Gregory D. Squires, ed., 2018).

16 Von Hoffman, *supra* Note 10. *See also* Peter Edelman, *Toward a Comprehensive Antipoverty Strategy: Getting Beyond the Silver Bullet*, 81 Geo. L.J. 1697 (1993).

CDBG program continues for now as an essential source of funding for community development initiatives.[17] The 1974 Act also created the federal Section 8 housing program, with subsidies for renters contributing to a growth in private low-income housing development.

Arguably in reaction to drawbacks of previous top-down approaches and coinciding with the curtailment of many War on Poverty programs, the 1970s and 1980s saw robust and widespread local activism to influence land use planning and public investment. This period witnessed growth in the volume of institutions and the variety of legal forms focused on local development. As illustrated by the CEI narrative, the community development corporation emerged as a foundational entity for locally based economic development. A CDC is typically a tax-exempt nonprofit organization chartered to revitalize particular disadvantaged neighborhoods by engaging in affordable housing and small business development, planning and advocacy, education and job training, or social services. The origin of CDC as a term of art is often attributed to the 1966 amendments to the Economic Opportunity Act to support community development corporations, followed by formation of dozens of early CDCs and the high-profile creation of the Bedford Stuyvesant Restoration Corporation in Brooklyn as a model. In subsequent decades, CDCs grew significantly in number and scale with substantial philanthropic funding, federal government support, and new state agencies for community development. Ancillary public policies enabled nonprofit CDCs to engage substantially in development, including IRS Revenue Rulings that expressly ruled community-based economic development to be a tax-exempt charitable purpose.[18] Today, close to 5,000 CDCs operate in urban and rural areas throughout the United States.

The proliferation of CDCs was accompanied by the emergence and growth in the late twentieth century of other community development institutions – regional housing development organizations, consumer cooperatives, land trusts, microenterprise funds, worker cooperatives, employee stock ownership plans, credit unions, community loan funds, community development venture capital organizations, and even community development banks. A common attribute across this landscape is a sort of "institutional hybridization," crossing boundaries among conventional enterprise forms, and integration of social and economic purposes. Thus, nonprofit CDCs increasingly pursued their goals through subsidiary or affiliated for-profit enterprises. Various forms of social enterprise proliferated, essentially re-making business corporations into catalysts for community change or even into more

[17] Brett Theodos et al., *Taking Stock of the Community Development Block Grant*, Urb. Inst. Apr. 2017.

[18] *See, e.g.*, Rev. Rul. 74-587 (ruling, inter alia, that a CDC designed to stimulate economic development in minority and low-income urban communities, support inner-city enterprises, and focus on community needs, qualified for tax exemption under I.R.C. § 501(c)(3)).

democratic institutions in their own right.[19] Community development organizations in this period connected with public and private entities in creative and sometimes complex legal structures, foreshadowing the emergence of more sophisticated community development finance.

Community Development Finance

Finance and financial transactions have been a critical component of community economic development throughout its history. CDCs and other local institutions assemble capital – from foundation grants and program-related investments, socially responsible investors and investment funds, bank loans, and government subsidies – and deploy this capital in support of housing and business development not otherwise driven by conventional market forces. In the context of cutbacks in antipoverty programs during the administration of President Richard Nixon and a push toward privatization of government functions during the Presidential administrations of Ronald Reagan and George H. W. Bush, the notion of market-based antipoverty approaches garnered bipartisan political support. This market orientation, shared by the subsequent administration of President Bill Clinton, gained ever greater purchase among community development leaders and practitioners as a politically viable strategy fueled in part by availability of federal support.

Over time, focus on the market and financial transactions grew more ascendant in the CED arena, from proliferation of community development loan funds to the emergence of community development banks and tax credit financing. A succession of federal policy initiatives reflected and helped to drive private market investment in community economic development. From the Community Reinvestment Act to the Low Income Housing Tax Credit and eventually the New Markets Tax Credit, local development organizations increasingly turned to evolving intermediary institutions with capacity, sophistication, and scale to tap new sources of capital.

Reflecting a shift in emphasis through the 1990s, CEI and some comparable organizations began to identify not just as community development corporations but as *community development financial institutions* (CDFIs). The notion of finance as central to the function of a CDC was hardly new, for CDCs acting as developers necessarily negotiated financing for their projects, raised funds for operations, and launched community development loan funds. But, advocates helped craft public policies and programs to more effectively tap private investment. CDFIs emerged as financial intermediaries to access, assemble, and channel financing to CDCs and other organizations engaged directly in economic development on the ground. The distinction in roles – CDC as developer and investor, and CDFI as financing entity

[19] Simon, *supra* Note 3 at 195–217. *See, e.g.*, David Ellerman & Peter Pitegoff, *The Democratic Corporation: The New Worker Cooperative Statute in Massachusetts*, 11 N.Y.U. Rev. L. & Soc. Change 441 (1983).

with a focus on lending – is not always precise, particularly in the case of hybrid institutions like CEI that are engaged in both roles. Nonetheless, a cohort of emerging CDFIs essentially helped build a new policy framework and practice to advance their social enterprise mission, complementing and in some cases helping to fuel CDC activity.[20]

The Community Reinvestment Act (CRA),[21] initially enacted in 1977 during the administration of President Jimmy Carter, later re-emerged as a factor in the growth of CDFIs. The CRA addresses how banks meet credit needs in low- and moderate-income neighborhoods in their lending areas. Its original justification included a perceived mismatch between deposits from local neighborhoods on the one hand and lending activity elsewhere on the other, at the expense of meeting local credit needs. It also aimed to discourage continued bank red-lining.[22] Federal bank regulatory agencies evaluate how banks meet the goals of the CRA and issue performance ratings that are among the factors in approval of proposed bank mergers. The importance of the CRA with respect to community development was magnified in 1989 when it was revised to require public disclosure of CRA ratings and in subsequent years when the Act and related regulations expanded CRA opportunities for a wider range of public welfare investments in targeted communities. These modifications in the CRA enabled CDCs to gain greater access to banking capital and to call the attention of banks to local needs. Through the 1990s and into the new millennium, the CRA helped fuel the growth of community development financial institutions, which increasingly served as intermediaries between CDCs and banks seeking favorable CRA ratings.

While the CRA applies to all federally insured depository institutions, a small subset of community development banks adopted lending policies expressly geared to local development. Most prominent among community development banks was the South Shore Bank (later re-named Shorebank), founded in 1973 in Chicago and identified publicly in the 1990s by President Bill Clinton as a model for community banking.[23] Despite later difficulties and ultimate demise in 2010, the South Shore Bank was influential in giving greater definition, prominence, and momentum to community development finance.

[20] James Greer & Oscar Gonzales, *Community Economic Development in the United States: The CDFI Industry and America's Distressed Communities* (2017) at 48–49 (characterizing the CDC model as a key building block of the CDFI movement), and at 77–86 ("A Brief History of the CDFI Movement").

[21] 12 U.S.C. § 2901–08 (2012).

[22] Darryl E. Getter, *The Effectiveness of the Community Reinvestment Act*, CRS Report for Congress (Jan. 7, 2015). Grassroots advocacy was and continues to be instrumental in the utility of the CRA, now reflected for example by the National Community Reinvestment Coalition. *See* National Community Reinvestment Coalition, www.ncrc.org/ (last visited June 22, 2018).

[23] Greer and Gonzales, *supra* Note 20 at 94. *See also* Rashmi Dyal-Chand, *Collaborative Capitalism in American Cities: Reforming Urban Market Regulations* 75–76 (2018) (overview of Shorebank).

Concurrently, a handful of national institutions emerged as a bridge between private capital and hundreds of local development organizations.[24] In 1978, Congress established the Neighborhood Reinvestment Corporation (still operating today as NeighborWorks America) to provide technical assistance to neighborhood housing organizations and to operate a secondary market for high-risk loans. In 1980, the Ford Foundation took the lead in creating the Local Initiatives Support Corporation (LISC) to assist and support CDCs with loans, grants, and technical assistance. In short order, it assembled millions of dollars from corporations, foundations, and federal agencies. LISC continues to operate today on a national scale and launched "Rural LISC" in 1995 to expand its reach to include rural communities throughout the nation. The Center for Community Self-Help in North Carolina grew from a local community development organization supporting worker-owned companies in the 1980s to, in subsequent decades, a national advocate for responsible lending, a billion dollar national credit union family, and a lender to numerous housing and job development projects. Other national institutions added momentum, including the Enterprise Foundation (now re-named Enterprise Community Partners), founded in 1982 to support low-income housing development.

A notable element of the shift toward community development finance was promotion and implementation of federal (and some state) tax credit programs to leverage private investment for affordable housing and enterprise development. After enactment of the Tax Reform Act of 1986, CEI and a growing number of nonprofit (and for-profit) developers began to make use of Low Income Housing Tax Credits (LIHTCs) authorized by the Act to support development of affordable housing.[25] In the subsequent decade, a cohort of CDFIs and others advocated for a new federal program to support not just affordable housing but broader enterprise and economic development. The Riegle Community Development and Regulatory Improvement Act of 1994, sponsored by US Senator Don Riegle of Michigan, created the Community Development Financial Institutions Fund (CDFI Fund) as a program of the US Department of Treasury. Its statutory purpose was to promote economic revitalization and community development in distressed neighborhoods, and it codified in federal law for the first time the term "community development financial institution."[26] In enacting the Riegle Act, Congress acknowledged widespread poverty in urban, rural, and Native American communities. The Act found explicitly that "community development financial institutions have proven their ability to identify and respond to community needs for equity investments, loans, and

[24] Von Hoffman, *supra* Note 10. *See generally* Local Initiatives Support Corporation, www.lisc.org/ (last visited May 28, 2018); Howard E. Covington Jr., *Lending Power: How Self-Help Credit Union Turned Small-Time Loans into Big-time Change* (2017).

[25] Low-Income Housing Credit, 26 U.S.C. § 42 (2012).

[26] Riegle Community Development and Regulatory Improvement Act of 1994, 12 U.S.C. § 4701 (2012).

development services."[27] It authorized funding to "certified" CDFIs that in turn would make use of their enhanced liquidity to raise and invest additional capital in targeted communities. Close to a thousand CDFIs are certified by the CDFI Fund today.

In the late-1990s, banks began to emerge as the dominant lenders to CDFIs, channeling substantial new capital investment for community development. Senator Don Riegle also co-sponsored the Riegle-Neal Interstate Banking and Branching Efficiency Act of 1994, which eliminated certain geographic restrictions on banks, allowing bank holding companies to acquire banks in any states and banks to merge across state lines. This legislation paved the way for a wave of bank mergers, resulting in formation of larger national banks with extensive branch networks operating in multiple states. It also provided that an interstate bank must receive a separate CRA rating for each state in which it has a branch and required that, before any expansion, the bank must undergo a review of its CRA compliance.[28] The 1994 establishment of the CDFI Fund and subsequent growth of CDFIs were boosted significantly by the concurrent changes in banking regulation and, consequently, substantial increase in CRA investments by banks.

CEI and other advocates envisioned and pressed for enactment of a new tax credit program, comparable to the LIHTC, but for business, industrial, and commercial development in distressed communities rather than exclusively for housing. Congress enacted the Community Renewal Tax Relief Act of 2000, which created the New Markets Tax Credit (NMTC).[29] This legislation authorized the CDFI Fund to administer tax credits to stimulate investment and economic growth in low-income urban neighborhoods and rural communities that lack access to the patient capital needed to support and grow businesses, create jobs, and sustain healthy local economies. CEI created a wholly owned for-profit subsidiary, CEI Capital Management, LLC (CCML), which served as a vehicle for using the new tax credit to leverage financing for community-based economic development. Today, CCML is one of the largest allocatees of New Markets Tax Credits in the nation – and the largest serving primarily rural America – and has utilized these credits to leverage several billion dollars of investment in transactions in disadvantaged communities nationwide.[30]

An entire industry of lawyers, finance specialists, accountants, and others has grown to implement and administer complex community development financial mechanisms, including tax credit transactions, and a sector of CDFIs has amassed

[27] *Id.*

[28] Patrick Mulloy & Cynthia Lasker, *The Riegle-Neal Interstate Banking and Branching Efficiency Act of 1994: Responding to Global Competition*, 21 J. LEGIS. 255 (1995) (recounting the history of geographical restrictions on American banks and changes under the Riegle-Neal Act).

[29] New Markets Tax Credit, 26 U.S.C. § 45D (2012).

[30] *See* COASTAL ENTERPRISES, INC., www.ceimaine.org/investing/cei-capital-management/ (last visited June 21, 2018).

experience in serial transactions. Evolving from its origin as the National Association of Community Development Loan Funds founded in 1986, the Opportunity Finance Network (OFN) today is a national network of over 200 CDFIs investing in low-income, low-wealth, and other disinvested communities. About 100 of these CDFIs (including most of the largest) are monitored and rated by Aeris, an information service launched by OFN in 2004 that provides data analysis and assessment of CDFIs to support investors' due diligence. The national CDFI Coalition has been the locus of policy advocacy for the field since 1992. It was instrumental in creating the federal CDFI Fund and played a role (with a kindred NMTC Coalition formed in 1998) in establishing and sustaining the New Markets Tax Credit program. NeighborWorks America, formed initially by Congress in 1978, has evolved to assist and evaluate community development financial institutions today.[31]

The world of community development finance has witnessed dramatic growth in scale and complexity and notable tools tapping private investment. Community development financial institutions have become intermediaries between private sector resources and grassroots initiatives, making expansive capital sources more accessible to CDCs, local developers, social entrepreneurs, and other local constituents. Federal incentives such as the Low-Income Housing Tax Credit and the New Markets Tax Credit have created robust private sector financing regimes and have been vehicles for investment of billions of dollars in disadvantaged communities.

From a policy perspective, this leveraging of substantial private investment has proven successful as measured by private dollars spent and affordable housing units built, jobs created or retained, and commercial enterprise in selected areas. But to the extent that policy makers perceive these programs as a substitute rather than a complement to more direct federal antipoverty measures, the result is arguably fewer policy initiatives – from a higher minimum wage and direct wage or housing subsidies, to job training or educational benefits and enhanced Medicaid coverage – that would raise the floor more expansively for the working poor and build a safety net for others in need. An apparent distancing of community development finance from the civil rights and grassroots origins of CDCs gives rise to continuing tensions. CEI seeks to address this issue by serving as a hybrid organization with both CDFI and CDC functions, attributes, and attitudes.

Tax Credit Transactions

The longstanding theme of private sector engagement in community development took shape increasingly around tax credits in the 1990s and since. Creation of the

[31] *See* Opportunity Finance Network, http://ofn.org/ (last visited May 28, 2018); Aeris, http://aerisinsight.com/ (last visited May 28, 2018); CDFI Coalition, www.cdfi.org/about-cdfi-coalition/history/ (last visited May 28, 2018); NeighborWorks, www.neighborworks.org/ (last visited May 28, 2018); NMTC Coalition, http://nmtccoalition.org (last visited May 28, 2018).

LIHTC in 1986 triggered growth in tax-favored finance transactions by enabling nonprofit CDCs like CEI (and for-profit developers) to tap private investment for affordable housing development. Driven in part by the tax incentive, banks and corporations substantially increased their investment in affordable housing transactions by using the LIHTC.[32] The turn to market mechanisms to alleviate poverty continued through the Clinton era, including designation in 1993 of selected low-income neighborhoods as "empowerment zones" with employers receiving tax incentives for hiring area residents and a menu of other tax benefits.

When the Riegle Act[33] created the CDFI Fund in 1994, it underscored the expanding finance thread in community development. It defined CDFI to include not only for-profit community development banks and community development credit unions (essentially, depository cooperatives) but also non-depository entities including nonprofit community development loan funds, micro-enterprise loan funds, community development venture capital funds, and, of course, CDCs. The function of CDFIs in complex finance transactions took a significant step forward with authorization in 2000 for the CDFI Fund to administer New Markets Tax Credits, with a scope of activity well beyond the LIHTC's affordable housing mission.[34] Selected CDFIs and other intermediary organizations have used the NMTC to stimulate investment and economic growth in targeted communities to grow businesses, create jobs, and sustain local economies.

Administered by the IRS, the LIHTC through tax expenditure has become the largest source of public subsidy for production and rehabilitation of affordable rental housing. Since enactment in 1986, the LIHTC has been the mechanism to finance over two million affordable rental units in more than 28,000 developments. In 2016 alone, its cost in forgone tax revenue was about $8 billion.[35] Similarly, the NMTC, jointly administered by the IRS and the CDFI Fund, has awarded around $45 billion in tax credit authority for community-based business and economic

[32] Low-Income Housing Credit, 26 U.S.C. § 42 (2012). Federal funding programs for housing development continued to leverage private investment in the years following the 1986 creation of the Low Income Housing Tax Credit. In the early 1990s, the federal HOME Investment Partnership Program was authorized to provide grants to state and local governments for affordable housing development, and the federal HOPE VI program provided additional funding to replace distressed public housing projects with redesigned mixed-income housing. *See The Legal Guide to Affordable Housing Development* (Rochelle E. Lento & Tim Iglesias eds., 2nd ed. 2013) (including a thorough chronology and analysis of federal policies for financing affordable housing development).

[33] Riegle Community Development and Regulatory Improvement Act of 1994, 12 U.S.C. § 4701 (2012).

[34] New Markets Tax Credit, 26 U.S.C. § 45D (2012); *cf.* Carol Steinbach, *The CDC Tax Credit: An Effective Tool for Attracting Private Resources to Community Economic Development*, Brookings Inst. Aug. 1, 1988 (analyzing results of a pilot program of tax credits for CDCs, a precursor to the NMTC a decade later).

[35] *The Effects of the Low-Income Housing Tax Credit (LIHTC)*, Research Brief (NYU Furman Center), May 2017.

development, leveraging substantial private sector investment in low-income communities.[36]

LIHTC and NMTC transactions are highly technical and require specialized and multi-disciplinary professional expertise. In the LIHTC program, the IRS allocates federal tax credits to state housing credit agencies based upon relative population. In a competitive process, nonprofit and for-profit developers apply to the state housing agencies for allocation of federal tax credits to reduce financing cost of affordable housing development projects. Criteria for these allocations are published in each given state's Qualified Allocation Plan and reflect priorities such as location, impact on meeting affordable housing needs, and capacity of the project sponsor. The tax credits serve as an incentive for private investors, ordinarily banks or corporations. Typically, the developer will form a limited partnership or limited liability company (LLC) with one or more investors through which it can provide these investors with tax credits in return for up-front equity investment. The developer or sponsor, often a nonprofit CDC, serves as the general partner with management authority and a minimal ownership interest. The investor or investors serve as limited partners, with substantial ownership interest but no management authority. The investors claim the tax credits over a ten-year period, passed through the limited partnership or LLC, to offset other taxable income. Certain rules to ensure that the housing remains affordable to low-income residents stay in place for fifteen years, violation of which can subject the investor to risk of IRS recapture of the credits. The housing property must remain affordable for thirty years, although the tax credit investor does not risk recapture in the latter half of this thirty-year period. LIHTC transactions become substantially more complicated when a syndicator combines multiple investors to form an investment fund involving a number of housing projects.[37]

Steps in a LIHTC transaction typically span two years, more or less, with the sponsor receiving a fee in exchange for development services and for taking the risk of lead-time work in advance of the tax credit allocation. Site selection and eventual real estate purchase option, initial assessment of the costs and hurdles ahead, and other due diligence is followed by local approvals from the municipality or other governing authority. At this stage, the developer might also negotiate tax increment financing (TIF), whereby the local government agrees to return to the developer as a

36 Community Development Financial Institutions Fund, www.cdfifund.gov/about/Pages/default.aspx (last visited May 28, 2018). The NMTC is a 39 percent credit – that is, an investor in a NMTC transaction is eligible to receive a tax credit, realized over seven years, in the amount of 39 percent of its qualified investment.

37 *Low-Income Housing Tax Credits: Affordable Housing Investment Opportunities for Banks*, Report (Community Developments Insights), Apr. 2014. In a certain category of affordable housing transactions, developers make use of tax-exempt Private Activity Bonds in conjunction with the LIHTC to attract further private investment. *See, e.g.*, Michael J. Novogradac, *Financing Affordable Housing: LIHTCs and Tax-Exempt Bonds Offer Options for Investors and Brokers* (CCIM Institute – www.ccim.com/cire-magazine/articles/financing-affordable-housing/?gmSsoPc=1).

partial rebate of property taxes an amount reflecting the increased property taxes arising from the new development. The sponsor then submits an application to the state housing credit authority, for both a tax credit allocation and a loan. If the application is successful, the housing authority issues a notice to proceed (with conditional allocation of credits), and the sponsor enters an extended use agreement to restrict its property to comply with the program requirements. Full architectural plans and updated pro forma financial statements accompany legal documentation for a construction loan, project construction, and eventual permanent financing and occupancy. This cursory description understates the legal complexity of such a transactional process, which might include well over 150 separate documents – for organization of legal entities, tax credits, and syndication; for construction loan, tax credit investment, and permanent financing; for title, survey, construction, environment, zoning, and other property matters; and for numerous opinions of counsel with a range of assurances and certifications.[38]

A NMTC transaction is similarly complex. The CDFI Fund certifies specially designated "community development entities" (or CDEs) to use tax credits to raise private capital for qualified low-income community investments, typically business and commercial real estate projects. CDEs compete roughly on an annual basis for a share of the year's total NMTC allocation. A CDE that receives an allocation of NMTCs through this competitive process then works to obtain investment from a bank or other for-profit investor in exchange for tax credits channeled through an LLC or limited partnership structure. The CDE in turn typically makes loans to "qualified active low-income community businesses." The tax credits, which the investor realizes over seven years, essentially allow for a lower interest rate for the community business or project. Like the LIHTC, many NMTC transactions involve syndication or multiple investors in a special investment fund and multiple or special-purpose CDEs. Deals are often layered with other tax credit programs, including state-level programs parallel to the federal NMTC program in more than a dozen states.[39] An intermediary organization like CEI ordinarily holds a number of potential projects in waiting and in varying states of progress, lists them as illustrative

[38] Descriptions here of steps in tax credit transactions are drawn in part from John Kaminski of the Portland, Maine, law firm Drummond Woodsum, who worked through a simulated LIHTC transaction, and from Charlie Spies and Tom Dolan of CEI Capital Management LLC, who worked through a simulated NMTC transaction, with my Economic Development Law class at the University of Maine School of Law in 2017.

[39] *New Markets Tax Credits: Unlocking Investment Potential*, Report (Community Developments Insights), June. 2013. For an explanation of a basic New Markets Tax Credit transaction, see Herbert F. Stevens, New Markets Tax Credits, *in Building Healthy Communities: A Guide to Community Economic Development for Advocates, Lawyers, and Policymakers* at 161–69. In addition to state-level New Markets Tax Credit programs in a number of states, historic tax credit programs exist at both the federal and state level to support preservation of historic buildings.

in its application for NMTC allocations, and selects the most viable or compelling projects for development if and when it receives a tax credit allocation.

Deployment of NMTCs enabled CEI to scale up dramatically through its subsidiary CEI Capital Management LLC. In a wide-ranging approach to building assets, CEI has deployed program-related investments from national foundations and loans from banks large and small, and has raised capital through its own private offering of fixed-income debt securities to individuals and institutions seeking community investment opportunities with positive social impact. CEI also has formed a series of venture capital subsidiaries to invest in emerging job-generating companies and as a complement to other CEI financing initiatives. A new subsidiary added in 2017, Bright Community Capital, focuses on environmental sustainability. It invests equity, debt, and tax equity in nonresidential solar projects in low- and moderate-income communities.

SUSTAINABILITY AND ACCOUNTABILITY

Scaling Up

Jeremy Nowak, former board chair of the Federal Reserve Bank of Philadelphia, frames two distinct phases in the evolution of CDFIs. A "proof of concept" phase began in the 1970s and continued through the 1990s, followed by a "steady growth" stage since 1999.[40] The first of these two phases was characterized, with some exceptions, by relatively small community-based lending institutions relying primarily on grants and loans from foundations, high-wealth individuals, and religious institutions. The critical innovation during this period of community development finance was to develop credible lending and risk management practices and to connect higher-risk borrowers with social investors; to "demonstrate the capacity to make loans and repay investors" and to "negotiate ... a practical space between markets and public purpose."[41]

The second phase of CDFI growth witnessed a sea change in financial scale. While foundation support continued, the federal government increased its use of public grants for community development finance, triggered by the 1994 creation of the CDFI Fund, amplified by the subsequent development of the NMTC program, and coupled with further growth and momentum in use of the LIHTC. In particular, direct capital placements in CDFIs by the US Department of Treasury – essentially unencumbered funds available for equity and for operations – boosted CDFIs to a scale much greater than typical community development loan funds capitalized primarily by debt. Foundation and government grants created an equity

40 Jeremy Nowak, *CDFI Futures: An Industry at a Crossroads*, Opportunity Finance Network, Mar. 2016.

41 *Id.* at 8.

base for CDFI expansion and leverage, putting them in a position to capitalize on the tremendous growth of community reinvestment by banks since the late 1990s.

Today, the notion of "impact investing" labels a new generation of socially responsible capital allocation by banks, pensions, mutual funds, foundations, endowments held by universities and religious organizations, wealth managers, and individuals. Ron Phillips, CEI's founder and former CEO, argues that impact investors today present tremendous potential for investment in community development organizations.[42] So-called philanthrocapitalism has captured the imagination of some extremely wealthy and high-profile figures.[43] A 2015 survey of private investors conducted by JP Morgan and the Global Impact Investing Network counted $60 billion in impact investments worldwide, and major asset management firms have increased their attention to impact investing.[44]

Although just a small fraction of total private investments, impact investing received a regulatory boost from President Barack Obama's administration that potentially will increase participation by foundations and pensions. In September 2015, the IRS issued a notice that foundations may dedicate mission-investments aligned with their charitable purposes, even if these investments fail to offer the highest return, lowest risk, or greater liquidity which, prior to the ruling, risked imposition of additional excise tax.[45] A month later, the US Department of Labor (DOL) issued an interpretive bulletin rescinding a 2008 ruling that subjected "economically targeted investments" by pension funds to additional scrutiny, a rule that chilled pension investments that considered social impact rather than simply risk and return. The bulletin clarified that social, environmental, and governance issues should be considered as factors directly influencing risk and return. Although the DOL back-pedaled on this issue in 2018, pension funds still have the capacity and authority for impact investing, provided there is no adverse effect on risk and

[42] Ronald Phillips, *Impact Investing and Community Development*, 25 ME. POL'Y REV. 63 (2016) (tracing the origin of the term "impact investing" to the Rockefeller Foundation's post-recession gathering of thought leaders a decade ago in Bellagio, Italy); *see also* Antony Bugg-Levine, Future of Community Development: How CDFIs Can Best Ride the Impact Investing Wave, *in Investing in What Works for America's Communities*; Ellen S. Seidman et al., *Making Sure There Is a Future – Capitalizing Community Development Financial Institutions*, URB. INST., May 2017.

[43] *See, e.g.*, John Cassidy, *Mark Zuckerberg and the Rise of Philanthrocapitalism*, THE NEW YORKER, Dec. 2, 2015; Eric Franklin, *Philanthrocapitalism: Exacerbating the Antidemocratic, Paternalistic, and Amateuristic Nature of Philanthropy*, LEGAL STUDIES RESEARCH PAPER (UNLV William S. Boyd Sch. L.), Dec. 2016; David Rieff, *Philanthrocapitalism: A Self-Love Story*, THE NATION, Oct. 1, 2015.

[44] Michael Etzel, *New Regulations Boost Social Impact Investing*, STAN. SOCIAL INNOVATION REV., Dec. 17, 2015; *see* GLOBAL IMPACT INVESTING NETWORK, http://thegiin.org/about/ (last visited June 22, 2018). *See also* Shena R. Ashley & Joycelyn Ovalle, *Investing Together: Emerging Approaches in Collaborative Place-Based Impact Investing*, URB. INST., May 2018.

[45] Internal Revenue Service, Notice 2015–62, regarding application of I.R.C. § 4944.

return on pension investments.[46] With about $9 trillion in pension assets, even modest changes by fund managers might materially affect the level of impact investing overall.

Nowak describes a third phase of "capital transformation" potentially emerging now in community development finance, primarily among the largest of CDFIs. This represents a further shift in identity and scale with greater recognition by and access to conventional capital markets.[47] A trend among the largest few dozen CDFIs in recent years has been geographical expansion, operating in a multi-state or national arena and hence diminished focus on place. One driver of this trend is national banks engaged in interstate banking and seeking to maximize reach in their multiple CRA target areas by investing in CDFIs. Other drivers are the imperatives of sustainability in any successful financial institution – gaining efficiencies through scale, mitigating risk through diversification, accessing a larger volume of deals to increase liquidity, or specializing in products that can be replicated in multiple markets.[48]

Although less connected to a particular locale, these larger CDFIs often work on projects through and in conjunction with locally based, less well-healed, and smaller CDCs and CDFIs. It is through these collaborations, in part, that larger CDFIs can maintain some community focus, encouraging local accountability and reducing risk by relying on a local partner to understand the politics and culture of the region, to know and monitor local project players, and to provide needed technical assistance at the grassroots. "Translation" of complex transactions and attention to local needs and values is facilitated by collaborators on the ground.

The increased scale of CDFI operations, while presenting challenges to local participation and accountability, is also an important factor in sustainability. Scale expands access to private capital, and CDFIs have managed to grow and tap private capital at a time of shrinking public expenditures. Even as Congress has reduced funding for other programs, CDFIs as a trade group constitute a strong lobby and thus far have managed to preserve the federal tax credits so critical to their work. The LIHTC has been impressive in its stability and resilience. The NMTC faces greater uncertainty, but it too benefits from bipartisan support. In late 2014 with support from the Obama administration, the NMTC received a five-year renewal to remain in effect until 2019, although it is still dependent upon annual fiscal allocations by Congress. Both of these tax credits survived passage of the so-called Tax Cuts and

[46] U.S. Dep't of Labor, Interpretive Bulletin 2015–01, regarding application of the Employee Retirement Income Security Act of 1974, §§ 403, 404. *Cf.* Field Assistance Bulletin No. 2018–01, U.S. Dep't of Labor (Employee Benefits Security Administration), www.americanbenefitscouncil.org/pub/b9d6b6e9-9702-485f-0654-f1eacoff79e2.

[47] Nowak, *CDFI Futures: An Industry at a Crossroads.*

[48] *Id. See also* Michael Swack et al., *CDFIs Stepping into the Breach: An Impact Evaluation – Summary Report*, Carsey Sch. Pub. Pol'y, Univ. of New Hampshire, Aug. 2014 (detailing both the relatively limited scope and the potential for growth in CDFIs).

Jobs Act, a major overhaul of tax law in late 2017. But impacts of this legislation on tax credit financing for affordable housing and community development finance are subtle and still unfolding. A substantial reduction in corporate tax rates, for instance, might combine with other changes in the tax law to reduce investor demand and thus reduce the volume of affordable housing production.[49]

CEI grapples with balancing its local focus and its national reach. It has evolved as a hybrid institution – a local institution serving and grounded in Maine, while extending its expertise nationally in rural development. The parent nonprofit is primarily engaged with Maine institutions, through its platform of housing finance and business lending, technical assistance, and related policy analysis and advocacy, coupled with national policy engagement. Much of CEI's activity around the nation is through subsidiary entities.

The CEI "family of enterprises" has come a long way since its origin as a local nonprofit CDC and looks very different today than it did in the 1970s. To manage its wide-ranging programs and growth in scale, CEI is staffed by close to ninety employees and bolstered by engaged volunteers serving on boards and committees of the parent entity and its subsidiaries. It continues to innovate, adapting to a changing context in the market, in sources of finance, in public policy, and in community needs. Its story is one of reinvention, adding new programs and entities from time to time and spinning off others. Its social justice mission, however, has remained consistent throughout its existence – to create quality jobs, environmentally sustainable enterprises, and shared prosperity. So, too, the evolution of community economic development has seen policy and politics, legal framework, technique, and context change significantly, with the touchstone of economic justice at its core.

"Community" in Community Development Finance

Limitations of community economic development have been well documented – from scattershot neighborhood projects in the urban core to inadequate attention to rural poverty, from multi-cultural and racial insensitivities to overly vague claims of empowerment. Fealty to philanthropic and public funders arguably reinforces resistance to confronting powerful conventional institutions. Impact on structural inequalities and segregation is modest at best. Professionalization of the field can

[49] *See* Alyssa Katz, *The Harm to Affordable Housing*, The American Prospect, (Summer 2018), http://prospect.org/article/harm-affordable-housing. *See also* Michael Novogradac et al, *Tax Reform and Its Consequences for Affordable Rental Housing*, 27 J. Affordable Hous. & Cmty. Dev. L. 107 (2018). In a throwback to Reagan-era "enterprise zones" and Clinton-era "empowerment zones," the 2017 tax act provides for designation of selected "opportunity zones" and offers a tax incentive for private investment in low-income communities. Taxpayers, for example, can defer capital gains tax on sales of property to the extent such gains are reinvested in a qualified opportunity zone. *Id.* at 118–21. *Cf.* Conor Dougherty, *Tax Overhaul Is a Blow to Affordable Housing Efforts*, N.Y. Times, Jan. 18, 2018.

distance organizations from their local constituents.[50] Many practitioners avoid or intentionally address and moderate these limitations in practice. But, awareness and documentation of these issues enables scholars and practitioners to measure expectations and success within defined boundaries – and to push against those boundaries for greater social impact.

The particular challenge of remaining accountable and accessible to local constituents persists in community development finance, especially with its growth in scale and its multi-layered financial structures. Revitalizing distressed urban and rural communities is the central mission driving many CDFIs. As previously noted, though, community economic development does not simply view the community as beneficiary of these efforts but also as agent. The technical and transactional complexity of community development finance can overshadow the progressive goals that motivate many actors in the field. The policies and practices can distance CDFIs from the very constituents at their core and from the activist origins of community development corporations.

Practitioners in the field suggest a concrete upside to tax-credit transactions, in both discipline and accountability. Over time, LIHTC and NMTC transactions have become standardized, replicable, and dependable deal structures and thus more able to attract banks and private capital into community investment. Furthermore, banks, investors, developers, government agencies, and other parties to these transactions have a shared interest in a successful outcome – from preserving tax credits through the multi-year life of such deals to assuring repayment of private loans or public bonds. Accountability to one another and to the integrity of the deal is built into the transactional documents, while multiple parties have an interest in enforcing necessary compliance. From this perspective, the web of transactional accountability can be more effective than direct and binary grants or contracts. And, the transactions often have a community development entity at their core, helping to negotiate and enforce provisions for community benefits embedded in the transaction.

CEI and a number of other organizations require participants in their tax credit projects to commit to community benefit agreements. A community benefit agreement might stipulate, for example, targeted workforce training and job creation, scholarships for local low-income students, reduced rent in a newly constructed building, or certain labor and environmental standards. A CEI project in rural

[50] *See* Michael Haber, *CED after #OWS: From Community Economic Development to Anti-Authoritarian Community Counter-Institutions*, 43 Fordham Urb. L.J. 2 (2016); Scott L. Cummings, *Community Economic Development as Progressive Politics: Toward a Grassroots Movement for Economic Justice*, 54 Stan. L. Rev. 399 (2001); Nicholas Lemann, *The Myth of Community Development*, N.Y. Times, Jan. 9, 1994. *See also*, *Maine Forest-Based Communities as a Live Case Study*, CEI Capital Management LLC Rural Economies Form (June 2017) (addressing particular challenges facing rural economies in community development); Simon, *supra* Note 3 at 219–27.

Baileyville, Maine, illustrates the application of such a mechanism. It used NMTCs to finance a retooling and expansion of St. Croix Tissue, a paper factory, and helped preserve jobs and create new ones. A community benefit agreement associated with the investment successfully required St. Croix to hire a certain percentage of workers from low-income households and to implement a systematic program of employer-specific workforce training.[51] This focus on job *quality*, not just quantity, reflects a strategic trend among a number of community development organizations. Rather than simply counting and celebrating the *number* of jobs created and retained, these institutions seek to leverage jobs that provide a living wage, basic benefits, career- and wealth-building opportunities, and a fair and respectful workplace.[52]

Both the LIHTC and the NMTC programs favor applicants that can demonstrate local project approval and benefit. The federal CDFI Fund certifies community development entities to administer NMTC allocations. Criteria for certification include a primary mission to provide investment capital for low-income communities or persons and accountability to residents of such communities through representation on the community development entity's governing board or advisory board.[53] Acknowledging particular challenges in *rural* America, Congress in 2006 required that "non-metropolitan" areas receive adequate allocation of investments from the NMTC.[54] Allocations of federal LIHTCs are made (generally by state housing authorities) pursuant to a given state's Qualified Allocation Plan, which defines criteria for allocation priorities. By federal statute, these criteria give preference to projects appropriate to local conditions, serving low-income residents, and contributing to concerted community revitalization plans, and the allocating agency must give notice to the chief executive officer of the relevant local jurisdiction (e.g., mayor of a town) with an opportunity to comment.[55]

The impact of CDFIs depends to some extent on their commitment to providing projects with not just financial investment but also technical assistance and

[51] Lori Valigra, *CEI Presents 'Opportunity Award' to St. Croix Tissue*, ME. BIZ (Mar. 15, 2017), www.mainebiz.biz/article/20170315/NEWS01/170319968/cei-presents-%27opportunity-award%27-to-st-croix-tissue.

[52] *See Moving Beyond Job Creation: Defining and Measuring the Creation of Quality Jobs*, INSIGHT AT PACIFIC COMMUNITY VENTURES, Apr. 2016; *Public Policy and Investments in Quality Jobs: Ideas for Policy Change*, INSIGHT AT PACIFIC COMMUNITY VENTURES, Mar. 2017. For an in-depth examination and analysis of workforce development strategy and job quality, *see* Steven L. Dawson, *The Pinkerton Papers Job Quality Series*, THE PINKERTON FOUND., 2016–2017, www.thepinkertonfoundation.org/paper_type/job-quality-series (last visited June 27, 2018). *Cf.* PARAPROFESSIONAL HEALTHCARE INSTITUTE, which promotes quality jobs in home health care, https://phinational.org (last visited June 29, 2018).

[53] I.R.C. § 45D(c)(1).

[54] Tax Relief and Health Care Act of 2006, in extending and modifying the New Markets Tax Credit, added language to "ensure that non-metropolitan counties receive a proportional allocation of qualified equity investments … " I.R.C. § 45D(i)(6). *See* Cynthia M. Duncan, Community Development in Rural America: Collaborative, Regional, and Comprehensive, *in Investing in What Works for America's Communities*.

[55] I.R.C. § 42(m).

development services. Such services ordinarily include screening and assisting enterprises prior to financing, to assure that they have the capacity to succeed and to minimize default risk. Also critical is ongoing business consulting and financial training that accompany financing and further reduce the likelihood of default. CDFI collaboration with banks, foundations, and other local institutions in packaging multi-layered financing arrangements, as well as engagement with regional government and advocacy organizations with respect to public policies, all combine to facilitate buy-in by and accountability to a web of stakeholders.[56] Meaningful impact, of course, requires attention to many other aspects of revitalizing low-income communities and their residents, not simply doing deals, and requires connection with the resources of broader regional economies and with levers of power.[57]

Driven in part by external funding dictates and the availability of compelling tax incentives, many CDFIs are focused on transactions and organizational growth, arguably at the expense of more fundamental economic and social change and at the risk that finance chills activism. This tension is hardly new. Looking back, the civil rights movement and welfare rights advocacy in the 1950s and 1960s, and subsequent expansion in community organizing, amplified the tension between activism and economic development.[58] In some cases this advocacy was at odds with economic development initiatives, as in those urban renewal projects that destroyed neighborhood housing. In other instances, though, organizing and advocacy essentially created the political space that allowed for community development initiatives. Expressly coupled with community development, grassroots activism also grounded some of these efforts with greater local accountability.

Apparent here is a conceptual distinction between community *development* and community *organizing*, and a critical tension between the two. Community organizing emphasizes broadly based grassroots efforts, in low- and moderate-income and often minority communities, to confront institutions of power, public or private. These powerful governmental or corporate institutions, from an organizing perspective, hold responsibility to implement policies and programs. The mission of community organizing is to pressure these institutions to act responsibly, essentially bringing the political power of mobilized citizens to bear on assuring equitable treatment and results. In contrast, community development focuses less on confrontation and more on building capacity within community organizations to implement policies and programs. By internalizing the mechanisms and provision of business and social services, this development approach shifts responsibility for implementing policy and programs to community institutions. Recalling early

56 *See* Brett Theodos et al., *Scaling Impact for Community Development Financial Institutions*, Urb. Inst., June 2016.

57 *See* Ellen S. Seidman, Integration and Innovation in a Time of Stress, *in Investing in What Works for America's Communities*.

58 *See* Cummings, *supra* Note 50.

tensions between direct action organizing and the emergence of CDCs in the 1960s and 1970s, community economic development today can be so tied into conventional financial and governmental institutions as to compromise its impact in confronting structural drivers of economic and political inequality. Fighting entrenched poverty requires advocacy for essential public benefits like health care and child care, living wage standards and supplements like the earned income tax credit, public transit, and opportunity for quality education, along with development of jobs and housing.[59]

There is a long history of difference and debate among community organizers and community development advocates.[60] Tension persists between institution-building and social change advocacy. But, borders between the two are often blurred, in rhetoric and practice, especially given overlapping constituencies, values, and goals. Community development practitioners cite themes of empowerment and social change in their work and indeed share these goals with other institutions engaged in organizing and advocacy. Emphasis on these themes, however, tends to invite criticism by measuring a community development institution's success against goals beyond its core practice.

Definitional clarity is important in measuring and evaluating impact. Community development and finance is essentially about bridging capital markets with community-based enterprise, about building community capacity and bringing business expertise to bear on urban and rural revitalization, and about modeling and pushing for social responsibility in finance and banking. By this standard, CDCs and CDFIs have performed well, developed innovative financial tools, and demonstrated positive impact in selected locales. By also holding true to their explicit social purpose, many of these institutions have moderated their assimilation into the mainstream financial system and distinguished themselves from conventional banks.

Moreover, community economic development as a strategy need not stand alone. CDFI alliances or collaborations with kindred organizing and advocacy partners, and meaningful connection with social movements, can be a key ingredient in the character and sustainability of community development finance. The distinction between community organizing and community development is real, but the two can co-exist. In the best circumstances, creative collaboration between organizing and development can be a potent combination.[61]

[59] *See* Peter Edelman, Our History with Concentrated Poverty, *in Investing in What Works for America's Communities*.

[60] Mike Miller, *Can the Debate Be Resolved? Community Organizing vs. Community Development*, ORGANIZE TRAINING CENTER REPORT (2009), www.organizetrainingcenter.org/writings.html.

[61] *See, e.g.*, INTERVALLEY PROJECT (IVP), www.intervalleyproject.org/ (last visited May 28, 2018) (explaining the InterValley Project, which is an organizing network of seven regional organizations that combine community organizing and development strategies); Greg LeRoy, Making Economic Development Accountable, *in Building Healthy Communities*; Barbara Bezdek,

COMMUNITY DEVELOPMENT PRACTICE AND THE LEGAL ACADEMY

"Most law reviews do not contain cartoons," read the lead in a *National Law Journal* article. "Then again, the Spring 1991 issue of the *Buffalo Law Review* ... is not like most law reviews."[62] As a law professor then at the State University of New York (SUNY) at Buffalo, I oversaw publication of a symposium issue of the *Buffalo Law Review* entitled "Buffalo Change & Community."[63] It was an interdisciplinary take on the Buffalo political economy in the early years of SUNY-Buffalo's curricular and clinical program in community development law and affordable housing finance. The *National Law Journal* and others took notice of this unusual enterprise – a scholarly law journal addressing the urban challenges in its own community. A series of Buffalo-subject political cartoons by Tom Toles (then a syndicated artist at the *Buffalo News*, now at the *Washington Post*) helped to underscore the departure from traditional scholarship, to make it more accessible to a popular audience, and – with his Pulitzer Prize just months before publication of the law review – to heighten public attention. By design, research for the law journal issue helped to shape our law school work in western New York, including scholarship, curriculum, and clinical legal practice in regional community economic development – and one of just a handful of law school transactional clinics at that time.

Fast forward to 2017, and we see the emergence and maturing of community development clinics alongside other outreach, civic engagement, and clinical practice by law students and faculty. Numerous law schools today house transactional clinics engaged in affordable housing finance, small business counseling, or community economic development, and legal scholarship increasingly addresses growth, innovation, and challenges in the field. A discussion group on "Community Development Law and Economic Justice – Why Law Matters" at the 2017 annual meeting of the Association of American Law Schools marked this robust attention in the legal academy.[64] The event brought together legal scholars from across the nation and across generations. It presented an opportunity to assess an array of new law school initiatives and strategies in the field, and to give further definition to "community development law" at a fluid moment in its history.

Although community economic development is not lawyer-driven, law and lawyers are pervasive in the field and particularly in financial transactions. In the

Digging into Democracy: Reflections on CED and Social Change Lawyering after #OWS, 77 Md. L. Rev. Endnotes 16 (2018).

[62] Ken Myers, *SUNY Buffalo's Law Review: Spring 1991 Issue Looks Home*, Nat'l L.J., Aug. 19, 1991.

[63] 39 Buffalo L. Rev. 313 (Spring 1991).

[64] Peter Pitegoff, *Community Development Law, Economic Justice, and the Legal Academy*, 26 J. Affordable Hous. & Cmty. Dev. L. 31 (2017) (introducing a symposium of ten short articles arising from the program on community development law and economic justice at the January 2017 annual meeting of the Association of American Law Schools).

policy arena, lawyers play a pivotal role in translating innovative ideas and best practices into workable laws and regulations and in arguing for their enactment. Many legislators who pass these laws or government agency leaders who administer them are trained in the law, as are many staff and board members in CDFIs. With respect to legal practice, structuring and negotiating a LIHTC or NMTC transaction requires specialized skill and training and lawyers with deep expertise. The practice implicates corporate law, tax, securities, contracts, land use, real estate, intellectual property, environmental law, regulatory compliance, and more. The National Economic Development and Law Center – founded in 1969 in Oakland, CA, and still operating today as the Insight Center for Community Economic Development – was an early mover in practicing and shaping law in this realm. Along with direct legal assistance, it served as a back-up center for community development lawyers nationwide in the emerging field. Such legal expertise today is widely dispersed in private law firms, CDFIs, local development organizations, public agencies, and law schools.

The legal academy plays a role in sustaining and advancing the discipline of community development law, through research and scholarship and through clinical and classroom teaching. The proliferation of transactional clinics engaged in affordable housing and community development around the nation brings the resources of the academy to bear directly upon neighborhood revitalization efforts. Similar to other law school clinical programs in a wide range of disciplines, these development clinics have a multiplier effect. Beyond direct impact on the ground, they are sensitizing new generations of lawyers to the skills and values of community development law. Today, roughly 140 transactional clinics, broadly defined, operate in American law schools – about 25 percent of them with a community economic development, affordable housing finance, or social justice focus.[65] Parallel efforts in classroom courses contribute to educating future lawyers about the roles they might play in revitalizing distressed communities. Law school curricula include courses expressly about affordable housing and community development, nonprofit organizations, poverty law, and economic justice, and law professors integrate related content in more conventional courses like corporation law and professional responsibility.

[65] Susan R. Jones & Jacqueline Lainez, *Enriching the Law School Curriculum: The Rise of Transactional Legal Clinics in U.S. Law Schools*, 43 Wash. Univ. J. L. & Pol'y 85, 93 (2014) (examining and broadly defining "transactional" law school clinics to include, in addition to affordable housing and community economic development clinics: small business and entrepreneurship, microenterprise, nonprofit organization, intellectual property, and arts and entertainment clinics); *see*, Patience Crowder, *Designing a Transactional Law Clinic for Life-Long Learning*, 19 Lewis & Clark L. Rev. 413 (2015); Praveen Kosuri, *"Impact" in 3D–Maximizing Impact through Transactional Clinics*, 18 Clinical L. Rev. 1 (2011); Lynnise E. Pantin, *The Economic Justice Imperative for Transactional Law Clinics*, 62 Villanova L. Rev. 175 (2017).

Analysis and critique of community economic development law appeared early on in scholarly law journals and has increased over time with growth in the field. Legal scholars have the space and purpose to provide policy analysis and reflection. Their research can spotlight best practices and build upon innovations. Outside the fray of practice, scholars can take a long view, identify trends, chronicle advances, and bolster the field by constructing a theoretical foundation and public policy rationale. The legal academy has a role to play as a repository of knowledge and expertise and as a modest contributor to sustainability.

Critical scholarship can identify shortcomings in the field, help keep community development connected with its activist roots, and reinforce economic justice values. Scholars, for instance, have highlighted structural issues of the LIHTC, including the potential capture of substantial "residual value" in the coming years by private developers of affordable housing as LIHTC property use restrictions begin to expire.[66] Scholars also have done well at articulating a rationale and vision of a more politically engaged and advocacy approach to community economic development, at positioning it within broader progressive movements, and at chronicling examples in practice.[67] A 2007 symposium issue of the *California Law Review*, for instance, presented an expansive definition of community, way beyond contained geographical spaces or institutions.[68] It explored the subtlety of the lawyer's role and responsibility in community economic development, of lawyer accountability and deference, and of the importance of integrating legal capacity within organizational actors.[69]

An emergent body of applied scholarship is and must be grounded by narratives of and engagement with the evolving practices in community development and the law. In 1991, following enactment of the Low Income Housing Tax Credit program and growth of related legal practice, the American Bar Association established its Forum on Affordable Housing & Community Development Law.[70] A permanent

66 Brandon M. Weiss, *Residual Value Capture in Subsidized Housing*, 10 HARV. L. & POL'Y REV. 521 (2016).

67 *See, e.g.*, Cummings, *supra* Note 50 (accounts, for instance, of integrating community economic development with living wage campaigns, worker cooperative development, community benefit agreements, and sectoral development strategies). *See also* Haber, *supra* Note 50; Bezdek, *supra* Note 61.

68 William H. Simon, *Introduction: Lawyers and Community Economic Development*, 95 CALIF. L. REV. 1821 (2007); Sameer M. Ashar, *Public Interest Lawyers and Resistance Movements*, 95 CALIF. L. REV. 1879 (2007).

69 Sheila R. Foster & Brian Glick, *Integrative Lawyering: Navigating the Political Economy of Urban Redevelopment*, 95 CALIF. L. REV. 1999 (2007); Jennifer Gordon, *The Lawyer Is Not the Protagonist: Community Campaigns, Law, and Social Change*, 95 CALIF. L. REV. 2133 (2007).

70 The American Bar Association, in addition to its large and wide-ranging practice-area Sections, creates smaller Forums to explore and monitor new areas of law as they emerge on a national scale. Other ABA Forums include: Air & Space Law, Communications Law, Construction Law, Entertainment & Sports Industries, and Franchising.

organization with a mission of education and professional development, the Forum in short order assembled a national membership of and conversation among lawyers and law professors involved in affordable housing and community development and today reflects a membership of more than 3,000 lawyers. Academic members, although outnumbered by practitioners, have nurtured a legal educators group throughout the life of the Forum. In a further link to the legal academy, the Forum reaches out to law students, holds panel discussions at law schools, and sponsors a law student writing competition, in a concerted attempt to attract new lawyers to the field. Early on, it established the *Journal of Affordable Housing & Community Development Law*, with law professors and lawyers serving as editors on a rotating basis, engaging law students in the editorial process, and working with the ABA for publication. The journal, published in three issues per year, is an explicit connection between legal scholars and lawyers practicing in community development finance.[71] The only law journal devoted exclusively to affordable housing and community development law, it does well at bridging theory, policy, and practice.

Underlying goals and values in community economic development have remained consistent over the past several decades. The context, however, is continually changing. As demonstrated by the history of Maine-based CEI, the strategies and mechanisms of community development need to keep pace with changes in the economic landscape, most recently with the continuing impacts of the 2008 recession. Organizations like CEI monitor and, indeed, help craft legal and regulatory policies in development finance, and contend with new technologies, global trade, climate change, and a fluid political economy. From growth in contingent employment and low-wage labor to emergence of a so-called gig economy,[72] from urban in-migration and gentrification to growing recognition of rural poverty, from extreme economic inequality and continued racial tensions to challenges faced by immigrants and sharp partisan divisions of the Trump era – community development practitioners and scholars have taken account and must continue to adapt as other issues inevitably arise. Research and practice in law schools can track and, in some

[71] Professor Tim Iglesias of the University of San Francisco School of Law states: "The *Journal* offers the space where good-willed legal practitioners, policymakers, and academics ... can foster mutual understanding and greater collaboration." Tim Iglesias, *Affordable Housing, Fair Housing and Community Development: Joined at the Hip, We Need to Learn to Walk Together*, 25 J. AFFORDABLE HOUS. & CMTY. DEV. L. 195, 199 (2017).

[72] *See, e.g.*, Steven Greenhouse, *On Demand, and Demanding Their Rights*, THE AMERICAN PROSPECT (Summer 2016) (on the gig economy, Uber, and a new chapter in American labor history); Steven Greenhouse, *The Whatchamacallit Economy*, N.Y. TIMES, Dec. 16, 2016; Harry Arthurs, The False Promise of the Sharing Economy, *in Law and the Sharing Economy: Regulating Online Market Platforms* (D. McKee et al, eds., 2018); Nestor M. Davidson & John J. Infranca, *The Sharing Economy as an Urban Phenomenon*, 34 YALE L. & POL'Y REV. 215 (2016).

cases, anticipate these changes and challenges. This academic enterprise in community development law is evolving in parallel with practice, including the growing sophistication and complexity in community development financial institutions and their legal innovations.

Attention in law schools to community development law suggests a valuable and promising track in the legal academy. Legal scholars and clinical professors are increasingly engaged in theory, policy, and practice in the field. Today, a symposium issue of a law review about the local political economy, with or without political cartoons, would hardly stand out as unique.

5

How to Increase Our Affordable Housing Stock

Robert Solomon[1]

INTRODUCTION – OUR NATIONAL HOUSING POLICY

The United States is facing a severe housing shortage. A recent McKinsey study found that in California alone 50 percent of households cannot afford market rate housing and virtually no low-income families can afford to pay market rates.[2] From 2009 to 2014, California real estate prices increased by 15 percent, while median income increased by 5 percent.[3] According to McKinsey, California ranks 49th for housing units per capita, with a current housing shortage of two million units and an estimated shortage of 3.5 million units by 2025. Los Angeles voters, facing a severe homelessness problem, approved a small tax increase, which may take people off the streets but is unlikely to create substantial numbers of new units.

California is not alone. Nationally, the inventory of homes for sale is near historic lows, resulting in housing costs rising much faster than income.[4] At the current rate of production, we will construct 8.7 million new units over the next ten years, with a projected need of 15 million additional units.[5] More than two-thirds of urban markets are facing housing pressures.[6] New housing starts in 2015 were 30 percent

[1] Clinical Professor of Law, University of California Irvine.

[2] Jonathan Woetzel et al., *Closing California's Housing Gap*, McKinsey & Co (Oct. 2017), www.mckinsey.com/global-themes/urbanization/closing-californias-housing-gap.

[3] *Id.*

[4] Lawrence Yun, *Four More Years? No Quick End in Sight for the U.S. Housing Shortage*, Forbes Magazine (Dec. 13, 2016), www.forbes.com/sites/lawrenceyun/2016/12/13/housing-shortage-for-how-long/#c3c81a25ee46.

[5] *Id.*

[6] Yuqing Pan, *Sold Out: These 10 U.S. Cities Have the Biggest Housing Shortages*, Realtor.Com (Jan. 16, 2017), www.realtor.com/news/trends/top-10-housing-markets-constrained-by-tight-inventory/?aid=11921783&pid=7597981&cid=aff_cj_rdcandrental_allaffiliates_cj.

below the historic average between 1970 and 2007,[7] and, while there is a building boom in multi-family apartments, most new apartments are aimed at the top of the market.[8]

Blighted housing, housing shortages, and homelessness are not new, but the United States has never had a coherent housing policy to address structural housing deficits, as opposed to a series of economic policies that affected housing, sometimes as unintended or incidental consequences. The Homestead Act of 1862, the greatest land give-away in US history, was about settling the West, not developing housing.[9] The intent of the Act was to create 160-acre farms, but when this proved inadequate in the arid West, a few landowners were able to accumulate enormous tracts of land at the expense of the original homesteaders. The Pacific Railroad Acts, also in 1862, did the same for the railroads and brought about the development of towns wherever the railroads placed their stations.[10] Since then, national efforts have focused primarily on providing incentives for homeownership for those who could afford it, while providing some rental housing for those who could not.

The National Housing Act of 1934,[11] which created the Federal Housing Administration and the Federal Savings and Loan Insurance Corporation, had the primary purpose of protecting financial institutions and a secondary purpose of spurring the construction industry during the depression. The United States Housing Act of 1937[12] authorized public housing, but with great deference to state and local enabling acts and a limited view of federal responsibility. The result was high concentrations of rental public housing in high-density urban areas, with a paucity of government-funded rental housing elsewhere. The Housing Act of 1949[13] tinkered at the edges of the 1937 Act, but offered little in the way of a national housing policy. When it comes to urban centers, our notion of urban renewal may have been based

7 Stockton Williams, *Understanding the Scope of the Housing Shortage in the United States*, UrbanLand (Aug. 22, 2015), http://urbanland.uli.org/development-business/housing-shortage-u-s/.

8 *Id.*

9 The Homestead Acts are a fascinating part of American history, with dramatic results throughout the West. See, for example, *The Homestead Act of 1862*, Nat'l Archives: Educator Resources (last updated Oct. 3, 2016); www.archives.gov/education/lessons/homestead-act or *About the Homestead Act*, Nat'l Park Serv. (last updated Apr. 10, 2015), www.nps.gov/home/learn/historyculture/abouthomesteadactlaw.htm.

10 As part of the various Railroad Acts, Congress granted 174 million acres of public lands as rights-of-way. *The Pacific Railway Act of 1862*, Our Documents (last visited Aug. 26, 2018), www.ourdocuments.gov/doc.php?flash=false&doc=32; http://cprr.org/Museum/Pacific_Railroad_Acts.html; www.loc.gov/rr/program/bib/ourdocs/PacificRail.html.

11 12 U.S.C. § 1701.

12 42 U.S.C. § 1437(a)(3) (the Act's Declaration of Policy states that "The Federal Government should act where there is a serious need that private citizens or groups cannot or are not addressing responsibly.").

13 42 U.S.C. § 1441.

on an idealized society, but the reality included building highways through neighborhoods and eliminating affordable housing in the name of slum clearance.[14]

Section 8,[15] started in 1973 by the Nixon administration as a market-oriented experiment, was a way to take the government out of the housing business by moving from supply-side to demand-side interventions. Since 1973, Section 8 and public housing have competed for a limited pot of federal funding. Section 8 is winning. Since we are talking about a limited pot, it will become harder to sustain public housing units and their number will inevitably diminish.

Each year, Section 8 gets a larger share of the pie and public housing gets less. In 2014, the Congressional Budget Office reported that the Housing Choice Voucher (the Section 8 portable voucher used to subsidize rent on the private market) received $18 billion in funding, Project-Based Rental Assistance (also direct payments to private landlords) received $12 billion, and Public Housing received $7 billion. The Low Income Housing Tax Credit,[16] which is the source of 90 percent of all affordable housing production in the United States, accounted for $7 billion in tax expenditures.[17] That is a total of $44 billion for affordable rental housing. Meanwhile, the tax expenditures to the middle class and wealthy totaled $130 billion in lost tax revenues through mortgage interest and property tax deductions.[18]

Even where programs exist, the federal government deemphasizes homeownership opportunities for the poor. The Housing and Community Development Act of 1992 authorized homeownership assistance to first-time buyers, but HUD did not issue regulations until 1998, and the final regulations did not become effective until October 2000.[19] There are over two million outstanding Housing Choice Vouchers,[20] but from 2004 to 2012, HUD reports only 19,960 homeownership

[14] *See* Jane Jacobs, *The Death and Life of Great American Cities* (1961); for a view of urban renewal in New Haven, CT, *see* Robert Solomon, *Building a Segregated City: How We All Worked Together*, 16 St. Louis U. Pub. L. Rev. 265 (1997).

[15] 42 U.S.C. § 1347; 24 C.F.R. § 982.

[16] 26 U.S.C. § 42.

[17] A tax expenditure is not an appropriation, but a deduction or credit that results in less income to the treasury. When it comes to balancing the budget, a tax expenditure has the same effect as an appropriation.

[18] *Cong. Budget Office, Federal Housing Assistance for Low-Income Households* (Sept. 2015), www.cbo.gov/sites/default/files/114th-congress-2015-2016/reports/50782-lowincomehousing-onecolumn.pdf.

[19] Edgar A. Olsen, *Promoting Homeownership among Low-Income Households*, The Urban Institute (Aug. 20, 2007), www.urban.org/research/publication/promoting-homeownership-among-low-income-households.

[20] Douglas Rice and Barbara Sard, *Decade of Neglect Has Weakened Federal Low-Income Housing Programs: New Resources Required to Meet Growing Needs*, Center on Budget and Policy Priorities 10–12 (Feb. 24, 2009), www.cbpp.org/sites/default/files/atoms/files/2-24-09hous-sec2.pdf.

closings, an average of 2,217 per year.[21] This is not a question of ramping up, because the numbers for 2011 and 2012, the last two years reported on the HUD website, averaged 1,554 homeownership closings per year.[22] With even a modest turnover rate for vouchers over a nine-year period, the homeownership utilization is less than 1 percent of Section 8 recipients.

Among the poorest households, renters are more than five times as likely as homeowners to be subsidized.[23] Looking at these and other numbers, one researcher concluded that "[s]everal pieces of evidence suggest that the current system of low-income housing assistance is biased against homeownership for the poorest households."[24]

The message is clear. The primary federal housing policy is to subsidize homeowners through the tax code and the provision of infrastructure. A much smaller effort is devoted to subsidizing *some* poor renters. The homeowner subsidy is an entitlement, meaning that anyone owning a home has the right to claim the tax benefits. The rental subsidy is limited to the lucky few, and people will line up overnight to secure the opportunity to obtain a Section 8 voucher.

The foundation of our housing policy is, and always has been, a reliance on market forces. The American housing market works relatively well. Most people are housed, most people have indoor plumbing, heat and hot water. All markets have a top and a bottom, and when we talk about market failure, our concern is to bring up the bottom of the housing market to a level of habitability. We may decry the waste and gluttony at the top of the market, and we may urge a reduction in tax benefits for mansions and second homes, but those are side issues. The real goal of housing advocates is a market that spreads the benefits of decent housing across all income levels. One of those benefits is the opportunity to build wealth through home ownership.

Markets are supposed to be self-adjusting, but the housing market has not kept up with need, largely because we have incentivized the market to provide for the top and, to a lesser extent, the very bottom. The wealthy do not have a problem in finding housing and a few people get new subsidized units, but a portion of society remains underserved. Forbes reported that a shrinking housing inventory "is the principal reason why home prices have been outpacing people's income growth for the past five consecutive years."[25]

Over the past decade, we have produced an average of 870,000 new units per year. At that rate, we will produce 8.7 million units over the next decade, when we

21 *Homeownership Vouchers*, Dep't of Hous. and Urban Dev. (last visited Aug. 27, 2018), https://portal.hud.gov/hudportal/HUD?src=/program_offices/public_indian_housing/programs/hcv/homeownership.

22 *Id.*

23 Olsen, *supra* Note 19, at 18.

24 *Id.* at 4.

25 Yun, *supra* Note 4.

need 15 million.[26] Jonathan Smoke, the chief economist at Realtor.com, reported that "[m]ore than two-thirds of the markets are seeing less inventory now than compared to a year ago."[27] The problem is worst on the West Coast, but is common in Midwestern cities and other urban markets.[28]

In this chapter, I propose ways to take advantage of market forces to provide incentives for affordable homeownership and affordable housing development. As I detail more fully in this chapter, manufactured homes, also known as mobile homes, offer an opportunity to expand affordable housing without increasing governmental subsidies. I believe it is critical that we treat manufactured housing for what it is – a source of affordable permanent homeownership, worthy of being treated as real property for purposes of taxation and financing. This could be accomplished with modest changes in the tax code to provide access to capital through the existing mortgage interest and property tax deduction, as well as a change in the Low Income Housing Tax Credit (LIHTC) to incentivize affordable homeownership in addition to the current program, which is limited to affordable rentals.

While the focus of this chapter is on manufactured housing, the reality of developing affordable housing is that we often need more than a single subsidy to make a project financially feasible. We need to use every tool in our toolbox, and at the end of this chapter, I discuss briefly how to incorporate other tools, including community land trusts, inclusive zoning, linkage fees, and shared equity homeownership programs, to increase opportunities to low-income homebuyers. Our primary focus should be on maximizing the potential of the LIHTC.

THE LOW INCOME HOUSING TAX CREDIT

In discussing the Low Income Housing Tax Credit, it is not my intention to provide a primer for syndicators. Banks do not need and have not asked for help. My goal is to consider the credit as a resource for community-based housing providers, and to explain the credit from their perspective. I believe that the LIHTC should be amended to provide incentives for affordable home ownership, which can have a substantial effect in ameliorating displacement in gentrifying neighborhoods by expanding low-income ownership and allowing urban residents to benefit from the increased value of real estate in those neighborhoods.[29]

[26] *Id.*

[27] Barbara Eldridge, *U.S. Housing Shortage Is Worst on the West Coast, New Study Finds*, Curbed (Jan. 23, 2017), www.curbed.com/2017/1/23/14345668/us-housing-crisis-shortage-seattle.

[28] *Id.*

[29] *State of New York City's Housing and Neighborhoods in 2015: Focus on Gentrification*, NYU Furman Center (May 9, 2016), http://furmancenter.org/files/sotc/Part_1_Gentrification_SOCin2015_9JUNE2016.pdf.

The Tax Reform Act of 1986 changed the landscape for both the rental and homeownership markets. The Act eliminated the tax deduction for consumer interest and created a new tax credit for investments in affordable housing. The tax credit is deep and the LIHTC is now the major vehicle for developing affordable housing, continuing the trend of privatizing the means of production without addressing the ongoing shortage of affordable units.

Although it is a supply-side tax expenditure program, the LIHTC moves the means of production from government to the private market. Unlike the individual mortgage interest deduction, however, the LIHTC is not open-ended. The LIHTC is allocated by state at $2.70 per capita.[30] State agencies are required to establish a Qualified Allocation Plan (QAP) to determine priorities, and the QAP must consider location, housing need, use of existing housing as part of a revitalization plan, the project sponsor, projects intended for eventual ownership, energy efficiency, and historic nature. A 2002 report prepared for HUD by The Urban Institute showed that half of the states established preferences for rural projects and virtually all emphasized geography.[31] Production is not based on need alone. There is political pressure to distribute projects throughout a state, especially since the total production is limited by the total tax credit allocation, which is a drop in the bucket in many jurisdictions. This may – or may not – be wise tax policy, but it is not wise housing policy.

Although subject to criticism, the LIHTC has its virtues. From 1987 to 2014, the LIHTC has resulted in 2.78 million housing units in 43,092 projects. The program is decentralized, with state and local LIHTC-allocating agencies determining local needs for almost $8 billion in annual budget authority for tax credits. The credits are used for acquisition, rehabilitation, or new construction of rental housing for lower-income families.[32] The results depend on private investment, and the LIHTC is, ultimately, a practice in behavioral economics, with the goal of keeping the return on investment high enough to entice investors without sacrificing the quantity and quality of housing production.

The LIHTC is popular in Congress, with the support of liberals who want more housing and conservatives who want to base subsidized housing on market forces, as well as create a lucrative investment opportunity. There is an argument that LIHTC returns are too high and the program too inefficient, but a rich body of literature on

[30] Michael Novogradac & Peter Lawrence, *Omnibus Spending Bill Contains Affordable Housing Credit Improvement Provisions*, Novogradac & Co, LLP: Notes from Novogradac (Mar. 21, 2018), www.novoco.com/notes-from-novogradac/omnibus-spending-bill-contains-affordable-housing-credit-improvement-act-provisions.

[31] Jeremy Gustafson & J. Christopher Walker, *Analysis of State Qualified Allocation Plan for the Low-Income Housing Tax Credit Program*, Dep't of Hous. and Urban Dev. (May 2002), www.huduser.gov/portal/Publications/pdf/AnalysisQAP.pdf.

[32] *Low-Income Housing Tax Credits*, Dep't of Hous. and Urban Dev. (June 6, 2018), www.huduser.gov/portal/datasets/lihtc.html.

these subjects already exists and I will not address those questions in this chapter.[33] Instead, since I urge maximizing the potential of the LIHTC, I start from the proposition that the program has succeeded when it comes to producing and maintaining affordable rental housing. I want to expand the program to include affordable home ownership.

The LIHTC offers a mechanism for private equity investment in affordable housing. A community group hearing this would likely have two questions: (1) what does that mean and (2) why would anyone want to invest in our project, which is unlikely to make a profit? The answer to both questions is that investors will earn tax credits, and for many people, especially those paying at the top marginal rate, tax credits are more valuable than earned income.

The marginal rate in our current tax code, starting in 2018, is 37 percent, which is applied to income over $500,000 for an individual or $600,000 for a married couple. That means that every taxable dollar over these amounts will be taxed at the 37 percent rate. In addition, the income will be subject to state tax, which in New York, New Jersey, and California (where many wealthy investors live) ranges from 8.82 to 13.3 percent at the margin. That means that many wealthy taxpayers will pay over 45 percent federal and state tax on some of their income. At a 45 percent tax rate, a taxpayer needs to earn $1.82 to put $1 in his pocket. With a tax credit, a taxpayer gets a dollar-for-dollar reduction of his taxes. If the tax is $100, a $100 credit reduces the tax to zero, while a $100 charitable donation would only reduce the tax to $55. In other words, the LIHTC offers a deep subsidy, which creates a strong incentive for private equity investment in affordable housing.

That explains why wealthy people love tax credits, but not how this results in their investment in affordable housing. That is the point at which markets take over. The market favors building housing for the rich over building housing for the poor for the simple reason that expensive housing provides greater returns for the investor. If a tax credit provides greater returns than other investments, the same capitalist system that ignored low-income people will find a way for the wealthy to access the tax credits and build affordable housing. Here's how it works.

Like so many things, it starts with land. Anyone who has a plan to build on land must have site control, which means that she must own or have a legal right to purchase or use the land. Site control can be as simple as an option to purchase, but

[33] There is a wealth of literature on the LIHTC, including many critiques. *See, e.g.*, Chris Edwards & Vanessa Brown-Calder, *Low-Income Housing Tax Credit: Costly, Complex, and Corruption-Prone*, CATO INSTITUTE (Nov. 13, 2017), www.cato.org/publications/tax-budget-bulletin/low-income-housing-tax-credit-costly-complex-corruption-prone (calling for repeal); Kristin Niver, *Changing the Face of Urban America: Assessing the Low-Income Housing Tax Credit*, 102 VA. L. REV. ONLINE 48 (2016), www.virginialawreview.org/volumes/content/changing-face-urban-america-assessing-low-income-housing-tax-credit (describing the LIHTC as a successful public–private partnership).

the builder must have some legal means of control. Good intentions and a good plan are not enough.

Without site control, all discussions are academic. Talking to an investor when you do not have site control would be like trying to sell a car you do not yet own. With site control, a builder may have access to the LIHTC, which is a valuable commodity, and people will pay for the right to claim those credits. That's where capitalism and the market, which have resulted in blighted housing, help to create new affordable housing. Like all profitable markets, there is a niche for those who build the bridge between the investors and the profit.

Money managers are in the highly competitive business of providing a high return on investments. Once the market determines that the LIHTC provides a higher return than comparable risks, the rest is a matter of execution, and money managers are quite good at that. Financial institutions create investment opportunities, and compete to draw investors to their products. In the case of the LIHTC, one can go online and see that US Bancorp, for example, advertises its "Tax Credit Syndications – Socially responsible investing that makes financial sense."[34] USB explains that

> Tax credits are used to induce investments from the private sector in support of projects that benefit distressed communities and populations; enable historic preservation; and provide clean energy. When an investment is made in a development entity or eligible project, investors receive tax credits that can be used to offset their own federal or state income tax obligations. In the case of USBCDC, some of the tax credits are used to offset U.S. Bancorp's own tax obligations, while others are made available to qualified investors in a practice referred to as 'syndication'.[35]

The National Equity Fund explains that "Tax-credit syndicators help bridge the gap between the various parties to affordable housing transactions. Syndicators raise money from investors and identify low-income housing projects in which to invest that capital. National Equity Fund® is particularly focused on building long-term relationships with partners."[36] You can find similar statements from Enterprise Community Partners,[37] Municipal Capital Appreciation Partners,[38] and dozens of others. Tax credits are a cottage industry and those involved in the industry are

[34] *Financing for Community Development*, U.S. Bank (last visited Aug. 27, 2018), www.usbank.com/commercial-business/tax-credit-financing.

[35] *Id.*

[36] *About LIHTC*, National Equity Fund (last visited Aug. 28, 2018), www.nationalequityfund.org/whoweare/aboutlihtc/.

[37] *The Low-Income Housing Tax Credit*, Enterprise Community partners (last visited Aug. 28, 2018), www.enterprisecommunity.org/financing-and-development/low-income-housing-tax-credits.

[38] *Success Using Low Income Housing Tax Credit Syndication*, Municipal Capital Appreciation Partners (last visited Aug. 28, 2018), www.themcapfunds.com/tax-credit-syndication.

doing the work of finding the investors and matching them with a LIHTC project. They do this is by collecting all of the investments into a pool and then "buying" tax credits.

"Buying" tax credits is a euphemism. The Internal Revenue Service (IRS) does not permit the credits to be sold. Instead, the syndicator, on behalf of the investors, will enter into a partnership with the owner, in which the syndication will purchase 99.9 percent of the project in exchange for 99.9 percent of the tax credits and other tax advantages, including depreciation and interest business deductions. While the cost of land acquisition is not eligible for such deductions, construction costs are.

People make investments for a variety of reasons, including social purposes, but the large majority of investments are based on risk and rate of return. There is risk in building affordable housing – contractors go bankrupt, housing management can be challenging, and the IRS can deny all or part of the tax credit – but these risks are controllable, and the return to the investor is substantial. Investors compare this investment to others, and determine how much they are willing to invest to get their expected rate of return.

To understand the incentive to an investor of a LIHTC investment, consider this example: Assume a project consisting of 100 units of affordable housing, with each unit costing $100,000 to build. This amounts to a total of $10,000,000 worth of eligible costs. According to the Comptroller of the Currency, a project like this has a 10-year credit at $9,000,000. (There are two separate credits applicable to different types of projects, known as the 9 percent credit and the 4 percent credit, but the credits are claimed over ten years, so they are computed based on 90 percent and 40 percent of eligible costs.) In addition, the Comptroller estimates depreciation and other real estate losses at $2,205,294, which produces a total of $11,205,294 in tax benefits for the investors.[39]

The amount the investors are willing to pay for the tax credits varies, but for the last several years, the price has exceeded 90 cents investment for each dollar of credit, and has often exceeded $1.00, because of the additional tax benefits that accompany the credit.[40] From January 2017 through April 2018, the investment was quite steady, ranging from .91 to .93 for every dollar of credit.[41]

At 90 cents on the dollar, this means the investors will invest $8,100,000 in the $10,000,000 project. For the 4 percent credit, which is less competitive, the tax credit still comes to $4,000,000, thus attracting an investment of $3,600,000. This is a simplified version, but we are talking about a substantial investment. For a

[39] *Office of the Comptroller of the Currency, Low-Income Housing Tax Credits: Affordable Housing Investment Opportunities for Banks* (Mar. 2014), www.occ.gov/topics/community-affairs/publications/insights/insights-low-income-housing-tax-credits.pdf.

[40] *LIHTC Pricing Trends*, Novogradac & Co, LLP (May 9, 2018), www.novoco.com/resource-centers/affordable-housing-tax-credits/data-tools/lihtc-pricing-trends.

[41] *Low-Income Housing Tax Credit Equity Pricing per Credit*, Novogradac & Co, LLP (May 9, 2018), www.novoco.com/atom/169786.

community organization starting with nothing beyond site control, this is like finding the pot of gold at the end of the rainbow.

These calculations are based on rental housing, for the simple reason that the LIHTC does not provide for homeownership opportunities. As a society, we say that our goal is to increase the pool of stakeholders and build wealth through homeownership, but our policy limits the pool. We provide incentives for developers to build affordable rental housing, with no provision for homeownership. It makes much more sense to expand the pool to include the working poor, by providing incentives for developers to build an infrastructure for affordable manufactured homes. In fact, the LIHTC provides a disincentive for affordable homeownership, since its success draws capital toward the LIHTC and away from investment in affordable homeownership. We could change this with a minor expansion in the statute, by allowing the LIHTC definition of eligible costs to include the infrastructure necessary to prepare a site for qualified homeowners.

As a practical likelihood, most, but not all, of those potential homeowners will be people who are otherwise priced out of the homeownership market. This adjustment will facilitate wealth-building for the working poor. Additionally, it will require only a small tax expenditure per unit and stretch the value of the LIHTC, resulting in a larger number of units.

One benefit of this structural change is that unlike the perverse incentives that led to the toxic loans of the 2007 crash, this plan uses market forces in two important ways. First, the market has shown that the LIHTC will draw private investment. Tax cuts will likely affect the amount that investors are willing to pay, but the LIHTC remains a valuable commodity. Expanding the credit to infrastructure-only projects will result in smaller financial packages, since the cost of building the units will be removed from the total costs. To benefit from the credit, these projects may need to be packaged differently. Perhaps they will draw a different investor or require a higher rate of return. In any event, the market will resolve these issues and, since the LIHTC is capped, the resolution will come at no cost to the Treasury. For every dollar invested in homeownership credit, we will have a net increase in the number of units, because we will be passing most of the cost onto the homebuyer.

Second, purchasers of manufactured housing are already participating in the market, and succeeding, even though the market is skewed against them.[42] Manufactured home buyers bear the burden of added transaction costs, which led several

[42] In a world of unintended consequences, the Dodd-Frank statute has added additional impediments in financing manufactured housing. Manufactured homes, which do not have the benefits of mortgages, are included in the CFPB definition of "residential mortgage loan," which makes the loans subject to the protections of Dodd-Frank. Jan Hollingsworth, *Dodd-Frank and Manufactured Home Financing: The Place Where Good Intentions and Unintended Consequences Collide*, MHL Living News (2015), http://manufacturedhomelivingnews.com/dodd-frank-and-manufactured-home-financing-the-place-where-good-intentions-and-unintended-consequences-collide/.

lenders to leave the manufactured home market, especially for loans under $20,000, because the added costs made the chattel loans unprofitable.[43] In a case study, Jan Hollingsworth found that one buyer, who had an optimal site for his new manufactured home, went through the borrowing process, only to end up with a $9,500 loan at 36 percent interest, with an additional $1,500 closing fee. The loan was still a bargain compared to the costs of his previous rental.[44] We need to even the playing field and bring these buyers into the mortgage finance system.

Policymakers have made some progress in this area. Several states – New Hampshire, Vermont, California, Oregon, and Minnesota – have recently implemented a pilot program under the US Department of Agriculture's (USDA's) Section 502 Direct and Guaranteed loans for manufactured homes in land-lease communities. The pilot program offers favorable financing terms for moderate, low, and very low-income buyers of energy-efficient manufactured and modular homes in resident-owned or nonprofit-owned land-lease communities in eligible rural areas. The USDA Section 502 Direct and Guaranteed programs offer eligible applicants 100 percent financing, affordable fixed rates, and a thirty-year mortgage term, with no private mortgage insurance requirement. Historically, until the introduction of the pilot program, the 502 program was not available for manufactured homes titled as personal property in land-lease communities.[45]

THE ROLE OF MANUFACTURED HOMES IN PROVIDING AFFORDABLE HOMEOWNERSHIP

Even after the market crash, homeownership continues to be part of the American Dream. A 2013 study by the Joint Center for Housing Studies of Harvard University concluded that "there continues to be a strong support for the association between owning a home and accumulating wealth."[46] Even as homeownership dropped from a high of nearly 70 percent in 2004 to a twenty-year low of 64.3 percent in 2014, owning a home has remained the primary means for low- and moderate-income people to build wealth, and homeowner net assets continue to outpace those of renters.[47] The study notes that there are risks to home ownership, and it is critical to

43 *Id.*

44 *Id.*

45 Kevin Walker, *Steps Forward: Delivery of Competitive Manufactured Home Financing in Land-Lease Communities, Especially with Long-Term Security of Tenure*, PROSPERITY NOW (Oct. 2016), https://prosperitynow.org/files/resources/steps_forward_10–2016.pdf.

46 Christopher E. Herbert et al., *Is Homeownership Still an Effective Means of Building Wealth for Low-Income and Minority Households? (Was It Ever?)*, HARVARD UNIVERSITY, JOINT CENTER FOR HOUSING STUDIES (2013) at 2, http://jchs.harvard.edu/sites/jchs.harvard.edu/files/hbtl-06.pdf.

47 Editorial Board, *Homeownership and Wealth Creation*, N.Y. TIMES (Nov. 29, 2014), www.nytimes.com/2014/11/30/opinion/sunday/homeownership-and-wealth-creation.html?_r=0.

identify conditions in which low-income owners are more likely to succeed.[48] It identifies the major factors for success as (1) the forced savings of an amortized mortgage, (2) appreciation, (3) favorable financing, (4) federal tax benefits, and (5) the ability to hedge against inflation.[49]

In the lead-up to the market crash of 2007, lenders provided high-risk loans, many of which were fraudulent, for low-income people to enter the home ownership market, with targeted programs backed by FNMA and GNMA. The failure of these programs has been well-documented.[50] In the aftermath of the 2007 collapse, credit markets have tightened and lower-income borrowers have been shut out of the housing market, especially in the context of home ownership. Low-income wage earners are lost in the current regime. They do not have sufficient access to credit to purchase real property and many do not qualify for subsidized rental units. Even if they do qualify, the number of units is so small as to make this process more of a lottery than a housing policy.

Yet counter to all expectations, low-income people are still purchasing homes, but they are manufactured homes. Manufactured homes, more commonly referred to as "mobile homes" and often placed in "trailer parks," are home to more than 22 million people.[51] The cost savings of a manufactured home compared to a site-built home are striking. According to a 2014 study by the Consumer Finance Protection Bureau, metropolitan area owner-occupants of site-built housing pay an average monthly housing cost of $1,505, while owner-occupants of manufactured homes spend an average of $686.[52] I use the word "homes" because these are structures in which people live and raise families, but for the purpose of the tax code and access to capital, manufactured housing is generally treated as personal property. This means that a resident owner is unlikely to obtain a mortgage to purchase and is not eligible to deduct interest payments as a tax deduction.

Because most owners of manufactured housing place their homes on rented land, manufactured housing is typically financed through chattel mortgages. A chattel mortgage is a loan on a moveable piece of property, like a car, boat, or trailer. Chattel loans tend to carry higher interest rates and fewer consumer protections than mortgage loans on real estate. Mobile home buyers do not get a deed. They get a certificate of title, as is issued for a car, for which they pay yearly fees. In 2015,

[48] *Id.* at 3.

[49] *Id.* at 4–5.

[50] There are literally thousands of articles about the causes of the housing bubble and its collapse. Virtually all include a discussion of sub-prime loans, teaser rates, banking deregulation, fraud, and the other factors that led to the 2007 collapse. For one example, see *The Origins of the Financial Crisis*, THE ECONOMIST (Sep. 7, 2013), www.economist.com/news/schoolsbrief/21584534-effects-financial-crisis-are-still-being-felt-five-years-article.

[51] Ann M. Burkhart, *Taxing Manufactured Homes*, 67 TAX LAW 909 (2014).

[52] *Consumer Finance Protection Bureau, Manufactured-Housing Consumer Finance in the United States* (Sept. 2014), https://files.consumerfinance.gov/f/201409_cfpb_report_manufactured-housing.pdf.

80 percent of new manufactured homes, representing the homes that were placed on rented land, were classified as personal property.[53]

Over a thirty-year term, a $150,000 mortgage loan on real estate at 7 percent will result in payments of $69,000 more in interest payments than a 5 percent loan.[54] These figures assume that the buyer has access to capital for a long-term real estate loan, which is generally not the case for buyers of manufactured homes. Because they do not have access to real estate mortgage financing, buyers of manufactured homes are paying car-loan interest rates on shorter-term loans than purchasers with a typical fifteen- or thirty-year home mortgage loan, resulting in even worse payment terms. For example, a thirty-year mortgage for $100,000 at 5 percent results in a monthly payment of $536.82. Reduce the term to six years and the monthly payment jumps to $1,610.49. Increase the rate to 7 percent and the monthly payment is $1,704.90.

The law of manufactured housing depends on where you place your home. If you buy a manufactured home and place it on your own land, and live there with your family, you are a homeowner. You can obtain a mortgage and deduct mortgage interest and property taxes as itemized deductions on your tax return. However, if you buy the same manufactured home, place it on rental land, and live there with your family, you are unlikely to be eligible for the mortgage deduction because you are unlikely to have a mortgage, as opposed to a consumer loan. Even though your home stops being mobile once it is placed down, your home is forever classified as a mobile home and you are classified as a renter in a mobile home park.

The tax code treats most owners of manufactured homes as if they lived in cars. There is a history to this. After the depression, many people purchased and lived in trailers, which had wheels and could be hitched up to a car and moved anywhere. As homes on wheels, the trailers were financed and taxed like cars. After a period of time, the wheels came off – literally. The next generation of manufactured housing, called mobile homes, were brought to a site, the wheels were removed, and the mobile homes were placed on a slab and connected to utilities. Many of them were attached to foundations. They were not very mobile, but the name stuck, as did their treatment by banks, the secondary mortgage market, and the Internal Revenue Service. Our current policy concerning manufactured homes is based on an old perception of trailers, hooked up to a truck and pulled away on the whim of their owners. It is a perception that is out of date, makes no sense, and is contrary to our national interest in encouraging homeownership and wealth-building.

The Bureau of the Census reports there are 9 million manufactured homes in the United States, 538,000 of which are in California. The homes come in a variety of sizes and shapes. Some have second stories and many have porches. Since 1976,

53 *The Facts about Manufactured Housing*, I'M HOME (2016), https://familypromise.org/wp-content/uploads/2018/03/Manufactured-Housing-Fact-Sheet_2017.pdf.

54 *Id.* at 8.

manufactured homes have had to comply with the National Manufactured Housing Construction and Safety Standards Act, a HUD-established national code.[55] Homes built under the HUD standards compare favorably to site-built housing on issues of durability and construction quality.[56] Moving them is difficult and expensive and, as a result, they are rarely moved. Like other homes, they are sold when the owners move elsewhere.

By every measure, manufactured home residents are poorer than owners of site-built homes. They have less income and fewer assets.[57] Yet, contrary to public perception, manufactured home residents move less than owners of site-built homes.[58] The primary threat to their continued stability is that 70 percent of them do not own the land on which their homes sit,[59] making them vulnerable to increased land leases and redevelopment.

However, both when owners of manufactured homes sell their homes and when they remain in them over a long period, current laws prevent such owners from achieving the same kinds of financial gains as those achieved by owners of site-built homes. While the mortgage market is dependent on a vibrant secondary market that frees up capital to increase the total volume of loans, thus facilitating the buying and selling of homes, the Manufactured Housing Institute reported that as of 2009 "the secondary market for personal property loans is essentially nonexistent."[60] This increases the pressure for short-term loans at high interest rates. There is a great deal of discussion about the secondary market, but as of this writing the discussion has not resulted in change.

In September 2014, the Consumer Financial Protection Bureau (CFPB) published a report, *Manufactured-Housing Consumer Finance in the United States*, analyzing the manufactured housing industry.[61] The CFPB found that as of 2012, more than two-thirds of all mortgage and chattel loans on manufactured housing met the definition of a "higher-priced mortgage loan" (HPML) as compared with only 3 percent of the loans on site-built homes. The CFPB also found that one in six of the loans charged such high rates and fees that the minimum monthly payment was a full $200 higher than it would be if it were merely subprime. As it currently stands, state and federal protections for homebuyers do not apply to these personal property loans.

55 42 U.S.C. §5402.
56 Walker, *supra* Note 45.
57 *Id.*
58 *Id.*
59 *Id.*
60 *Id.*
61 *Consumer Finance Protection Bureau, Manufactured-Housing Consumer Finance in the United States* (Sept. 2014), https://files.consumerfinance.gov/f/201409_cfpb_report_manufactured-housing.pdf.

In other words, taking the five key factors for building wealth from the Harvard study discussed earlier,[62] i.e. (1) the forced savings of an amortized mortgage, (2) appreciation, (3) favorable financing, (4) federal tax benefits, and (5) the ability to hedge against inflation, manufactured housing homeowners do not have an amortized mortgage; are unlikely to benefit from appreciation, in part because the next buyer will not be able to get a long-term mortgage; cannot get favorable financing; and get no tax advantage. The only advantage is that their home is a hedge against inflation. But even that advantage is limited by the fact that they are subject to land rent increases, which are much more volatile than property tax increases, not to mention the broader problem of being treated by the law as renters.

The last point is critical. The financial and legal structures treat manufactured homes as personal property, and personal property is not protected in the same fashion as real property. It is much easier to repossess a manufactured home than it is to foreclose on a mortgage. Worse, a manufactured home owner is subject to eviction for nonpayment for failure to pay the ground rent or other charges assessed by the landlord. Since the homeowner does not have the capital to move the home, eviction often results in abandonment.

In the best of circumstances in the case of eviction, the homeowner will secure a buyer. The buyer, like the seller, will likely be unable to obtain a mortgage, as opposed to a chattel loan. Since chattel loans have higher interest rates and shorter terms than mortgages, the monthly payments for a chattel loan are higher than for a mortgage in the same amount. Because the buyer must also pay a ground rent, the added higher monthly cost of a chattel loan serves to depreciate the value of the manufactured home, for the basic economic fact that the buyer's purchasing power is suppressed by the higher debt service. In short, because of the buyer's lack of access to capital in the form of a mortgage, the seller is forced to sell at less than full value.

Even then, the buyer, as a new tenant, must be approved by the landowner, who may refuse to accept the new homeowner, and then offer the current owner a low-ball purchase price. In many cases, the homeowner has no choice but to accept. Not only does the manufactured housing homeowner not have the benefits of the many protections offered to the homeowner through mortgage foreclosure law but he is also particularly vulnerable to eviction from the land, which can wipe out any accumulation of wealth he may have managed through homeownership. Because the cost of moving a manufactured home is prohibitive to many owners, there is little flexibility in negotiating a sale.

When it comes to manufactured housing, developers of affordable housing are in the same position as manufactured housing homeowners. If a housing developer buys a manufactured home and places it on the developer's land to rent to a low-income renter, the rental property will qualify under the LIHTC for a ten-year tax

[62] Eldridge, *supra* Note 27.

credit of 90 percent of the cost of the home and the infrastructure. A developer can buy hundreds of the same homes, and investors will be delighted to pay for the opportunity to invest in the project, for the benefit of sharing the tax credits. However, if a developer builds the same infrastructure to rent space to low-income *owners* of manufactured homes, the developer will not be eligible for a tax credit, because he developed the land but not the homes.

This is a serious problem. Since 90 percent of all affordable housing in the United States is built with investments through the LIHTC program, we are excluding some of the neediest homeowners from the benefits of the LIHTC, which effectively means we are excluding them from living in a decent environment. This situation is particularly bad for low-wage workers, who cannot afford to purchase land, and often own manufactured homes.

While manufactured housing has been situated primarily in rural and suburban areas, improvements in construction and appearance make these flexible structures ideal for urban infill and vacant lots. Casey J. Dawkins and C. Theodore Koebel, writing in the Journal of the American Planning Association, found that the number of manufactured units in a community is not determined by the market, but by regulatory restrictions like permits, snow load standards, fire codes, zoning codes, subdivision regulations, and architectural design standards.[63] As manufactured housing continues to improve its design and quality standards, simultaneous with the recent movement toward smaller houses,[64] the time has come to remove these artificial barriers.

A PROPOSAL FOR CHANGE

I propose two changes to the tax code and one change in lending practices, which I believe will be a natural consequence of the tax changes. First, the LIHTC should be amended to allow the tax credit to be used for the development of infrastructure for affordable housing, with the actual housing being owned by a qualified low-income owner. The qualification of the homeowner would remain the same as currently set forth in the LIHTC, which is based on median income. Under the new, improved credit, there would be no distinction between manufactured homes and homes built on site. Both could be owned by a homebuyer and fully eligible for the mortgage interest and property tax deductions. Second, the IRS should treat manufactured housing as real property, even when it is sited on rental property. The

[63] Casey J. Dawkins & C. Theodore Koebel, *Overcoming Barriers to Placing Manufactured Housing in Metropolitan Communities*, 76 J. AM. PLAN. ASS'N 73–88 (2009), http://dx.doi.org/10.1080/01944360903401052.

[64] *See, e.g.*, Shelley Little, *Why Houses Are Getting Smaller*, FRESHOME (Sept. 11, 2014), http://freshome.com/2014/09/11/why-houses-are-getting-smaller/; Lis King, *Downsizing to Smaller Homes Is the New Trend*, TALLAHASSEE MAGAZINE (June 30, 2014), www.tallahasseemagazine.com/downsizing-to-smaller-homes-is-the-new-trend/.

notion that the manufactured house is a vehicle is outmoded and ignores the reality of the modern manufactured home. A structure that is treated as real property when it is placed on an owner's land should be treated the same when it is placed on rented land. Finally, lenders should issue mortgages for manufactured homes, regardless of siting, as long as they are attached to the land.

How the Tax Credit Could Work for Affordable Homeownership

My law firm represents a group of forty families living in a mobile home park with substandard electrical, water, and sewer services. The park owner did not have a permit to operate it as a mobile home park. The residents, largely farmworkers, own their mobile homes, which are not mobile. Many of the homes are in terrible condition and could not survive a move. In any event, moving a mobile home costs upwards of $10,000, and it makes much more economic sense to sell to the next occupant. Because the homes are treated as trailers for financing purposes, buyers have little to no access to capital. Thus, the homes are usually sold within a family, to a friend, or through seller financing, which consists of a bill of sale and a promise to pay.

We represented the residents in litigation against the owner for failure to maintain the park in a habitable condition. The major problems included unhealthy well water, inadequate sewage, and an inadequate and dangerous electrical system. We settled the litigation with an agreement for a resident-approved entity to purchase the property for $225,000, a distressed price, based on the cash-flow value of a fully-permitted park, reduced by the cost necessary to bring the park to permitted standards. We formed a single-purpose entity to purchase the park. After a great deal of effort, we obtained a conditional permit to operate the park and financing to purchase it. That left us with an estimated $1.5 million in costs to bring electric, water, and sewer to habitable standards.

If the developer could obtain an additional $1 million, it could rehabilitate the existing homes. In other words, the developer would take forty uninhabitable homes in a park, with an unsafe and unhealthy infrastructure, and replace them or bring them up to habitable standards at a total cost of $2,725,000, or $68,125 per unit, including infrastructure. As it happens, there is adjacent housing, with an additional forty families with similar conditions, and the bulk of the cost could be amortized among eighty, not forty, families. Excluding the $225,000 for land purchase, the remaining $2.5 million would be eligible for the LIHTC if the landlord, and not the residents, owned the units. At a 9 percent credit, the project could generate an investment of $2,025,000; at a 4 percent credit, it could generate an investment of $900,000. However, because the residents own the units, under current law the entire project is ineligible for tax credits, even if each of the residents is low-income and would qualify as a LIHTC resident.

There is vacant land next to this park. The developer could spend $2 million on that land to build the infrastructure, including electrical, water, and sewer hookups, to prepare sites on which the manufactured homes would be placed. Forty low-income homeowners could bring their manufactured homes to this site, at a development cost of $50,000 per unit. With the tax credit, this would be an attractive investment. Without the tax credit, the project would need a deep governmental subsidy, which is unlikely to happen.

This is a lost opportunity on many levels. Under current law, a developer seeking tax credit investors is limited to developing rental housing. The developer will need to purchase or build units in addition to the infrastructure. The cost per unit will be multiple times $40,000, which means fewer units. If LIHTC applies, the tax expenditure will be larger, resulting in fewer total affordable units. The renters will lose the opportunity to build wealth through home ownership. A simple change to allow LIHTC to be used for the limited purpose of building infrastructure for manufactured housing resolves all of these negative effects of current law. The intent of LIHTC is to provide incentive for the private market to build affordable housing. We need to modify existing law to create more units.

How the Tax Code Works for the Rich (And Should Work for the Poor): Land Trusts

While the LIHTC is a powerful vehicle for incentivizing private investment in housing, the current permitted use of the tax credit does not expand homeownership. With minor changes and no additional loss to the treasury, Congress could expand the number of affordable units and encourage greater home ownership. To succeed on the ground, especially in an urban setting, where development costs are high and cheap land is rarely available, success will likely depend on the ability to use the LIHTC in conjunction with other tools. Developing affordable housing usually involves "subsidy layering," and the LIHTC is one of several possible subsidies. The land trust is another tool and, used in conjunction with the amended LIHTC, could be a powerful tool in urban areas.

The University of California, Irvine has created a successful land trust, approved by the IRS, to subsidize housing for its employees. While the UCI model is based on its unique and fascinating history, the basic idea is easily replicable.

The Homestead Act of 1862 is a classic example of the unintended consequences of well-intentioned public policy. The Act was supposed to create small farms, but had a very different result, due to a false assumption about access to water in the West. The theory was that people would be drawn to the West by offers of 160 acres of free land, and would farm and settle the land, simultaneous with the development of the railroads. The settlers found that 160 acres, ample acreage for a farm in the fertile east, was not sufficient in the arid west. This led to false claims, mass forced sales of failed farms, and homestead claims made more to control water than to control land. The result was the accumulation of enormous amounts of land in a few hands. In California, the system was complicated by the Mexican land grants, some of which were challenged by homesteaders.

Eventually, Congress recognized the Mexican land grants, and James Irvine and two partners formed the 185-square-mile Irvine Ranch. In 1959, seeking to develop the City of Irvine, the Irvine Company donated 1,000 acres to the University of California and sold another 500 acres for housing. The Regents of the University of California formed the Irvine Campus Housing Authority, and ICHA applied for and received status under the Internal Revenue Code as a Section 509(a)(3) supporting organization to the Regents. ICHA's purpose is to supply housing to UCI's employees.

Because of its 509(a) status, ICHA is able to piggy-back onto the Regents' tax-exempt status and operate as a tax-exempt entity, a beneficial status for which ICHA would not otherwise qualify. ICHA has built out 300 acres in a community known as University Hills, with 1,066 for-sale homes and 360 rental units. It is the largest, on-campus, for-sale workforce housing community in the country. The housing is limited to the UCI workforce. It is subsidized by land owned by the Regents, a state actor that controls selling price, buying price, and rules and regulations.

The legal structure has important similarities to mobile home parks. ICHA retains ownership of the land, but qualified buyers can purchase the homes, and lease the land. Because the homes are built on-site, as opposed to manufactured housing, the homeowners have all the benefits of an income tax deduction for mortgage interest and state property taxes, as well as a long-term mortgage. Thanks to ICHA's tax exemption and the state subsidy, including free land, this results in housing costs to consumers of roughly 50 percent of market value.[65]

This system is effectively a government-subsidized, tax-exempt land trust for employees with incomes too high to qualify for traditional housing subsidies. ICHA holds the land in trust for the Regents of the University of California in order to provide subsidized housing to well-paid professors. It is, in fact, a brilliant system, taking advantage of the tax code to lower the cost of housing in support of the University's educational purpose.

We can use the same concepts, in conjunction with the LIHTC, in urban settings. The basic idea of a land trust is that the trust, usually formed as a tax-exempt entity, holds the land as a steward for the public good, including affordable housing. There are only 243 land trusts in the United States, and the largest, in Burlington, Vermont, leases land to approximately 500 homeowners.[66] But the concept is an ideal way

[65] The author lives in University Hills and is a beneficiary of this structure.

[66] Alana Semuels, *Affordable Housing, Always*, The Atlantic (July 6, 2015), www.theatlantic.com/business/archive/2015/07/affordable-housing-always/397637/.

to provide community ownership of land. A land trust can keep rents affordable, provide homeownership opportunities, and prevent displacement.

As one successful model, Dudley Neighbors, Inc. (DNI) is a community land trust started in 1988 as an offshoot of Dudley Street Neighborhood Initiative. DNI was designated as an Urban Redevelopment Corporation by the State of Massachusetts and has the power of eminent domain. DNI acquires empty lots from private and public sources, and working with for-profit and nonprofit developers, has created more than 225 affordable units.[67] The National Community Land Trust Network provides technical assistance to over 100 CLTs across the country.[68]

My law firm also represents an urban community land trust in Santa Ana, California. According to the 2010 census, Santa Ana is the fifth densest city in the United States, right behind Boston and ahead of Chicago. This is extraordinary considering that unlike other cities high on the list, Santa Ana is built horizontally, with little high-rise housing. Our client's first priority is to acquire small parcels of land to develop community gardens, pocket parks, and affordable housing. If our client, as the land owner, develops rental housing, its projects will qualify for the LIHTC. If it sells the housing to low-income purchasers the project will not qualify, even if the deed limits equity and restricts resale to a qualified low-income buyer. If our client develops the infrastructure to allow homeowners to place manufactured homes on prepared sites, the project will not qualify for the LIHTC, and the homeowners are unlikely to secure long-term financing and will likely pay a higher interest rate than if they purchased a home. The homeowners will not be eligible to deduct their mortgage interest. However, combining the land trust model with the proposed LIHTC reforms, our client could build the infrastructure for housing units using tax credits but sell the housing units to qualified buyers. The buyers would enter into a ground lease, as in the mobile home parks, but would have the benefits of homeownership.

While the land trust offers particular advantages in expanding the LIHTC, we should not stop there. There is no reason the proposed changes in the tax credit should not include common property interests, especially as a means to renovate blighted buildings in urban areas. In addition to the benefits of turning renters into owners, the tax credit in such settings can be used to provide a hedge against gentrification. This model is easily adaptable to common-ownership structures in urban areas, where ownership may mean a cooperative or condominium in a multistory building. In that situation, the community land trust can choose to retain an ownership position equal to its subsidy. The CLT provides a subsidy to the purchase price, which is often the largest impediment for a first time buyer.[69] The down payment is secured by a second mortgage, which is paid at the time of resale, along

[67] *History of DNI*, Dudley Neighbors, Inc. (last visited Aug. 29, 2018), www.dudleyneighbors.org/background.html.

[68] Melora Hiller & Brenda Torpy, *Annual Report*, Nat'l Community Land Trust (2013), http://cltnetwork.org/wp-content/uploads/2014/10/2013-Network-Annual-report.pdf.

[69] *Id.*

with a percentage of the appreciation. Those funds can be recycled to another low-income borrower.[70]

Under current law, a developer could qualify for the LIHTC by developing rental affordable rental units within existing buildings. These units are set aside and must be rented to qualified low-income renters. This is an expensive proposition, requiring a deep subsidy, often through a combination of LIHTC and Section 8 subsidies. The proposed LIHTC change would allow the developer to use the credit for common area building improvements, including building systems like HVAC, electrical, and plumbing, while selling the units to qualified low-income buyers. Because the tax credits will reduce the total development costs, the individual units can be sold to qualified buyers at a below-market price. Because the sale price will reduce the per-unit development cost, the overall cost will be reduced, as will the LIHTC per-unit subsidy. As with the mobile home and land trust models, the result will be more units, with the opportunity for low-income people to build wealth. In addition, this may be a highly effective anti-gentrification strategy.

The gentrification issue is complicated, especially when it comes to displacement, but there is no question that gentrification results in increased real estate values and higher rents. In an extensive study of New York City neighborhoods, NYU's Furman Center found that "The share of recently available rental units affordable to low-income households declined sharply in gentrifying neighborhoods between 2000 and 2010–2014."[71] There is no magic to this finding. Every unit rehabbed and occupied by a higher-income person is a unit lost to a lower-income person. Unless controls are in place, low-income renters and buyers can never outbid those with higher incomes, and displacement becomes inevitable.

Currently, long-time owner-occupants can share in appreciated value only by selling and moving, and renters are priced out of the market. There is evidence that residents who survive gentrification do so by frequent moves to cheaper housing as they are priced out of the market. Their choice is to pay rent at a level they cannot afford or move to less attractive housing. As a neighborhood gentrifies, this can lead to multiple moves. Including ownership under the LIHTC umbrella can provide a mechanism for local residents to share in the appreciated value of their neighborhood at a low comparative cost.[72] If we are serious about creating more homeownership for low-income people, the cost of rehabilitating existing

[70] *Id.*

[71] *Report Analyzes New York City's Gentrifying Neighborhoods and Finds Dramatic Demographic Shifts*, NYU Furman Center (May 9, 2016), http://furmancenter.org/thestoop/entry/new-report-analyzes-new-york-citys-gentrifying-neighborhoods-and-finds-dram.

[72] For a fuller discussion of gentrification, *see* Kalefa Sanneh, *Is Gentrification Really a Problem?*, The New Yorker (July 11 & 18, 2016), www.newyorker.com/magazine/2016/07/11/is-gentrification-really-a-problem; For a study of gentrification in New York City, supporting the proposition that gentrification results in increased rents, *see Report Analyzes New York City's Gentrifying Neighborhoods and Finds Dramatic Demographic Shifts*, NYU Furman Center (May 9, 2016), http://furmancenter.org/thestoop/entry/new-report-analyzes-new-york-citys-gentrifying-neighborhoods-and-finds-dram.

substandard housing before or early in a period of gentrification is a lot cheaper than starting from scratch.

CONCLUSION

As the United States comes to grips with its housing shortage, we risk leaving behind whole segments of our population. This need not be the case. With minor structural changes, we can use existing tools to support existing manufactured housing, create infrastructure for new manufactured housing, and expand opportunities for community and individual ownership. We need to work toward a participatory environment in which community members not only stay in gentrifying neighborhoods but share in increased value. We know that tax credits can produce high-quality affordable housing, based on twenty years of history with the LIHTC. We also know that people who cannot afford to buy on-site housing can afford to buy manufactured housing.

The tax code and market tools, which have benefited wealthy portions of our society, can be used with great effectiveness to expand homeownership to many who are traditionally at the bottom of the market. This is not a farfetched idea. We have all of the necessary tools for success. Now we need to work together to build the communities we all deserve.

PART III

The Legal Academy and the Urban Core

6

Focused Ethnography

A Methodological Approach for Engaged Legal Scholarship

Tonya L. Brito, Daanika Gordon** & David J. Pate Jr.****

INTRODUCTION

It is July 2015 and I am meeting another researcher from our study team at the county courthouse at 8:15 am. We are observing child support enforcement hearings together in family court. On the floor where the family court commissioners hear cases, we meet up and walk toward the check-in desk. The physical space resembles the type of waiting room you might find in a low-income neighborhood health clinic, with worn, white linoleum flooring and plastic chairs lining the walls. The check-in desk is staffed by court administrative staff. Today there are two middle-aged, Black

* Jefferson Burrus-Bascom Professor of Law, University of Wisconsin Law School. The authors thank Amanda Ward, Jia-Hui Stefanie Wong, Garrett Grainger, Chloe Haimson, Sarah Ishmael, and Rachel Johnson for their many insights and contributions during our collaboration on the study described in this chapter, Alec Fischer and Sofia Jonas for their valuable assistance with case files, and Jennifer Hanrahan for her exemplary administrative assistance. We thank the participants in the UW Law School Wednesday Workshop series, A2J Empirical Methods Workshop, Midwest Law & Society Retreat and the members of Professor Brito's writing group, Gwyn Leachman, Mitra Sharafi, and David Schwartz, for their generous comments on earlier drafts of this chapter. This study is supported by two research awards provided by the National Science Foundation (NSF) under Grant No. SES-1323064 and Grant No. SES-1421098. This study would not have been possible without the support of NSF and our other funders, including the University of Wisconsin Law School, the Institute for Research on Poverty, the Sheldon B. Lubar Research Chair, the University of Wisconsin-Madison Graduate School, the University of Wisconsin-Milwaukee Spaights Endowment, and the University of Wisconsin-Milwaukee Fromkin Award. We acknowledge with appreciation the assistance of the officials of the courts where we conducted this research. Finally, we are especially grateful to the many participants in this study who have been willing to share their experiences and perspectives on access to justice for low-income litigants in child support enforcement proceedings.

** Ph.D. Student, Sociology Department, University of Wisconsin-Madison.

*** Associate Professor of Social Work, Helen Bader School of Social Welfare, University of Wisconsin-Milwaukee.

women,[1] one whom we've encountered frequently during our site visits. The other woman turns to her and asks if she should let us pass. "Yes, they are with the university."

We walk into the child support court hearing room and see that Dorothy Knight, the court clerk, has brought in two wooden chairs for us in anticipation of our arrival.[2] Dorothy is seated at her desk and the commissioner that day is Elaine Schmidt, a White woman who looked to be in her early 40s with shoulder-length blond hair. She is wearing a black sweater with a long gold necklace. The government attorney that day is Kevin Graves, a lean, middle-aged White man with thinning, white hair. He is wearing a grey suit and a lavender dress shirt with a matching patterned tie.

The hearing room is small, square, and cramped. There is a wood table in the middle of the room, where the litigants and lawyers sit. Our two seats are squeezed into a corner, between the clerk's desk and a row of filing cabinets and shelves that line the adjacent wall. The low ceiling combined with the commissioner's bench, which is elevated on a dais and appears to take up at least a quarter of the room, gives the room a claustrophobic feel.

Graves, who represents the child support agency, is seated at the table along with the parents (i.e., litigants). The father, Eric Bracy, is a heavy-set, light skinned Black man wearing boxy glasses, sneakers, khaki shorts, and a large and bright orange shirt. He looks to be in his mid-30s to mid-40s and he has a goatee. He is seated in the middle, between Graves and the custodial mother, Lisa Gill, a Black woman who is also heavier and about the same age as Mr. Bracy. She has on grey pants and a red V-neck shirt. Her hair is straightened and dyed to an amber color. She wears it pulled back in a short ponytail. Like most cases we have observed, neither of the parents is represented by an attorney.

The room is quiet when we enter; the commissioner, clerk, and attorney all have their eyes on their computer screens and are silently working. Gill v. *Bracy is before the court for a review hearing and it gets started just as we are getting settled. Commissioner Schmidt begins by directing questions at Mr. Bracy at a near rapid fire pace. "Do you have a job? How long have you had a job? How are you doing in the job? What do you anticipate your check being?" We learn that at an earlier hearing the court referred Mr. Bracy to the Jobs Program. He has a letter with him that indicates that he now has a job as a subcontractor with a transportation agency. His current monthly order is $250 plus a $15 repay for his accrued child support debt, which exceeds $3,000. Mr. Bracy hadn't made a payment in July and states that he hadn't been paid in July. She asks Mr. Bracy if he could make a payment that day and he replies that he could pay $75.*

Commissioner Schmidt then addresses attorney Graves and asks for the state's request. Graves explains that because Mr. Bracy was a contractor, they could send a wage assignment to his employer, but it would be ignored. He requests that the case be set out for another review. Graves does not look at Mr. Bracy, instead keeping his eyes on his paperwork. Dorothy, the clerk, stares at her computer screen as well and keeps typing. She also does not look at Mr. Bracy.

[1] Following the tradition in critical race theory whose founders have noted that "Blacks, like Asians, Latinos, and other 'minorities,' constitute a specific cultural group and, as such, require denotation as a proper noun," we capitalize "Black" as a racial descriptor in the United States. *See* Kimberlé Williams Crenshaw, *Race, Reform, and Retrenchment: Transformation and Legitimation in Antidiscrimination Law*, 101 HARV. L. REV. 1331, 1332 n.2 (1988).

[2] All participant and location names are pseudonyms.

The commissioner asks Ms. Gill, the mother, if there is anything she wants to say. Ms. Gill had been sitting silently, not engaging with Mr. Bracy in any way, and now she directed a frustrated account to the commissioner: "every time you'll find him working, he'll quit. He has a lot of connections where people can write him things. He doesn't participate in anything with the kids; his mother does, because she loves the kids, but he's here with a bunch of foolishness. He's telling a tale and he does this every time." While she is speaking, Mr. Bracy listens and shakes his head. He keeps quiet but his foot starts tapping.

"When I try to be civil with him and talk to him, he doesn't participate. I have the girls and he comes to the school and dogs me. This is a waste of my time because I have to pay someone to watch the kids while he pulls one over on the court. I'm tired of going through this. I'm going back to school. Eric makes a lot of money a month. I try to be civil with him, but I can't talk to him. He's very disrespectful to me." Mr. Bracy snorts, stops shaking his head, and looks at the commissioner. "I can't understand why he can't be made to do what he's supposed to do." Though Ms. Gill speaks forcefully, her voice inflected with frustration, she doesn't look at Mr. Bracy, instead addressing her remarks to the commissioner. Mr. Bracy sits silently beside her, his hands folded over his chest.

Commissioner Schmidt responds, explaining that they have had two hearings in the family court commission and the next step would be to go before the judge, who can incarcerate him. She explained, "typically, we try to get him paying before it gets certified to the judge. I know there was a substantial warrant out there prior to the 2015 dates." She looked at the file and noted that "we were here in 2008, so it's been a while."

Then she asks Graves what Mr. Bracy had paid to date and what the state's request was. Graves responds: "Since unemployment ran out, he only made two payments: $100 over a couple of months." When Commissioner Schmidt asked, "What is the State's request?" Graves answers, "Because he's an independent contractor, the state asks for another review." Graves does not look at Mr. Bracy while he is talking.

Ms. Gill asks if she could say one more thing. She says, "I'm not saying that I want him incarcerated because it'll do damage to the kids, but I'm saying that Eric is very smart when it comes to manipulating the courts and I feel like $250 with twins is no money to pay when I'm doing everything." When she says that he manipulates the court, Mr. Bracy shakes his head. Commissioner Schmidt tells her, "you may be right, but we can't do anything about increasing this unless you file a motion. We're asking him to bring in documentation of everything he's earning and then it would be up to you to file a motion to modify child support." Ms. Gill responds, "thank you, yes ma'am." There is a minute of quiet as the legal actors worked on their respective forms. Graves hands Mr. Bracy a form to sign and the commissioner says, "Good luck to you Mr. Bracy." After the parents leave the hearing room, the next case is called in.

Members of our research team produced the above in-person, ethnographic account of a child support enforcement hearing as part of our data collection plan for a qualitative study investigating the civil justice experiences of noncustodial parents in child support enforcement proceedings. The research team utilized focused ethnography as its methodological approach when conducting the court observations. Most of the parents in these cases are no- and low-income Black fathers who lack attorney representation and owe both current and past due child support, often in the thousands of dollars. We examine how their cases are handled by the judges and attorneys they encounter and how they navigate the civil process in proceedings where they face a variety of increasingly punitive enforcement measures, including civil incarceration for failure to pay support. This social phenomenon is widespread, with county jails across the United States incarcerating poor fathers who lack money to pay the support they owe (Brito, 2012).

Our study investigates two primary questions: How do lawyers matter? And are there more limited forms of legal assistance that provide a suitable alternative to attorney representation? We seek to enhance understanding of how attorney representation and other more limited forms of legal assistance affect civil court proceedings for low-income litigants. We examine how different legal assistance models shape legal access in the context of child support enforcement proceedings. Broadly, our study involves an in-depth exploration of the legal processes in these cases, focusing on court interactions and examining them from multiple perspectives and over an extended period of time. This approach explores the meaning people draw from legal interactions as well as the complexity of the relationship between process and outcomes. An earlier publication from this project, which draws from both our ethnographic and interview data, provides an empirical exploration of racialized access to justice issues within family courts, particularly the consequences that result from the ostensibly color-blind manner in which the proceedings are carried out (Brito, 2015).

There are a variety of different methodological approaches researchers can employ when gathering empirical data. In this chapter we present focused ethnography as a qualitative empirical approach that is well suited to legal scholars studying justice-related problems in urban settings. Focused ethnography is an effective methodology for engaged scholarship addressing the legal mechanisms and challenges underlying urban poverty. We begin by explaining why ethnography is a desirable choice for legal researchers studying these issues. The chapter then introduces focused ethnography as a type of ethnography, describes its elements, explains how it compares to immersive ethnography, and examines existing studies utilizing focused ethnography.

We then describe the elements of focused ethnography through a detailed discussion of the methodological choices we made in designing and implementing our access to justice empirical project, a study that investigates a widespread problem impacting low-income families in the urban core. By so doing, we describe the kinds of research questions, sampling strategies, data collection and analysis methods, and techniques of evaluating rigor characterizing focused ethnography. We also discuss the practical constraints that shaped decisions about methods. In providing this concrete example, we hope to demonstrate how legal scholars can apply this methodological tool to their own research. The chapter concludes with a discussion of the important ethical issues that need to be anticipated in all phases of the research process in ethnographic studies of legal issues impacting the urban core and individuals living in poverty. By describing the utility of focused ethnography, particularly in the courtroom setting, and emphasizing the unique ethics issues that exist in this field of research, we hope that this synthetic work provides a useful roadmap for legal scholars who are interested in engaged research addressing the intractable problems of the urban core.

Focused Ethnography and the Urban Core

Why apply focused ethnography to the study of legal systems operating in the urban core? Ethnographic observations, unlike conventional doctrinal legal scholarship and other empirical methodologies, generate original, unique, and essential empirical data on legal proceedings that are largely invisible. Legal systems in the United States operate on multiple tracks depending, in part, on whether the litigants are corporate entities, affluent individuals represented by counsel, or low-income pro-se litigants. Proceedings involving the latter group take place in municipal and lower courts and operate "underneath" and on a parallel track to civil court proceedings involving parties with greater power and resources. The proceedings are highly, sometimes painfully, consequential for the individuals involved; yet, there is a notable lack of transparency and accountability in these courts. As discussed more fully later in this chapter, their cases have low levels of public visibility and oversight, fail to generate an adequate public record documenting the proceedings, and judicial accountability through review by a higher court is rare.

Though the proceedings are ostensibly public, in practice public access to the courtroom is circumscribed by local custom. For example, in the six jurisdictions we studied, only named parties and their lawyers were permitted access to the courtroom. Friends and family members accompanying litigants to court were told to wait outside the courtroom. Court access rules are enforced by low-level bureaucratic gatekeepers. In each of our field sites, the research team had to negotiate initial access to the hearings and, over the five-year period we collected data, maintaining access required considerable renegotiation. Indeed, the hearing room described in the preceding ethnographic account lacks seating for *any* members of the public. Additional chairs were temporarily brought in for members of our research team when we conducted observations.

These cases remain further hidden from view due to the skimpy public record they produce. The child support hearings we observed are "off the record." In the vast majority of hearings, there is no stenographer present recording the words spoken during the proceedings. The hearing is not audio recorded and made available for later transcription. The only public records of the hearing are the clerk's brief, typed notation on the case civil docket sheet that reports the hearing outcome and the one-page, check-a-box court order signed by the judge. These case records are incomplete accounts in that they convey a small part of what transpired in court. Civil artifacts of this sort lack the rich detail needed to fully examine, understand, and critique the experiences of the many thousands of low-income, unrepresented litigants who appear daily in our urban courts.

The court experiences of the low-income families in child support court are similar to the experiences of many litigants in the nation's lower and municipal courts. Urban municipal courts handle a high volume of city ordinance violations such as traffic tickets, disorderly conduct, domestic violence, vandalism, housing violations, drunken driving, and the nonpayment of civil fines and fees. In municipal court, ordering the defendant to pay a monetary fine is the primary outcome imposed. When defendants do not pay, the judge may suspend their driver's license or incarcerate them. In recent years there has been increased scrutiny of urban municipal courts' use of incarceration to recoup revenue from court fines and fees. In 2014, National Public Radio reported that forty-eight states have passed on to defendants and offenders fees and fines that consist of payment for electronic monitoring, probation or supervision, public defender or legal costs, jail room and board, and increased civil/criminal fees (Shapiro). Further, a 2015 Department of Justice (DOJ) report on Ferguson, Missouri, in the wake of the Michael Brown murder, shed national attention on municipal courts' returning to use of debtors' prisons (United States Department of Justice, Civil Rights Division). The report documented that the city of Ferguson collected $2.6 million in court fines and fees. The investigation found that this practice, which generated about 21 percent of Ferguson's total budget, was an organized effort by the city government to raise revenue and that it imposed unnecessary harm, primarily on Black residents.

Conventional approaches to legal scholarship are not well suited to studying these types of troubling justice experiences in urban courts. Doctrinal analysis, which dominates legal scholarship, interprets and analyzes legal texts, such as constitutions, statutes, regulations and judicial opinions. Judicial opinions, particularly at the appellate level, explicate the legal issues under consideration, the applicable law, the parties' positions, the evidence considered, the legal reasoning underlying the court's ruling, and, in some instances, offer in-depth perspectives on the social context in which the case is decided. Conventional legal scholarship employing doctrinal analysis of case law typically produces a restatement or recasting of a particular area of law.

This scholarly approach is an ineffective strategy for engaged scholarship addressing the legal challenges underlying urban poverty. Unlike courts of appeals, lower courts that preside over poor people's legal problems typically do not produce written opinions that lend themselves to doctrinal analysis. Moreover, low-income, unrepresented litigants rarely appeal lower court decisions, meaning that review by a higher court and issuance of a detailed written decision is similarly highly unlikely. When appellate review routinely does not take place, decisions of those lower courts are the final word and judicial accountability is undermined.

Simply put, researchers interested in understanding and transforming the legal systems at play in the urban core need to "be there." They must be present in the setting, get close to the individuals and legal processes involved, and – with their observations – collect original data that document otherwise hidden justice-related events as they are happening in their social setting. Qualitative fieldwork, focused ethnography in particular, is a useful and accessible tool to accomplish this goal because it consists of a set of interpretive, material practices that make the world visible (Creswell, 2013: 43). Fieldwork tends to be problem-focused, and one of the primary features of qualitative research is an emphasis on social justice. Rather than take as a given the conventional wisdom about how courts operate, it is important for engaged scholars to get in those inaccessible spaces and observe what is hidden and otherwise taken for granted.

In terms of data collection, ethnography usually involves the researcher's physical presence in a social setting, community, and/or people's lives for an extended period of time. Researchers situate themselves in a natural setting – the field at the site where people experience the issues or problem under study – and people's actions and accounts are examined in this everyday context. The researcher sets out to watch what happens in the field, listen to what those present say, observe how people behave in this natural setting, collect documents, photographs, and other artifacts, and ask questions of those present. The questioning can be informal, in situ conversations or more formal interviews, or both. In short, the ethnographer aims to collect whatever data are available that shed light on the subject of inquiry and the issues that are emergent. The closeness and detail of this type of ethnographic fieldwork gives researchers a deep appreciation of the complexities and contradictions of socially relevant problems.

Participant meanings, in particular, are an important element of inquiry. Rather than privilege the meaning that researchers bring to a project or the meaning drawn from academic literature, the focus is on learning the meaning that people hold about the problems or issue under examination. Observational fieldwork is critical, however, because it provides contexts for understanding what people say and at the same time carries data collection beyond what people say (and the explanations they provide). It allows the researcher to see patterns of behavior, the scripts that people follow and sometimes deviate from, and the structures that constrain action. It allows the researcher to "compare words to action" and to collect data on phenomena taking place in the field site that people have not shared in interviews, potentially because they have not noticed them or because they do not fit their explanatory scripts (Orne and Bell, 2015: 100).

Ethnography provides an analytical approach to making sense of data. Data collection and data analysis are not separate steps that take place independent of each other (Rose, 2015: 144). The ethnographic researcher follows an iterative path of both collecting and analyzing data to develop an increasingly detailed and contextualized understanding of the issue or problem under investigation. "The analysis of data involves interpretation of meanings, functions, and consequences of human actions and institutional practices, and how these are implicated in local, and perhaps also wider, contexts" (Hammersley and Atkinson, 2007: 3). The iterative analytical process also informs subsequent data collection and further analysis.

Critical Ethnography and Social Change

Many ethnographic researchers today employ a critical orientation that centers social justice and seeks to change systemic inequities. The critical ethnographer's social justice agenda is in response to systems of power (whether hidden or obvious) and unjust and oppressive social conditions that marginalize individuals and communities. "In contrast to critical approaches, traditional social science research, through claims of value neutrality, often serves the ideological function of justifying the positions and interests of the always-already powerful" (Rose, 2015: 151). Critical inquiry questions and ultimately rejects the traditional use of social science research methodologies "as colonizing apparatuses to 'fix' social 'problems'" (Pasque and Pérez, 2015: 159). Critical perspectives are instead focused on investigating issues of race, gender, and socioeconomic status (and their interaction) and how systems of injustice become institutionalized.

Ethnography is particularly well suited to a critical approach; "specifically, research questions that address processes at the 'community, neighborhood, and urban scales – quite often at the edges of formal institutions and legality – render ethnographic methods particularly germane.'" (Rose, 2015: 151, quoting Fairbanks and Lloyd: 6). The critical perspective must be "embedded" throughout the research process, from initial conception of the project and research questions to design to data collection and analysis to writing and presentation to dissemination of study findings (Pasque and Pérez, 2015: 163). Ethnographic researchers can pursue this by working closely with communities to develop research questions that address their lived experiences and concerns, use methodological approaches that respect the dignity and privacy of community members, being constantly reflexive in their analysis, and engaging in action-oriented dissemination of research findings that is deliberately directed at social change.

Legal scholar and critical ethnographer Bernadette Atuahene's dissemination strategy exemplifies how the purposes of critical ethnography can extend far beyond the typical scholarly goal of academic publications. For her recent book, *We Want What's Ours: Learning from South Africa's Land Restitution Program*,[3] she conducted 150 interviews of South Africans who were displaced from their homes and property during colonialism and apartheid and who received some form of compensation through the South African land restitution program. The study also included interviews with land commissioners and other government workers responsible for administering the program. Her book explores the economic, political, psychological, and social impacts of receiving compensation. She publicized her study findings through South African and US media outlets through her numerous guest appearances on television and radio programs in both countries. She placed several op-eds about the book in major South

[3] Bernadette Atuahene, *We Want What's Ours: Learning from South Africa's Land Restitution Program* (2014). United Kingdom: Oxford University Press.

African and US newspapers like *Business Day, Mail & Guardian, Cape Times, City Press, LA Times*, and the *NY Times*. Professor Atuahene also directed and produced an eighteen-minute short documentary film called *Sifuna Okwethu (We Want What's Ours)* about one South African family's fight to regain their land stolen by apartheid authorities. The film, which put a human face to the issues that surfaced in the book, was widely viewed as an official selection at the Montreal Black Film Festival, the Pan African Film Festival in Los Angeles, the New York African Film Festival, and the Chicago International Film Festival, and won an audience award at the Africa World Film Festival. In addition, she distributed her findings to diverse audiences by screening the film and presenting her findings in nonacademic settings, including bookstores, churches, museums, think tanks (Council on Foreign Relations, Chicago Council on Global Affairs, Wilson Center in DC, Institute for Justice and Reconciliation in Cape Town, Human Sciences Research Council in Pretoria), government agencies (South African Land Claims Commission, US State Department), the Chicago Public Library, the Chicago Cultural Center, and the World Bank. Finally, Professor Atuahene also published a well-received policy report based on the study's main findings, and the South African Deputy Land Claims Commissioner later announced that the Commission had implemented 90 percent of the evidence-based policy recommendations she made for subsequent rounds of the reform process. Professor Atuahene's example sets a new standard for disseminating research findings beyond the academy in furtherance of a critical, social justice agenda.

FOCUSED ETHNOGRAPHY IN SOCIOLEGAL RESEARCH

Sociolegal scholars who utilize qualitative methods often engage in targeted, intensive data collection through observation in highly specific settings, including law offices, mediation sessions, and courtroom hearings. In this chapter, we suggest describing these observations as "focused ethnography" (Knoblauch, 2005). Focused ethnography is a set of techniques and methods that have been used to study situated action in local settings. The term "focused ethnography" is not new. Neither are the techniques associated with the term; indeed, many researchers have employed the methods of focused ethnography while characterizing their research with broad labels such as "participant observation," "qualitative methods," and "ethnographic methods."

Explicating the methodology of "focused ethnography" is nevertheless a useful exercise. Ethnographic methods exist along a continuum that includes considerable variation in elements such as the scope of the field under study, the relationship between theory and data, the time spent in the field, the relationships established with research participants, the mode of data analysis, and the presentation of research findings. Considering these elements of ethnography along a continuum – with immersive ethnography at one end and focused ethnography at the other – can structure the decision-making of researchers and provide a means of assessing methodological rigor on a project's own terms.

Focused ethnography provides a methodological toolkit with a unique set of epistemological and practical advantages and can be usefully applied to research in the sociolegal field. In this section we briefly outline past efforts to define focused ethnography, identifying projects in other fields that have explicitly relied on the method in addition to canonical sociolegal studies that employ similar methodologies by other names. We discuss issues of rigor and evaluation in ethnographic research, noting the advantages and drawbacks of focused ethnography and offer suggestions on how to enhance rigor.

What Is Focused Ethnography?

A number of factors complicate efforts to define focused ethnography. First, scholars who have previously sought to define focused ethnography do not wholly concur on the elements that constitute the method. Second, studies that self-describe as focused ethnographies do not rely on a consistent set of techniques. Finally, many studies employing methods that fall under the umbrella of focused ethnography do not identify themselves as such. While we explore these challenges in more detail later, we begin by presenting a broad definition of focused ethnography that reflects the consensus found in existing literature: focused ethnography emphasizes targeted, intensive data collection in highly specific social settings around structured events or activities. As such, focused ethnography is a set of techniques and methods that have been used to study specific contexts in a world that is increasingly socially and culturally differentiated (Knoblauch, 2005; Higgenbottom et al., 2013).

Focused ethnographies take up the study of "small elements of one's own society" (Knoblauch, 2005: 5). The emphasis on targeted, intensive observation suggests that investigators delimit their cases and sites in relation to specific researchable questions. Some scholars argue that focused ethnography is distinguished through its emphasis on applied or problem-oriented research questions. For instance, McElroy et al. (2011) suggest, "the trademark of the approach is the goal of taking action on the issue being studied" (19). While suitable to applied research projects, focused ethnography can also be applied to basic research that aims to test and further develop social scientific theory by identifying causal processes (Otterbein, 1977, cited in Banks, 1993).

In either applied or basic research, scholars often begin by developing questions from existing theory and experiential knowledge and then enter the field to test their theoretical propositions or gather systematic data on a pre-identified phenomenon. Thus, the field of study is closed, as opposed to open (Erickson, 1977; Knoblauch, 2005; Higgenbottom et al., 2013). From this starting point, researchers engage in short-term, targeted field visits, often taking an observer role. Knoblauch (2005) describes data collection and analysis as characterized by "intensity" – often, multiple researchers iteratively analyze the same data and the researchers supplement field notes with audio or visual recordings. This intensity facilitates a precise analysis of the actors, relations, and interactions that converge in relation to a situationally specific problem.

Existing Focused Ethnographies

Research that explicitly identifies itself as focused ethnography is common in studies of nursing, in the sociology of science, and in workplace studies. Often, these kinds of studies take a particular site – a laboratory, a clinic, a school – and aim to understand the practical and discursive activities that occur within the site in relation to a specific problem. In this broad sense, these studies are unified as focused ethnographies. However, researchers employ diverse methods under this umbrella. Here we describe three studies that identify as focused ethnographies in order to illustrate the heterogeneity in frequency, duration, and specificity of focus of observations characterizing focused ethnographies.

In their study, "Implementation of a Case Coordinator Role: A Focused Ethnographic Study," Neal et al. (1999) examine the creation of a new case coordinator position in an inpatient psychiatric unit. This coordinator role aimed to organize and facilitate the activities of a multidisciplinary treatment team, which included nurses, physicians, occupational therapists, social workers, and administration personnel. The study evaluated the development and implementation of this role in relation to the existing culture of the unit. The authors define focused ethnography as "a time-limited, exploratory study of a particular phenomenon" that seeks "meaning-in-context" data (349). In conducting the focused ethnography, each researcher (on the team of three) spent at least eight hours observing in the unit, in increments ranging from half an hour to two hours. Observations captured "routine unit activities, multidisciplinary team meetings, and team members' interactions with patients" (350). The project began from a foundation of shared knowledge, as the research team comprised doctoral students in nursing, and sought to address a context-specific problem by evaluating the efficacy of this new professional position.

Little (1982) investigates the impact of the organization of the school as a workplace on teachers' engagement, comparing successful versus unsuccessful schools in the study, "Norms of Collegiality and Experimentation: Workplace Conditions of School Success." She describes the study as a "focused ethnography drawing on prior work to give substantive guidance and on the methodological resources of ethnography to generate new discovery and to add depth" (326). The project included six schools ranging in "successfulness" (based on standardized achievement scores). Little conducted interviews with over 130 teachers and administrators and conducted observations in the classrooms of eighty teachers, in staff meetings, and in various spaces on each school's campus. Though the frequency and duration of observations are not specified, the number of teachers included in the sample indicates that the study sought breadth across many teachers rather than depth in relation to a few.

Finally, Miller et al. (2008) ask, "what are the existing emotion work considerations for nurses working within an interprofessional context in a hospital setting? How does emotion work facilitate or impede nursing in this context?" in their study, "Nursing Emotion Work and Interprofessional Collaboration in General Internal Medicine Wards: A Qualitative Study." The study employs "focused field observations" and cites Knoblauch (2005) in relation to these techniques. The authors describe observations in three hospitals: "researchers were unobtrusively positioned throughout [general internal medicine] wards during brief, focused field visits. Descriptive data were recorded on verbal and nonverbal uni- and interprofessional interactions during unstructured (ward) and structured (scheduled meetings) activities" (335). The team observed 156 hours of unstructured activity between the three wards and 27.5 hours of structured activity. In addition, the researchers conducted five one-hour long shadows of nurses as they worked. Finally, the project incorporated data from semi-structured interviews with fifty nurses.

This diversity of methods indicates that there is an equivocal understanding of what constitutes a focused ethnography. These studies incorporate some, but not all, of the elements of focused ethnographies identified by Knoblauch (2005) and Higgenbottom et al. (2013). Likewise, many studies that share the features of focused ethnographies may not explicitly frame themselves as such or reference a core set of methodological foundations. Knoblauch suggests that these studies nevertheless share a "family resemblance" based on sharing a number of the features described in this section.

Focused Ethnographic Techniques in Sociolegal Studies

We suggest that focused ethnographic techniques can be usefully employed in sociolegal research and, in fact, canonical studies in the field that rely on observation already share in the family resemblance of focused ethnographies. This is, in part, because the courtroom setting and the legal hearing are both amenable to the methods of focused ethnography: They bring together a specific set of actors who have gathered in relation to a pre-defined problem – the disposition of a case. Legal settings narrow the scope of investigation because the legal process itself identifies the particular salient categories and social problems that enter into a space of structured interaction. Researchers can follow cases as they evolve over time or move between institutional contexts. This bounds the field of investigation in predictable and structured ways.[4]

While few sociolegal studies identify themselves as focused ethnographies, many rely on observation as a means of data collection. These observations fall along a

[4] While the legal setting presents certain advantages, it is not without practical challenges. Some dockets may group cases of interest together, but, in many other instances, cases may be randomly scattered across the court's calendar. This can frustrate the goal of focused ethnography, unless the research team is prepared to go to court hearings one by one.

continuum, with some resembling the narrative accounts produced by a single researcher through long-term immersion and others incorporating the techniques of focused ethnographies – most commonly, collaboration between multiple researchers and targeted data collection. We identify three works of sociolegal scholarship and briefly discuss how aspects of the methods align with the techniques of focused ethnography.

Sarat and Felstiner (1986) characterize their study, "Law and Strategy in the Divorce Lawyer's Office," as an "ethnographic account of lawyer-client interaction in divorce cases" (94). The authors began by selecting a site of substantive and theoretical interest. As Sarat describes, "divorce seemed particularly promising as an area in which to work because of the interplay of the usual stuff of law – money, property, rights – with emotions. Even when the legal rules say that divorce is no fault we thought that emotions might play a large part in the work of divorce lawyers. We were interested to see how the emotional context influenced the way lawyers and clients interact" (Halliday and Schmidt, 2009: 189). The research occurred over a thirty-three-month period in which the authors followed forty divorce cases from the initial interview through the end of the case. The authors describe, "we followed these cases by observing and tape-recording lawyer-client sessions, attending court and mediation hearings and trials, and interviewing both lawyers and clients about those events" (95). In total, the authors tape-recorded 115 lawyer–client conferences. They tracked cases over time by requesting notification from legal secretaries or directly contacting lawyers. Sarat and Felstiner conducted observations independently, though they audio-recorded hearings and exchanged the recordings after each hearing. In analyzing the data, the authors and three graduate student researchers read the transcripts from the hearings. Felstiner describes, "we'd all read the cases. We'd each figure out what was going on in the cases, how we were going to interpret the cases, what they told us about the kind of things we were interested in. Then we'd all sit down together and talk about it" (Halliday and Schmidt, 2009: 195).

This study exemplifies a focused ethnography in many regards: The researchers selected a specific context and interaction, lawyer–client conferences, and utilized technology to capture micro-interactional dynamics. The project entailed targeted data collection in relation to the specific problems that lawyers face in orienting their clients to the realities of the legal system. The authors selected a theoretically interesting type of case – in which extralegal emotions may be entangled with legal imperatives – and purposively observed relevant hearings. The use of audio files and transcripts permitted a research team to collaboratively analyze the data, reflecting the intensity in data collection and analysis described by Knoblauch and Higgenbottom et al. Through these techniques, the authors identified the interactional mechanisms by which lawyers communicate norms around trial versus negotiation proceedings and identify for the client only those aspects of their identities that will be legally relevant.

Sarat and Felstiner revealed both the lawyers' and the clients' perspectives on lawyer–client interactions in divorce cases. They observed that lawyers repeatedly tried to focus the client's attention on pursuing a satisfactory resolution of what the lawyers believed are the primary legal issues, i.e., dissolution of the marriage and property division, while their clients more commonly tended to focus on their emotional agenda, ambivalence about the end of the marriage, and desire for moral vindication. Their study also examined the consequences of those two competing perspectives. Most of the lawyers they observed invested considerable effort in client management activities. This meant that the lawyers would try to "cool out" their clients by shifting their orientation to the case. Lawyers helped their clients to come to accept that the legal process is equipped to deal with the financial realm of their dispute but not the emotional realm, and to begin to view the case in instrumental terms. In their effort to nudge their clients toward settlement (rather than an adversarial trial), the lawyers in the study shared with their clients their expert knowledge of how the legal system actually worked in their communities. The attorney–client interactions that Sarat and Felstiner observed through their focused ethnography alerted them to the divergence between the realities of divorce practice as experienced by lawyers and the clients' competing agendas, expectations, and sense of justice. The methodological approach they utilized made it possible for them to mine the rich data of these interactions, dialogues, and behaviors to produce scholarship that extends far beyond legal doctrine to a legal realist account and analysis of the competition and accommodation that lawyers and clients engage in over the course of divorce litigation.

Sally Merry's (1990) *Getting Justice and Getting Even* also draws upon techniques and methods characterizing focused ethnography. Merry explores legal consciousness and the experiences of working class people who bring their personal problems to the lower courts. The data derives from two projects; the first examined the kinds of disputes people brought to court and how mediation functions. Merry and her collaborator, Susan Silbey, compared mediation programs and courts in Salem, Massachusetts, and in Cambridge, Massachusetts, between 1980 and 1983. The project relied on five kinds of observations: (1) observations of 118 mediation sessions (observed by two researchers), (2) observations of court hearings, (3) quantitative analysis based on caseloads, (4) interviews with 124 people having gone through mediation, (5) an ethnographic study of three neighborhoods in Salem. Merry describes this final ethnographic component of the study:

> We did an ethnographic study of three small neighborhoods in Salem in which several of the conflicts occurred. This study included a survey of 93 residents of these neighborhoods; the survey asked them how often they had the kinds of problems we saw in mediation and what they did about them. The survey was part of a more intensive ethnographic study which included long conversations with several of the residents of these neighborhoods ... In addition, I spent hundreds of hours observing court proceedings, including hearings in front of clerk-magistrates; talking informally to court personnel, mediators, and mediation program staff; and doing general historical and ethnographic work on Salem and Cambridge (18).

The second study, conducted with Ann Marie Roucheleau from 1981 through 1984, examined a parent/child mediation program through observations of mediation sessions for 51 youth, observations of court proceedings for the same families, and follow-up interviews with 128 participants.

Like the Sarat and Felstiner study, the ethnographic component of Merry's research aligns with the elements of focused ethnography in many regards. According to Merry, she used the case as her unit of analysis and sought to observe the process of disputing as it is "rooted in the social system" (Halliday and Schmidt, 2009: 132). In order to do so, her observations focused on mediation sessions and lower court hearings – specific locations that are guaranteed to capture the interactions and dynamics of interest. Merry also hired local research assistants to conduct some interviews. She reported feeling challenged because ethnography traditionally has studied villages and she was studying more complex suburban neighborhoods. In her research setting, she could not conduct the ethnographic work by just "sitting there" and relied on her research assistants as both informants about the neighborhoods and interviewers. She described the combination of her own observations and the use of research assistants as "provid[ing] me with a lot of good insight into these neighborhoods. In a way it was collaborative and was really quite productive for getting a feeling about the neighborhood" (Halliday and Schmidt, 2009: 134). While this does not entirely approximate the data sessions described by Knoblauch, Merry's use of a research team facilitated intensity in data analysis. Though she only wrote about the cases that she herself observed, Merry's research assistants provided much-needed context for her ethnographic data. According to her, they were "very valuable in providing [her] with a framework of how typical a case is, how often it happens, [and] what the larger structure is within which these things happen." (Halliday and Schmidt, 2009: 135).

In her 2016 book, *Crook County: Racism and Injustice in America's Largest Criminal Court*, Nicole Gonzalez Van Cleve employs multiple data collection techniques, including those resembling focused ethnographic methods. Van Cleve examines the co-construction of race and law in criminal courtrooms in Cook County, Illinois. While the research began with a cumulative nine months of participant observation, with Van Cleve serving as a clerk with the Office of the Illinois State Attorney and the Office of the Public Defender, she additionally included interviews with legal actors and "supplemental qualitative work" (Van Cleve, 2016: 4). In this supplemental component of the project, Van Cleve oversaw 130 "court watchers," who gathered data in all 25 Cook County courtrooms over the course of two years. Van Cleve describes her motivation for this segment of the work: "While ethnographers often tout the methodological advantage of close personal observations, an ethnographic account of a large organization can lack breadth of coverage and vision" (4). The use of multiple researchers in the same setting permitted Van Cleve to address "matters of scope and reliability," investigating activity over time and across courtrooms (5). Van Cleve provided the court watchers with three hours of training prior to observations and standardized data collection though the use of a rubric. Court watchers observed in courtrooms for one-hour periods, rotating among five or six courtrooms on a given site visit. The methods of this part of the study remarkably resemble those of focused ethnography.

Employing Focused Ethnography along a Continuum of Ethnographic Inquiry

Focused ethnography exists along a spectrum of ethnographic inquiry and, as the aims of a project evolve over time, researchers may find that an adjustment to the research design is warranted. To consider that range, it is helpful to examine the features of focused ethnographies in relation to the elements of immersive ethnographies. By the standards of immersive ethnography, the researcher is expected to embed herself in the field for an extended period of time, form close relationships with participants, and develop expertise on the entirety of the social world under study. The researcher engages in an inductive process in defining the scope of investigation and individually analyzes data to produce written accounts of the local meanings attached to beliefs and practices. The credibility of a project is evaluated based on the ethnographer's ability to convey her status as a trusted associate with access to the inner workings of the social collectivity (Higgenbottom et al., 2013).

The elements of immersive ethnography are succinctly captured in the following chart from Higgenbottom et al. (2013).

Focused ethnography	Anthropologic ethnographies
Specific aspect of field studied with purpose.	Entire social field studied.
Closed field of investigation as per research question.	Open field of investigation as determined through time.
Background knowledge usually informs research question.	Researcher gains insider knowledge from participatory engagement in field.
Informants serve as key participants with their knowledge and experience.	Participants are often those with whom the researcher has developed a close relationship.
Intermittent and purposeful field visits using particular timeframes or events, or may eliminate observation.	Immersion during long-term, experiential-intense fieldwork.
Data analysis intensity often with numerous recording devices including video cameras, tape recorders, and photo-cameras.	Narrative intensity.
Data sessions with a gathering of researchers knowledgeable of the research goals may be extensively useful for providing heightened perspective to the data analysis, particularly of recorded data.	Individual data analysis.

Some ethnographic studies fit neatly into either the immersive or focused ethnography categories. To illustrate the contrasts between them, one can compare David Sudnow's (1967) book, *Passing On: The Social Organization of Dying* to the Neal et al. (1999) piece, "Implementation of a Case Coordinator Role: A Focused

Ethnographic Study," discussed previously. Sudnow spent one and a half years observing full-time in two hospitals, describing the institutional arrangements, routine activities, and normative understandings accompanying death and dying. He aimed to fully outline the otherwise "undescribed social organization of 'death work'" (v). In contrast, Neal et al. drew on semi-structured interviews with key informants and thirty-minute to two-hour observations of activities within a psychiatric ward (totaling around twenty-four hours of observation) to identify the practical and symbolic challenges surrounding the creation and implementation of the case coordinator role. These studies can be contrasted in the specificity of their scope and the forms of their data collection. The first is characterized by long-term immersion and seeks to describe all aspects of an institutional context. The second uses acute short-term visits to capture information relevant to a highly specific problem.

We emphasize that focused ethnography and immersive ethnography are not mutually exclusive practices. Many studies transcend these ideal-typical constructions, potentially moving from one end of the continuum to the other as a research project develops, or employing methods that fall on either side of the divide at a given point in the research process.[5] For instance, researchers may begin in a highly specific setting, but expand into other sites within the social field in order to contextualize findings from targeted observations. Or researchers engaged in immersive, long-term participant observation may begin to conduct targeted observations around specific phenomena once such phenomena become theoretically interesting. This fluidity on the continuum between immersive ethnography and focused ethnography thus reflects the evolving aims of a project.

We reproduce Higgenbottom et al.'s (2013) distinctions in order to emphasize that the design and implementation of ethnographic research includes a considerable number of choices. We hope that explicating the elements of focused ethnography broadens the array of ethnographic tools and cultivates resources for decision-making that are attentive to the fit between research questions and methods and attuned to the realities of the research process. These realities include great variation in the resources available to individual researchers or research teams. While a project's aims structure choices about methods, researchers must also make decisions in relation to practical and institutional constraints. In order to judiciously engage in data collection, researchers must account for the time they intend to spend in the field, travel to field sites, potential incentives for participants, the need

5 Distinguishing between focused ethnographies and immersive ethnographies is also rendered more challenging due to scholarly conventions around publication. While many immersive ethnographies may indeed begin with an open field of investigation and pursue a grounded theory approach, scholarly articles are often written as though researchers engaged in a highly deductive and theory-driven process. The writing conventions around framing new empirical research in relation to existing theory and previous findings results in the possible exclusion of detail regarding the realities of the fieldwork. Descriptions of immersive ethnographies are most likely to be found in the methodological appendixes of books, rather than articles.

for further methodological training, and opportunities to involve graduate students in the research process, to name a few potential considerations. The elements of focused ethnography suggest practical practices that vary considerably from those of immersive ethnography. Researchers visit sites intermittently and for short intervals of time; focused ethnographies often incorporate a broader sampling frame and include contact with a greater number of actors; the method encourages the use of a research team – multiple scholars, potentially including students – in data collection and analysis. These characteristics suggest that focused ethnographies can be a valuable mode of research design in light of common institutional imperatives and constraints.

Evaluating and Enhancing Rigor in Focused Ethnography

The techniques of focused ethnography and immersive ethnography provide different sets of practical and epistemological advantages and shortcomings. As Van Cleve's study demonstrates, often these methods can be used in complementary ways. In this ideal-typical depiction, immersive ethnographies are well-suited for inductive empirical investigations of an unfamiliar social world. They often provide rich narrative data that capture the cultural beliefs that govern behavior within the field under study. However, they are time and resource intensive and often a sole researcher is responsible for data collection and analysis, making verification efforts more challenging. By contrast, focused ethnographies are well-suited for hypothesis-testing projects driven by an experiential or theoretical knowledge of the field prior to entry. While they do not capture the full range of interactions and contexts present in the larger social field, they are more targeted in their resource deployment, scheduling site visits in relation to the problem of interest rather than seeking full immersion. Focused ethnographies permit the inclusion of multiple researchers in data collection and analysis, enhancing intersubjectivity by testing whether different researchers identify similar patterns and phenomena in the data.

Along this continuum, the plausibility of ethnographic accounts can be enhanced in a number of ways. Researchers can situate the project in relation to existing theory and the empirical findings of other studies, bolstering explanatory claims (Burawoy, 1998; Timmermans and Tavory, 2012). Researchers can also triangulate – studying the same phenomenon through two or more sources of data; this allows researchers to enhance the reliability and validity of findings by checking for consistency in the conclusions drawn from each source. Researchers can also compare a process or phenomenon across sites to test whether explanatory accounts hold up in different settings (Tavory and Timmermans, 2013).

In addition to these means of bolstering explanatory accounts, researchers can also actively test the rigor of their findings by identifying plausible alternative accounts and negative cases (Duneier, 2011). As they develop explanations of the social phenomenon at hand, researchers can be blinded to potential alternatives and disconfirming evidence. Avoiding these pitfalls and ensuring that the offered explanation is the most accurate requires attention to "phenomena that are inconvenient for the line or theory that has emerged from the fieldwork" (Duneier, 2011: 8). This attention guards against possible sources of bias or lack of nuance that may arise as researchers analyze their data.

Finally, researchers can enhance rigor through transparency around their decisions and their roles as a sampler, observer, and interpreter. Reflexivity requires researchers to critically examine how their social location shapes the research questions they ask, the populations they study, and the interpretations they apply to data. Biography, political motivations, education, and disciplinary habitus all shape scholarship (Sprague, 2005; Emirbayer and Desmond, 2012). Transparency requires that researchers account for decision-making processes that influence the production of research findings and provide rich data that allows the researchers' interpretations to be tested against alternatives (Katz, 1997).

Focused ethnographic techniques provide certain advantages – and limitations – in terms of these standards of rigor. By deriving questions from existing theory and experiential knowledge, researchers often select specific field sites and enter them with an eye out for the kinds of evidence they'll need to test their assumptions. One of the primary risks in such work is that the initial case selection and sampling frame omits other important sites or cases that are germane to the phenomenon of interest. Once in the field, researchers risk a tendency to focus on confirming evidence that validates their existing knowledge. These risks can be mitigated through reflexive attention to the preconceptions that researchers bring to a project. Researchers can usefully focus data collection on disconfirming or negative cases from day one, truly beginning with a theory-testing premise. They can also remain open to the possibility of incorporating new field sites and modifying or expanding the sampling frame to include cases that test the strength of explanatory accounts.

Focused ethnography has strengths in its various means of triangulation: It is conducive to multi-method research design; conserving the researcher's resources by limiting the time observing in the field often permits collection of other forms of data, for instance, through interviews, surveys, or content analysis. This complementarity facilitates triangulation. Targeted data collection also permits comparative work by allowing researchers to expand to multiple sites and to compare explanatory accounts across contexts. Finally, as focused ethnography is conducive to the use of research teams, design and implementation of projects requires active communication around issues of sample, observation, and interpretation. The use of multiple researchers to cultivate intensity in data analysis encourages intersubjectivity by exposing the same data to the potentially divergent interpretations of multiple researchers. Focused ethnographies can thus seek internal validity by testing the rigor of explanatory accounts across field sites, across data sources, and across researchers' interpretations.

THE ELEMENTS OF FOCUSED ETHNOGRAPHY

We outline the elements of focused ethnography using the example of our study, described earlier, which empirically examines the civil justice experiences of *pro se* noncustodial parents in child support enforcement proceedings. As noted previously, many nonpayers of child support are low- or no-income noncustodial fathers, and nonpayers risk civil incarceration for contempt if they are found to be willfully disobeying a court order. Enforcement hearings thus have important access to justice implications – they implicate the range of procedural protections that low-income litigants have access to, and they reflect the response of the legal process to systemic issues of poverty. While indigent litigants have no guaranteed right to representation in civil cases, the Supreme Court held in the 2011 *Turner* v. *Rogers* decision that litigants must be provided with adequate procedural safeguards to protect against erroneous civil incarceration. This project investigates the processes that shape substantive results in child support enforcement hearings by comparing a jurisdiction that provides counsel to indigent litigants in civil cases and a jurisdiction that offers more limited forms of legal assistance. We also explore the meaning people – including litigants, attorneys, and judges – place on these legal events.

We use the example of this project to describe the kinds of research questions, sampling strategies, data collection and analysis methods, and techniques of evaluating rigor characterizing focused ethnography. We also discuss the practical constraints that shaped decisions about methods. In providing this concrete example, we hope to exemplify useful tools – those of focused ethnography – that scholars can apply to their own research.

Research Questions and Case Selection

As suggested, focused ethnographies aim to describe experiences within the cultural context of specific sub-groups that are embedded within a broader set of shared social understandings. Questions develop from experiential or theoretical knowledge of the field and generally attend to a specific kind of situation or problem. This suggests that the research process begins closer to the deductive side of the continuum (though processes of induction and deduction are likely to characterize different stages of the research, as researchers discover evidence that disconfirms their explanatory account, develop new accounts, test those accounts, and revise them in relation to the data). Researchers select questions, site, and cases from a premise of familiarity with the field under study. In this project, the broad research question asks: Under what circumstances, and in what ways, does legal representation matter in child support proceedings? And are there more limited forms of legal assistance that provide a suitable alternative?

This research question derives from the existing knowledge of the research team, headed by a professor of law and a professor of social welfare. In addition to knowledge of the legal and social service fields stemming from professional practice, the principal investigators (PIs) bring their disciplinary training to bear by situating the project at the intersections of family law and structural theories of poverty. In addition, the team includes graduate student members with training in law, education, and sociology. This diversity of academic perspectives and professional experiences contributes to the researchers' understanding of child support enforcement proceedings as a substantively and theoretically important site of interaction.

The ethnographic component of the project reveals how parties construct social meaning in the context of a specific legal process. The study investigates the narratives that legal professionals and litigants draw upon in coming to conclusions about whether or not a noncustodial parent has the ability to pay a support order. By seeking variety in the circumstances and processes that result in determinations of the ability to pay, the project describes the roles of various legal actors and the experiences of represented versus unrepresented litigants. The substantive foundations of the project require a comparative design. Thus, observations took place in multiple jurisdictions in two states. Each state utilizes a distinct model of legal representation that is of interest: full representation in State A and the provision of legal assistance short of full representation in State B.

In contrast to an immersive ethnography, which typically would focus entirely on a single site, our site selection is driven by previous research that identifies variations in legal assistance as a determinative factor in access to justice. In fact, the project began with exploratory fieldwork, including court observations and interviews in six field sites. However, the researchers decided to modify the ethnographic data collection plan by conducting a focused ethnography in two field sites after an anonymous reviewer of the co-PIs' NSF proposal suggested the method. A focus on two sites permits more in-depth analysis of the child support enforcement process in these two counties. Site selection was also informed by considerations of access – in both sites, researchers can see court calendars in advance and have the opportunity to observe all aspects of the litigation process, including negotiation sessions prior to hearings in one of the field sites. Narrowing the study to two sites meant that observations captured place- and institution-specific dynamics that may not reflect patterns across jurisdictions within the same state. Nevertheless, the comparison between these two sites usefully describes how litigants navigate the legal system in the context of two different models of legal assistance and with what substantive results. The research examines *how* attorneys matter and contrasts this to a description of how legal assistance short of full representation operates in the context of enforcement proceedings.

Sampling and Sample Size

After site selection, focused ethnographies rely on purposive sampling, which seeks participants that have specific knowledge or experiences of interest, rather than a random sample from the total population of the site. Within cases, researchers strive to achieve variation in order to capture the full range and extent of a phenomenon. This means that relationships in the field are generally more broad than deep. In contrast to forming close and long-term relationships with participants, often following them across contexts, focused ethnographies are characterized by context-specific observation, thus generally limiting both the time and the place in which participants are observed. This is not to say that researchers cannot develop close, longitudinal ties to participants in a focused ethnography. However, as site visits are intermittent and purposeful, and as the researcher often acts as an observer, rather than a participant-observer, interaction between researchers and participants can be comparatively bounded.

In the context of this project, researchers aimed to observe all of the legal actors who are directly involved in enforcement proceedings in each of the two sites. These actors include judges, Child Support Agency attorneys, family court commissioners, and defense attorneys, as well as court administrative staff. The team also aimed to observe the range of litigants who come before the court in child support cases. This sampling strategy captured the individuals who have context-specific experience and knowledge that is germane to the question of the role of legal assistance in these proceedings. In order to access variety in the circumstances and processes of enforcement hearings, the researchers scheduled multiple, sequential site visits and observed (in most instances) in half-day increments over three-day periods. Prior to observation, the team identified relevant cases by examining court calendars in advance and attending those hearings related to enforcement for nonpayment of child support.

Site visits included observations of informal negotiation processes, hearings before the Family Court Commissioner, and hearings before the district court judge. The team returned to the field sites intermittently for four years and ten months (including earlier exploratory visits) until reaching a point of saturation, in that continued data collection ceased providing new or useful information. In the State A county courthouse field site, the research team collectively observed for 340 hours and observed proceedings for 490 cases. In the State B county courthouse field site, the research team collectively observed for 161 hours and observed proceedings for 154 cases.

Data Collection and Analysis

Data collection and analysis in focused ethnography is characterized by intensity. This often means that multiple researchers simultaneously gather data or that audio or visual recordings supplement observations to enhance accuracy. Though the project required building relationships with legal actors and litigants, researchers aimed to act as passive observers during enforcement hearings. These court proceedings are technically open to the public and, while this openness could be nominal, it nevertheless provided a foundation for access that is not available when entering private institutional settings. Generally, members of the research team sat on the benches available to the public and took notes throughout the hearings.

During observations, researchers used a data collection guide that draws attention to the dynamics that are germane to the research question. This guide was developed and refined during exploratory site visits and captures elements of the courtroom environment, the specific kinds of narratives and evidence presented during hearings, and the nature of interactions between various legal actors and litigants. All members of the research team engaged in observations at both field sites, providing a foundation of shared knowledge that facilitated informed data analysis. Though the project does not rely on audio or visual recordings of the ethnographic field, the team supplemented field notes with transcripts of the hearings when they were available. In order to increase the trustworthiness of the data, two researchers gathered data on each site visit.

In analyzing data, researchers engaged in an iterative, cyclical, and self-reflective process. "Data sessions," in which multiple researchers review and analyze the same data, enhanced the intersubjectivity of interpretation. While analysis draws on common practices including open-coding, identifying outliers and negative cases, and writing memos, focused ethnography benefits from the transparency in data collection and analysis that accompanies team projects. Sharing information and making collective decisions requires that researchers openly discuss and negotiate these aspects of the research process.

Data collection and analysis occurred in a simultaneous and iterative process. The team engaged in ongoing coding of existing data and staggered site visits, allowing insights from analysis to inform the data collected on future trips. New substantive findings were incorporated into the project's analytical framework. Focused ethnography permits this dialogic process – with theory and empirical findings developing in relation to each other – because the intermittent and targeted nature of site visits provides ample time to engage in concurrent analysis. At several junctures during data collection, the team paused our efforts for a few months in order to analyze our existing data and identify emergent themes, new lines of inquiry, and areas for follow-up that informed the next stage of data collection.

After individual field site visits, researchers debriefed and cross-checked their observations; the researchers debriefed each site visit a second time with the entire research team. Each researcher wrote detailed field notes based on the jottings taken during the hearings, incorporating analytical insights about those observations that were shared by other team members during our debrief sessions. Two researchers separately and independently coded each written piece of data and then critically reviewed each other's work, discussing and reconciling coding differences. This team approach heightened reliability by enhancing exposure to multiple interpretations of the data.

Maintenance of Rigor

Focused ethnographies often incorporate other sources of data to facilitate triangulation. This can bolster the trustworthiness and rigor of findings if they are replicated through the use of multiple methods. Triangulation also provides valuable insight into how particular methods shape findings, identifying possible sources of bias. Focused ethnography is particularly conducive to multi-method design for a number of reasons. The team approach facilitates large-scale data collection and potentially incorporates members with different forms of methodological expertise. The intermittent and targeted nature of site visits suggests that members of the research team have the time and ability to pursue other avenues of data collection. The legal setting often facilitates access to other data sources: case files, hearing transcripts, and the potential to meet and interview or survey both legal actors and litigants.

In this project, we supplement observations with publically available case file data and, when available, hearing transcripts. Examining case files allows the team to situate the hearing within the broader context of an ongoing case. The transcripts provide an account of verbatim exchanges during the hearing. Field notes supplement transcripts with data on the nuances of courtroom dynamics – nonverbal reactions, tone of voice, impressions about demeanor, etc. These various data sources provide context that elucidates process and interaction in enforcement proceedings.

As with many other sociolegal studies, this project relies on a multi-method design. The focused ethnographic component is only one prong of the project, which additionally includes 145 interviews with legal professionals and child support plaintiffs, and longitudinal interviews with a sample of 40 child support defendants. Interviews capture the meanings that these various groups of actors attribute to the enforcement process. They allow the team to compare the stated motivations, beliefs, and values of legal actors to their behavior during the hearings, and they identify the understandings of the legal process that litigants bring as they navigate them. Reliance on interviews, field notes, case files, and documents allows the team to test explanatory accounts across these data sources.

ETHICAL CONSIDERATIONS, THE URBAN CORE, AND FOCUSED ETHNOGRAPHY

Ethnographic study of legal issues impacting the urban core and individuals living in poverty raises unique and important ethics issues. Ethical considerations in research with human subjects broadly ask if the research process protects the rights of participants and produces benefits, while minimizing harms (Murphy and Dingwall, 2001). In the aftermath of the profound maltreatment and gross violations of rights at Nuremberg and Tuskegee, these abstract ethical principles have been widely codified and institutionalized (NIH, 2011). The Belmont Report, for instance, identifies respect for persons, beneficence, and justice as guiding protections for research participants. Researchers realize these principles through ensuring informed consent, assessing risks and benefits, and selecting subjects with the fair distribution of benefits and burdens in mind (United States, 1979). The Belmont Report – though originally developed to guide medical research – has served as a foundational guide for many institutional review boards that oversee ethnographic studies. While efforts to institutionalize ethical principles have ambiguities and limitations, we do not delve deeply into this.

Instead, this section first outlines the special considerations that arise when a study includes participants from the urban core. It then describes how ethical principles play out in immersive versus focused ethnographies based on the distinct character of the researcher–participant relationship in each. Though ethical considerations pervade all aspects of the research process – from study design to the politics of representation in publication – these two methods diverge considerably in how researchers relate to participants in the field. We take this topic up as a mere starting point, with the hope that this brief discussion encourages further reflection on the ethics and politics of focused ethnography in the urban core.

Power Dynamics in Ethnographies of the Urban Core

Urban ethnographies may present distinct ethical challenges, as the power differentials between researchers and participants from the urban core can be vast. Researchers bring with them the advantages of their institutional positions. They are well-educated and credentialed. They consume and produce forms of knowledge that are considered legitimate and mainstream. Often – given the make-up of the academy – they experience other privileges based on race and class identities. This can position researchers as closer in educational background and social location to the powerful actors – attorneys, social workers, police officers, and the like – who regulate and surveil residents of the urban core. This position can impact a range of things, from access and relationship building, to the presuppositions and biases that researchers may hold. Researchers must consider the implications of working with participants who may experience multiple forms of marginality – poverty, racial subordination, neighborhood segregation, and institutional neglect. Navigating informed consent, risks and benefits, and justice in this context is a challenging, but crucial, undertaking.

Ethnographers who study the urban core are often motivated by a desire to give voice to the disadvantaged – to represent their struggles, to reveal the constraints imposed upon them, and to effect social change for their benefit. Yet, it is more than this political motivation that accounts for the longstanding tendency for ethnographers to "study down" (Nader, 1972). Researchers studying the disadvantaged derive certain practical benefits from their dominant position. Compared to powerful entities and individuals, marginalized communities and people have less capacity to engage in gatekeeping. Researchers can often easily access information about residents of the urban core, even if they fail to form meaningful relationships in the field. The various forms of state supervision that target the urban core – for instance, those of the criminal justice system or the welfare bureaucracy – make many details of residents' lives available (Bowman, 2009). In addition, researchers can often "show up" in social settings of interest. Ethnographers of the urban core may struggle to navigate access amid informal pressures of suspicion, social distance, or perceived danger. Yet, the street corner (Liebow, 1967), the cafeteria (Duneier, 1992), and "the ghetto" (Anderson, 1999) remain physically accessible in ways that the boardroom, the research laboratory, and the police precinct are not. Comparative ease of access and a dominant–subordinate relationship that favors the ethnographer make it more challenging for marginalized individuals to avoid being research subjects.

Power differentials between the ethnographer and participants present additional difficulties in ensuring participants' rights to autonomy and self-determination. Even if researchers are meticulous about reviewing consent forms, explaining the research in lay terms, and re-consenting participants as a project goes on, aspects of the research process will remain opaque. Ethnographers may not fully communicate to participants the research objectives, nature of fieldwork, and processes of data analysis. This can happen for many reasons. On the one hand, research projects evolve and change, particularly when using an inductive or grounded approach. On the other hand, research design and data analysis are informed by highly specialized and disciplinary knowledge from the outset. This knowledge is not commonplace. Only 3 percent of the population attains a doctorate or professional degree (US Census Bureau, 2011). In contexts like the urban core, where residents are affected by deep inequalities in educational experiences long preceding access to graduate school, ensuring that research participants understand the implications of their participation can be a project in and of itself.

Ethnographers of the urban core face another set of complicated considerations in relation to the products of their research. Unintended consequences – and harms – can accompany the publication of study findings. Substantially, in research on the urban core, "ethnographic studies typically increase knowledge of the adaptive behaviors that actors use to accommodate structural and institutional pressures. By uncovering such behaviors, ethnographers offer tools for those with power to control or manipulate those without" (Murphy and Dingwall, 2001: 341). Researchers have little control over how their work is interpreted or represented by the broader public; it may be leveraged for political purposes in unexpected ways. As a foundational example, Oscar Lewis (1966) aimed to situate the lives of the poor within structural and economic conditions of free-enterprise, pre-welfare state capitalism. Lewis suggested that a "culture of poverty" was a coping mechanism produced by these social conditions. Yet, the culture of poverty concept was subsequently interpreted as a primary cause of inequality, resulting in policy interventions that targeted the "pathologies" of minority families, rather than the underlying structural sources of social dislocation (e.g., Moynihan, 1965 as an example; Greenbaum, 2015 on the consequences).

In addition, participants can be jarred by how they are represented in a research product. For instance, Carlson (2010) describes her experiences conducting member checks with five participants in a qualitative study. She notes that sharing verbatim transcriptions of interviews often resulted in participants' embarrassment, be it over grammatical errors or the personal nature of the interview content. Scholars also derive professional benefits from the work that are not shared by participants – book royalties, promotions and salary increases, social status, and prestige. If such benefits come at a cost to participants, then the research process itself has reproduced the exploitative relations that urban core residents experience in many other contexts.

Many urban ethnographers have made notable efforts to ensure self-determination and benefits for research participants. For instance, Mitchell Duneier shared the royalties from his book *Sidewalk* (1999) with the homeless book vendors he studied. In a methodological appendix, Duneier also describes reading aloud the manuscript to those featured in it to allow participants to make an informed judgment as to whether they wanted to be depicted in the book. Despite the value of these efforts in theory, Duneier describes their limitations in practice: "I practically had to beg people to concentrate on what I was saying. It also did not help that they now knew they would share in the profits, a factor that sometimes made them feel less motivation to listen carefully, on the assumption that I could be trusted" (348). He then goes on to quote at length an exchange with a participant – Keith – that occurred during this process of member checking. Illustrating the limitations of informed consent even in this inclusive method, Keith comments before hearing the relevant excerpts: "Just give me the contract, Mitch. I told you. I'm signing. I'm just proud to be in the book. All this reading and everything is completely unnecessary 'cause I'm just proud to be in the book" (349). Duneier nevertheless goes on to read segments of the text featuring Keith aloud. Reflecting on the experience, he writes, "the effort to be respectful by showing the text to the person in it sometimes turns out not to seem very respectful at all. In this case, I ended up insisting that the individual listen to me, and imposing my agenda on someone who seemed annoyed at my efforts" (348). There is no cure-all for the ethical dilemmas accompanying research on the urban core, just a difficult terrain that scholars must navigate with as much attention as possible to protecting the rights of participants and minimizing the harms they may experience.

Navigating this terrain is crucial to ensuring that such research produces benefits. Studies of the urban core often successfully document the consequences of deindustrialization, institutional racism, carceral policies, and many other structural and institutional pressures on the lived experiences of those most affected by them. This knowledge is critical. Without it, we willfully ignore subaltern narratives and fail to seek alternatives to economic and social policies that harm vulnerable individuals, families, and communities. Focused ethnography is a tool that can be applied to research on the urban core. Because it takes a different methodological tack than immersive urban ethnographies, it presents altered sets of ethical considerations.

Below, we outline these considerations through the example of our own focused ethnography of child support enforcement hearings.

The Researcher–Participant Relationship in Ethnography

In prototypical immersive ethnographies, a lone researcher forms close personal relationships with participants. These relationships can be expansive, transcending many aspects of a participant's day-to-day life as the researcher seeks to understand the entire social field. Close relationships between the researcher and participant are often the foundation of rich interpretive data. Yet, they can also muddle consent and self-determination. Expansive involvement in activities across many sites may make it difficult for participants to know what, exactly, the researcher is attending to and turning into data. Long-term, immersive relationships also often blur the boundaries between the ethnographer's roles as researcher and friend. While some have argued that developing more intimate relationships disrupts the power hierarchy between the researcher and participants, others have suggested that this makes participants more vulnerable (Wolf, 1996). Participants can be more likely to disclose private information or experience a sense of loss or betrayal when the ethnographer leaves the field (Murphy and Dingwall, 2001). Risks and benefits are complicated by the formation and dissolution of close personal bonds that transcend contexts. Yet, these features are central to the immersive ethnographic method.

By contrast, focused ethnographies center on specific events and interactions. They are therefore bound by time and place. This means that focused ethnographies are often institutionally mediated. Instead of following select participants across sites, researchers are attentive to the many actors who converge in a single site. Institutional spaces are characterized by their own power dynamics and hierarchies, and researchers must position themselves carefully within them. Researchers can find themselves studying down, up, and sideways simultaneously – encountering participants with high levels of professional and social status in addition to those with few such privileges (Bowman, 2009). The researcher's ability to navigate this space is enabled by their role as a passive observer. Relationships are generally impersonal, rather than close. This reduces the role ambiguity described earlier. Participants are likely to understand the researcher as an observer, rather than as a friend, confidant, or colleague. Yet, even with this clarity, researchers must be attentive to their position and the ways it can reinforce social hierarchies, particularly those that marginalize participants from the urban core.

Sociolegal research that uses focused ethnography to examine the legal experiences of litigants from the urban core can take place in formal legal settings like lawyer–client meetings, mediation sessions, and courtroom hearings. In these sites, actors negotiate both the symbolic meaning and material consequences of the law. Judges, attorneys, and other legal actors wield their legal knowledge and authority with the capacity to impose life-altering orders of fines and incarceration. Litigants encounter a complex system – filled with unfamiliar procedures and jargon – that they must navigate, often with few resources and little assistance. When researchers seek to document these dynamics, they must negotiate both practical and ethical considerations in relation to a broader array of differentially empowered participants.

Researchers generally need to cultivate and maintain working relationships with institutional actors for the sake of access. In formal legal settings, these actors can include lawyers, judges, clerks, and bailiffs, who typically request accounts of researchers' presence, even if proceedings are open to the public. In addition to the imperative of access, researchers may develop ongoing and familiar relationships with institutional actors due to repeated data collection visits taking place over an extended period of time. For instance, in our study of child support enforcement proceedings, the research team returned to two courthouses regularly over a five-year period. While relationships with legal professionals varied – with few taking on the status of key informants – many recognized members of the research team, and their comfort level and willingness to informally share information increased over time. Team members answered questions about the study and reciprocated when legal actors engaged them in casual, friendly conversation. Though these kinds of interactions do not approximate the close personal relationships that often occur in immersive ethnographies, they nevertheless require researchers to abide by the formal and informal professional norms within the research site.

Doing so may position researchers as more socially proximate to legal professionals than to litigants. Litigants may thus see the researchers as another party complicit in the scrutiny and, in some cases, humiliation that they are subjected to in legal proceedings. Our research team worried about this during site visits. We observed hearings where judges or family court commissioners actively shamed noncustodial parents, insinuating shortcomings that cut to the core of their moral character and, in the case of fathers who owed support, their masculinity. For instance, during a hearing, a judge addressed a litigant by telling him: "My job is to get you independent, self-sufficient and cut you lose. If you need a babysitter, I can send you to the jail. They will babysit you 24/7. It's not my job to babysit you. You are a grown man, and it's up to you." In these moments, team members witnessing these "degradation ceremonies" remained silent, trying to minimize interference in the interaction. Such a passive approach was challenging. In the short term, the researchers tried to preserve the dignity of litigants through subtle body language and expressions that disavowed degrading treatment. In the long run, we reminded ourselves and each other of the importance of bearing witness to the experiences of litigants from the urban core and shedding light on the processes that jeopardize their access to justice.

In spite of the challenges of navigating the social space between legal actors and litigants, focused ethnography is only nominally intrusive. Researchers often act merely as observers. This means less access to participants' broader life experiences, though participants may nevertheless have to share personal information in settings like court hearings. While researchers need to be attuned to privacy and confidentiality when dealing with this information, participants do not face the same risks that accompany the sharing of intimate information or the challenges of disengaging in the context of a relationship to the researcher that feels close and personal. In our study, all observed hearings were open to the public and did not require participants' consent. Though observations do not generate direct benefits to litigants, they are also unlikely to cause harms. The risks that litigants faced – for instance, disclosing personal or embarrassing information – existed regardless of the researchers' presence. Public access to these proceedings is a basic tenet of our democratic system. Its purpose is to ensure the accountability of court officials and promote a fair judicial system. Though in practice public access was often mediated by bureaucratic gatekeepers, the presence of observers in a hearing is not unprecedented and the information that litigants share in this context would be available to the public. Nonetheless, to protect the confidentiality of the individuals we observed in public court proceedings, we decided to alter their names and other identifying information and use pseudonyms in our publications.

Researchers have a duty to reduce harm and honor the rights of respect, self-determination, and justice for all participants. In sites that include participants from diverse and divergent backgrounds, this requires a high degree of reflexivity. Researchers must evaluate their own social locations, political orientations, affinities, and sympathies and ask how their status and feelings shape representations of research participants. They must interrogate tendencies to depict heroic or villainous figures, to give space to particular narratives, and to present some perspectives at face value, while deeply theorizing and interpreting others. These tendencies are infused with political implications. Throughout the project, the team has engaged in sustained group and one-on-one dialogues of these issues, illuminating a full range of considerations and collaborating on how best to proceed in our interactions with participants in the field.

Additionally, scholarly representations of participants often either reproduce or subvert hegemonic ideas of whose experiences get to be heard and valued (and by whom). While there is no easy answer to questions around the politics of representation, the team approach in focused ethnography facilitates reflexivity in data collection and analysis. Our study team has frequently discussed how our individual backgrounds – including disciplinary training, professional experience, and personal attributes like gender, race, class, and sexual orientation – inform our individual approaches to research and relationships with participants. Including diverse team members has enabled the group to approach the data from many angles. For instance, individual team members spearhead conference papers that reflect their own theoretical and empirical interests, refined through dialogue with the group. These papers address topics including how legal actors navigate the morally ambiguous terrain of child support enforcement, how noncustodial fathers understand their roles as parents, and how litigants think about the role of counsel in these proceedings. Through pursuing the data from varied and relational angles, the team has sought to understand both litigants and legal actors by honoring the integrity of their narratives, while recognizing that their experiences are embedded in historical, structural, and institutional contexts characterized by power inequalities.

In sociolegal research on the urban core, focused ethnography is a methodological tool that allows researchers to access the sites and interactions where litigants and legal processes converge. Focused ethnography, through its style of targeted data collection in institutional settings, has the capacity to mitigate some of the risks that traditionally affect immersive urban ethnographies. Researchers enter into institutional spaces as one of many actors embedded in a network of power relations, rather than through a dominant–subordinate relationship to participants. They employ minimally intrusive data collection strategies and generally avoid the risks accompanying role ambiguity by acting as passive observers. Yet, focused ethnographies of urban core residents in legal contexts raise differing sets of questions about reflexivity and representation. This discussion of ethical considerations in such research has aimed to identify some of the potential pitfalls and promises of focused ethnography as a method.

CONCLUSION

In the context of this study, focused ethnography provides a means of accessing the narratives that legal professionals and litigants deploy as they interact while navigating civil proceedings. The comparative nature of the study allows us to evaluate contrasting models of legal assistance by identifying substantive differences in process across counties. Thus, the study contributes to our understanding of *how* different models of legal assistance shape substantive outcomes. The bounded nature of enforcement proceedings lends itself to targeted data collection; focused ethnography permits rigorous investigation of the processes involved in these hearings, while providing feasibility advantages that account for resource constraints.

However, the evolution of this project has required corresponding developments in methods. The research team initially began with a relatively closed field of study, aiming to observe contempt cases in child support proceedings. However, the team soon realized that a full understanding of the phenomenon of child support enforcement required the expansion of data collection to all enforcement proceedings related to nonpayment of child support. In addition, the study expanded beyond the courtroom. In order to situate contempt within the broader context of child support enforcement, the research team collected interview and ethnographic data from various sites affiliated with the process. These sites included the public defender's office, courthouse libraries, legal aid clinics, temp agencies, and community organizations providing job placement services.

Employing a team-based focused ethnographic approach in our study contributed to our understanding of the dynamics at play in lower court proceedings involving *pro se* litigants from marginalized communities. Through our targeted examination of family court proceedings, we learned how *pro se* litigants navigate the legal system, when, how, and why they are most likely to stumble in their efforts at self-representation, and what types of legal interventions might prove most useful. We came to appreciate that the legal actors we observed in these cases themselves experience a complex set of challenges and constraints, and, not surprisingly, they do not approach the cases in a monolithic manner. Rather, the judges, lawyers, and family court commissioners produce justice in a variety of ways, depending on how they understand their role and their perception of the litigants and cases they preside over. We also developed a deep understanding of how judges and family court commissioners address the complicating factors of race, poverty, and gender that surface in the cases. We learned how systems of oppression that exist outside the courtroom are often replicated inside the courtroom, most notably through legal processes that reproduce poverty in families that are already experiencing considerable economic insecurity. Team members arrived at these findings collaboratively and collectively over a five-year period of iterative data collection and analysis, essentially involving thousands of conversations ranging from team members' one-on-one conversations in the field immediately following a court observation to our regular, weekly team meetings, where we debriefed the results of our most recent data collection efforts and engaged in a wide-ranging and reflexive analysis of both the data and our experiences in the field. The methods and techniques of focused ethnography were instrumental in helping us to conduct the study and produce this knowledge, given the substantive aims of the research project and the practical constraints that structure data collection and analysis.

FOCUSED ETHNOGRAPHY, REFERENCES

Elijah Anderson, *Code of the Street: Decency, Violence, and the Moral Life of the Inner City* (1999). New York: Norton.

Bernadette Atuahene, *We Want What's Ours: Learning from South Africa's Land Restitution Program* (2014). United Kingdom: Oxford University Press.

Cyndi Banks, *Women in Transition: Social Control in Papua New Guinea* (1993). Canberra, Australia: Australian Institute of Criminology.

Dina Bowman, "Studying Up, Down, Sideways and Through: Situated Research and Policy Networks." In *The Future of Sociology: Proceedings of the Annual Conference of the Australian Sociological Association*, edited by S. Lockie, D. Bissell, A. Greig, M. Hynes, D. Marsh, L. Saha, J. Sikora, and D. Woodman (2009). Canberra: Australian National University.

Tonya Brito, *Fathers behind Bars: Rethinking Child Support Policy toward Low-Income Noncustodial Fathers and Their Families*, 15 Iowa Journal of Gender, Race & Justice 617–73 (2012).

'*I Do for My Kids*': *Negotiating Race and Racial Inequality in Family Court*, 83(6) Fordham Law Review 3027–52 (2015).

Michael Burawoy, *The Extended Case Method*, 16(1) Sociological Theory 4–33 (1998).

Julie Carlson, *Avoiding Traps in Member Checking*, 15(5) The Qualitative Report 1102–1113 (2010).
Kimberlé Williams Crenshaw, *Race, Reform, and Retrenchment: Transformation and Legitimation in Antidiscrimination Law*, 101 Harvard Law Review 1331–87 (1988).
John W. Creswell, *Qualitative Inquiry & Research Design: Choosing among the Five Approaches*, 3rd ed (2013). Los Angeles: Sage Publications.
Mitchell Duneier, *Slim's Table: Race, Respectability, and Masculinity* (1992). Chicago: University of Chicago Press.
Sidewalk (1999). New York: Farrar, Straus and Giroux.
How Not to Lie with Ethnography, 41(1) Sociological Methodology 1–11 (2011).
Mustafa Emirbayer and Matthew Desmond, *Race and Reflexivity*, 35(4) Ethnic and Racial Studies 574–599 (2012).
Robert P. Fairbanks and Richard Lloyd, *Critical Ethnography and the Neoliberal City: The U.S. Example*, 12(1) Ethnography 3–11 (2011).
Frederick Erickson, *Some Approaches to Inquiry in School-Community Ethnography*, 8(2) Anthropology & Education Quarterly 58–69 (1977).
Susan Greenbaum, *Blaming the Poor: The Long Shadow of the Moynihan Report on Cruel Images about Poverty* (2015). New Brunswick, NJ: Rutgers University Press.
Simon Halliday and Patrick Schmidt, *Conducting Law and Society Research: Reflections on Methods and Practices* (2009). Cambridge: Cambridge University Press.
Martyn Hammersley and Paul Atkinson, *Ethnography: Principles in Practice* (2007). New York: Routledge.
Gina Higgenbottom, Jennifer Pillay, and Nana Boadu, *Guidance on Performing Focused Ethnographies with an Emphasis on Healthcare Research*, 18(17) The Qualitative Report 1–16 (2013).
Jack Katz, *Ethnography's Warrants*, 25 Sociological Methods and Research 391–423 (1997).
Herbert Knoblauch, *Focused Ethnography*, 6(3) Forum: Qualitative Social Research 44 (2005).
Oscar Lewis, "The Culture of Poverty" in *American* 215(4): 19–25 (1966).
Elliott Liebow, *Tally's Corner: A Study of Negro Streetcorner Men* (1967). Boston: Little, Brown.
Judith Little, *Norms of Collegiality and Experimentation: Workplace Conditions of School Success*, 19 American Educational Research Journal 325 (1982).
Theresa McElroy, Alexis Davis, Cynthia Hunt, Jigmet Dadul, Tsering Stanba, and Charles Larson, *Navigating a Way Forward: Using Focused Ethnography and Community Readiness to Study Disability Issues in Ladukh, India*, 33(1) Disability and Rehabilitation 17–27 (2011).
Sally E. Merry, *Getting Justice and Getting Even: Legal Consciousness among Working Class Americans* (1990). Chicago: University of Chicago Press.
Karen-Lee Miller, Scott Reeves, Merrick Zwarenstein, Jennifer Beales, Chris Kenaszchuk, and Lesley Gotlib Conn, *Nursing Emotion Work and Interprofessional Collaboration in General Internal Medicine Wards: A Qualitative Study*, 64(4) Journal of Advanced Nursing 332–43 (2008).
Daniel Patrick Moynihan, *The Negro Family: The Case for National Action* (1965). Office of Policy Planning and Research, United States Department of Labor.
Elizabeth Murphy and Robert Dingwall, The Ethics of Ethnography, pp. 339–51 in *Handbook of Ethnography*, edited by P. Atkinson, A. Coffey, S. Delamont, J. Lofland, and L. H. Lofland (2001). London: Sage.

Laura Nader, Up the Anthropologist: Perspectives Gained from Studying Up, pp. 284–311 in *Reinventing Anthropology*, edited by D. Hymes (1972). New York: Pantheon Books.

National Institutes of Health, "Protection of Human Research Participants." *NIH Office of Extramural Research.* (2011). Retrieved from https://phrp.nihtraining.com/files/PHRP.pdf.

Joyce Neal, Twila Brown, and Wilaiporn Rojjanasriraj. 1999. *Implementation of a Case Coordinator Role: A Focused Ethnographic Study.* JOURNAL OF PROFESSIONAL NURSING 15(5): 349–355.

Jason Orne and Michael Bell, *An Invitation to Qualitative Fieldwork: A Multilogical Approach* (2015). New York: Routledge.

Keith F. Otterbein, *Comparative Cultural Analysis: An Introduction to Anthropology*, 2nd ed. (1977). New York: Holt, Rinehart & Winston.

Penny A. Pasque and Michelle Salazar Pérez, Centering Critical Inquiry : Methodologies that Facilitate Critical Qualitative Research, pp. 139–70 in *Critical Qualitative Inquiry: Foundations and Futures*, edited by G. S. Cannella, M. S. Pérez, and P. A. Pasque (2015). California: Left Coast Press.

Jeff Rose, Ethnographic Research for Social Justice: Critical Engagement with Homelessness in a Public Park, pp. 129–60 in *Fostering Social Justice through Qualitative Inquiry*, edited by C. W. Johnson and D. C. Parry (2015). California: Left Coast Press.

Austin Sarat and William Felstiner, *Law and Strategy in the Divorce Lawyer's Office*, 20 LAW & SOCIETY REVIEW 93–134 (1986).

Joseph Shapiro, "As Court Fees Rise, the Poor Are Paying the Price." NPR. (May 19, 2014). Retrieved from https://perma.cc/YZE5-DLGD.

Joey Sprague, *Feminist Methodologies for Critical Researchers: Bridging Differences* (2005). New York: Altimira Press.

David Sudnow, *Passing On: The Social Organization of Dying* (1967). Prentice-Hall.

Iddo Tavory and Stefan Timmermans, A *Pragmatist Approach to Causality in Ethnography*, 119(3) AMERICAN JOURNAL OF SOCIOLOGY 682–714 (2013).

Stefan Timmermans and Iddo Tavory, *Theory Construction in Qualitative Research: From Grounded Theory to Abductive Analysis*, 30(3) SOCIOLOGICAL THEORY 167–86 (2012).

United States, *The Belmont Report: Ethical Principles and Guidelines for the Protection of Human Subjects of Research* (1979). National Commission for the Protection of Human Subjects of Biomedical and Behavioral Research.

United States Census Bureau, *Educational Attainment: Five Key Data Releases from the U.S. Census Bureau* (2011). Retrieved from https://perma.cc/Q67Y-EZ3F.

United States Department of Justice, *Investigation of the Ferguson Police Department.* Civil Rights Division. (Mar. 4, 2015). Retrieved from https://perma.cc/28JR-DZ5F.

Nicole Gonzalez Van Cleve, *Crook County: Racism and Injustice in America's Largest Criminal Court* (2016). Stanford, CA: Stanford University Press.

Diane Wolf, *Feminist Dilemmas in Fieldwork* (1996). New York: Routledge.

7

Legal Education, Democracy, and the Urban Core

*Kathleen S. Morris**

INTRODUCTION

In February 2017, just a few months before he died following a battle with cancer, the renowned urban political theorist Benjamin Barber participated in a panel discussion in which he made a compelling case for the growing economic and political power of cities.[1] The panel was framed as a response to the inauguration of Donald Trump, but Barber's take on the place of cities in democracy stretched far beyond any one election:

> In the 19th and 20th centuries, local meant parochial. Local meant backwards. Local meant reactionary. The fundamental balance between national and local has been inverted ... Every progressive policy you can look for – whether it's the minimum wage, whether it's the defense of rights, whether it's the defense of immigrants – is now an urban one, a local one. And national government has become reactionary, not universal. It's not just the United States. National governments are increasingly parochial, and cities are increasingly cosmopolitan. It's exactly reversed, which gives cities a whole new role.[2]

* Professor of Law, Golden Gate University School of Law. Many thanks to editors Peter Enrich and Rashmi Dyal-Chand; the participants in the 2015 "Tackling the Urban Core Puzzle" conference at Northeastern University School of Law; and research assistant Sherri Bridgeforth. This chapter has benefitted from ongoing conversations about cities and legal education with Heather Gerken, Jill Habig, Ludovic Blain, Kweli Kitwana, Anthony Niedwiecki, and Waymon Hudson. I dedicate this chapter to San Francisco Deputy City Attorney Buck Delventhal, a towering figure among local public lawyers.

1 *See* Richard Florida, *If Cities Ruled the World*, CityLab (Apr. 26, 2017), www.citylab.com/equity/2017/04/the-need-to-empower-cities/521904/ (published panel discussion between Richard Florida, Jonathan Haidt, and Benjamin Barber). For an essay discussing Barber's contributions, *see* John Nichols, *Benjamin Barber: A Brilliant Thinker Who Saw the Future*, The Nation (Apr. 25, 2017), www.thenation.com/article/benjamin-barber-a-brilliant-thinker-who-saw-the-future/. Barber founded the Global Parliament of Mayors; his scholarly contributions included *Jihad vs. McWorld* (1996), *If Mayors Ruled the World* (2013), and *Cool Cities* (2017).

2 *See* Florida, *supra* Note 1.

For the purposes of this chapter, I take two points from Barber's comments. First, those engaged in the study and advancement of American democracy should treat cities and their governments not as parochial "laboratories of democracy" but as sophisticated, potentially powerful ends in themselves. Second, at a time of intense national and statewide political polarization in the United States, those hoping to better the lives of poor and marginalized people should increase their focus on cities.

To these two points I would add two more. First, the United States is experiencing a golden age of American protest, largely led by young adults. Americans have been taking to the streets to ignite much-needed conversations about race and police violence; sexual assault and gender equality; anti-immigrant attitudes and policies; anti-Muslim discrimination; workers' rights; health care; public education; and gun violence. In a few years, many of these young adults will be ready to consider whether, and *why*, they should attend law school.

Second, during the Trump era, lawyers have become more highly visible as leaders and defenders of democracy and the rule of law. Many of the lawyers involved in high-profile court clashes with the Trump administration are staking out their positions from inside city, state, and federal governments. City lawyers are increasingly engaged in high-profile political, legal, and media battles in defense of urban constituents' values against interference by state governments, the Trump administration, and corporations. Having recognized the growing importance of cities as law and policy platforms, conservative and progressive[3] legal organizations alike are increasing their focus on cities.[4]

Considering these trends, law schools have an exciting opportunity to renew their support for and influence on American democracy and government from the ground up by plugging into the rising energy in city governments. Section I summarizes the rise of cities in politics, public interest law, and legal scholarship. Section II explains the central role American lawyers have always played in maintaining a healthy democracy, and how cities fit into that historical context. Section III describes how law schools can powerfully and visibly assert themselves as champions of democratic institutions by turning more of their attention to cities.

[3] By "conservative" I mean a person who favors limited intervention into markets, limited income redistribution, and a preference for private over public ownership of community services and facilities. By "progressive" I mean a person who favors more intervention into markets, more active income redistribution, and a preference for public over private ownership of community services and facilities. A progressive may favor policies like a relatively high minimum wage, increased taxes on the wealthy, strong rent control, transparent government, broad community participation in government, aggressive enforcement of labor and employment laws, aggressive consumer and environmental protection, aggressive civil rights protection and enforcement, equal geographic access to quality housing and public education, equal geographic access to parks and public facilities, affordable health care, clean air, clean water, and meaningful economic opportunity for rich and poor alike.

[4] *See, e.g.*, the American Legislative Exchange Council (ALEC), the State Innovation Exchange (SiX), the New American Leaders Project, Democracy for America, Mobilize America, Sister District, and the Public Rights Project.

THE RISE OF CITIES IN POLITICS, PUBLIC INTEREST LITIGATION, AND LEGAL SCHOLARSHIP

The Political Rise of Cities

Why and How Cities are Rising Politically

Cities are growing in population, in what Richard Schragger has called an "urban resurgence."[5] City populations, property values, and economic firepower are rising, in part because, with so many younger skilled workers wanting to live in urban areas,[6] corporations, in order to attract top talent, are relocating to cities.[7] As small and medium-sized cities grow, their law and policy concerns invariably become more complex.[8] For these groups of cities to thrive amid this growth, they will need an increasingly sophisticated cadre of elected and appointed officials and city law offices.

Moreover, as cities grow in population, their voting majorities can be expected to shift in a more progressive direction compared to state and federal majorities.[9] While our national and state governments may whiplash back and forth from "red" to "blue," our nation's growing cities will offer an increasingly stable platform for political progressives.[10]

In light of the political and economic rise of cities, activists across the political spectrum are turning more of their attention to the role of cities in law and policy

[5] *See* Richard Schragger, *City Power: Urban Governance in a Global Age* 19 (2016) (describing the "urban resurgence" in detail and urging a view of cities as natural ends in themselves rather than mere competitors for corporate largesse). *See also* Richard Schragger, *Is a Progressive City Possible? Reviving Urban Liberalism for the Twenty-First Century*, 7 HARV. L. & POL'Y REV. 231, 238 (2013) (discussing the barriers to creating progressive cities).

[6] *See* Richard Florida, *When It Comes to Skills and Talent, Size Matters*, CITYLAB (July 6, 2017), www.citylab.com/equity/2017/07/when-it-comes-to-skills-and-talent-size-matters/531411/ ("[t]alent and skill unequivocally have concentrated in larger cities and metro areas ... Generally speaking, larger cities attract more educated people, not just those with college degrees, but those with advanced degrees.").

[7] *See, e.g.*, Henry Grabar, *Trouble in America's Country Club*, SLATE (June 2, 2017), www.slate.com/articles/business/metropolis/2017/06/something_is_wrong_with_connecticut.html (describing how this trend is affecting the State of Connecticut).

[8] For the purposes of this chapter, a "small" city has a population under 25,000, a "medium" city has a population between 25,000 and 500,000, and a "large" city has a population of more than 500,000.

[9] *See* Paul A. Diller, *Reorienting Home Rule: Part 1 – The Urban Disadvantage in National and State Lawmaking*, 77 LA. L. REV. 287, 288–90 (2016) (describing the tensions between progressive policies city voters prefer and the relatively conservative policies their state and federal counterparts prefer).

[10] *See* David A. Graham, *Red States and Blue Cities: A Partisan Battle Intensifies*, THE N.Y. TIMES (JULY 6, 2017), at A1 ("At a time when Democrats are out of power from the White House, both chambers of Congress, the majority of governor's offices and three-fifths of the country's state houses, their ideas have at least one reliable outlet. Democrats still control most of the country's biggest cities.")

debates. Conservative cities in "blue" states are publicly aligning themselves with the Trump administration.[11] Progressive cities in "red" states are tackling issues that the federal or state governments may have rejected or abandoned.[12] They are enacting local policies designed to result in more progressive income redistribution,[13] increased government supervision of markets,[14] and the repair of economic and social disparities based on class, race, gender, sexual orientation, and disability.[15]

Because cities tend to trend "blue" as they grow, the growth of cities has particularly profound strategic implications for those seeking to improve the lives of economically and politically marginalized groups. Benjamin Barber specifically noted the global promise of city governments as platforms for improving the lives of poor people, and called on progressive organizers to understand that, while they may feel isolated from all governments, they have and should reach out to their natural allies in city governments:

> There is an institutional and constitutional haven for resistance, defined by cities, which have resources, money, citizens, and the power to do something. In other words, it's not just us, the citizens of the United States who got outvoted in the electoral college. It is rather the most ancient political institutions in our world, [cities]. All their institutional powers – their resources, their capacities, their lawyers – are in a position to mount an ongoing, systematic, institutional resistance to Trump and everything he stands for. It's not just, "He acts, we protest." It's the confrontation of power with power – of national power with urban power.[16]

[11] *See, e.g.*, Sarah Holder, *As California Protects Immigrants, Cities Revolt*, CityLab (Apr. 3, 2018), www.citylab.com/equity/2018/04/california-cities-fight-their-sanctuary-state/556973/ (describing how cities in San Diego and Orange Counties are pushing back against the State of California's immigration policies, aligning themselves with the US government's immigration policies).

[12] For example, as the Trump administration continues to roll back environmental, civil rights, education, and labor standards enforcement (*see* Jessica Huseman & Annie Waldman, *Trump Administration Quietly Rolls Back Civil Rights Efforts across Federal Government*, PBS Newshour (June 16, 2017), at 12:45 p.m., www.pbs.org/newshour/rundown/trump-administration-quietly-rolls-back-civil-rights-efforts-across-federal-government/), cities are moving into those gaps. *See, e.g., What Mayors Want*, CityLab (Apr. 5, 2018), www.citylab.com/life/2018/04/what-mayors-want/557312/ ("Mayors are increasingly focusing on issues like climate change, immigration, and infrastructure that have traditionally fallen to federal and state governments").

[13] *See* Gretchen Morgenson, *Portland Adopts Surcharge on C.E.O. Pay in Move vs. Income Inequality*, The N.Y. Times (Dec. 7, 2016), www.nytimes.com/2016/12/07/business/economy/portland-oregon-tax-executive-pay.html?_r=0 (discussing Portland's so-called millionaire tax).

[14] For example, cities are more likely to prefer "single payer" health care than states as a whole or the federal government. *See* Sarah Gamard, *Cities Fear Obamacare Repeal, Warm to Single Payer*, Politico (Jul. 24, 2017), www.politico.com/magazine/story/2017/07/24/mayors-support-obamacare-single-payer-health-care-215414.

[15] *See* Graham, *supra* Note 10 at A1 (describing city-state tensions on multiple social issues); *see also City vs. State: The Story So Far*, CityLab, www.citylab.com/equity/2017/06/city-vs-state-the-story-so-far/530049/ (summarizing current legislative battles between cities and states over the minimum wage, economic development, equal protection, environmental regulation, firearms regulation, and immigration).

[16] Florida, *supra* Note 1.

For cities to fulfill their promise as governance platforms, they need to be staffed up with sophisticated elected and appointed officials and public lawyers. But what would such sophistication look like? What are city governments exactly, what do they do, and what do their officials and lawyers need to know?

The Vast Portfolios of City Governments

City governments have vast governance portfolios because they serve two distinct, yet overlapping, functions: They are both public corporations and units of representative democracy. As public corporations, city governments create and operate a complex range of public works and services like transportation systems, waste collection and disposal systems, ports, airports, power systems, water systems, buildings, bridges, streets, sidewalks, homeless shelters, public housing, schools, libraries, museums, and parks.[17] As units of representative democracy, city governments are charged with figuring out how to improve constituents' lives and effectuate laws and policies that do exactly that.[18] They plan and zone public and private land; raise revenue (through taxation, bonds, loans, permitting, and ticketing); create and operate local enforcement agencies; oversee elections; enforce civil and criminal laws; and, through executive policy making and daily judgment calls, largely "run" the federal and state constitutions.[19]

In terms of collective scale, local governments give urban constituents a lot to work with. As of 2014, the United States had nearly 90,000 local public entities that employed more than 13 million workers and spent $1.5 trillion.[20] Localities (that is, cities, counties, and districts) have the institutional ability to tax and spend locally, and/or partner with private entities, to build excellent public schools, public transit, integrated affordable housing, affordable health care, beautiful parks and other green spaces, playgrounds, museums, and arts institutions.

[17] *See* Frederick A. O. Schwarz, Jr., *Lawyers for Government Have Unique Responsibilities and Opportunities to Influence Public Policy*, 53 N. Y. L. SCH. L. REV. 375, 376 (2008/2009) (describing city activities based on experience in the New York Corporation Counsel's Office); Kathleen S. Morris, San Francisco and the Rising Culture of Engagement in Local Public Law Offices, *in Why the Local Matters: Federalism, Localism, and Public Interest Advocacy* 51, 52–53 (Kathleen Claussen, Adam Grogg, Rachel Deutsch, & Ethan Frechette eds., 2010) (describing city activities based on experience in the San Francisco City Attorney's Office). For a brief overview of city attorney office activities nationwide, see the website for the International Municipal Lawyers Association, www.imla.org (last visited May 1, 2018).

[18] I first articulated the dual role of cities and their law offices in *supra* Note 17.

[19] *See* Alec C. Ewald, *The Way We Vote: The Local Dimension of American Suffrage* 3 (2009) (explaining that local civil servants are the front line constitutional interpreters).

[20] *See U.S. Census Bureau, Annual Survey of Public Employment and Payroll Summary Report* (Dec. 19, 2014), www2.census.gov/govs/apes/2013_summary_report.pdf (reporting the number of state and local governments and their employees). *See also* Urban Institute, *State and Local Expenditures*, www.urban.org/policy-centers/cross-center-initiatives/state-local-finance-initiative/projects/state-and-local-backgrounders/state-and-local-expenditures (last visited Apr. 29, 2018).

Cities also provide unique platforms for public engagement. Constituents can engage more directly and intensively in policy development at the local level than they can at the state or federal levels. As a former head of New York City's law office once wrote of the profound relationship between city governments and their constituents:

> Every day, city government touches people in the most intimate and immediate ways: their safety, their schooling, their health, their sanitation, their housing, their transportation, and their daily jobs. Directly and frequently, the city affects the lives, the aspirations, and the pocketbooks of millions of people and tens of thousands of businesses.[21]

Great American city leaders and activists of the past, like Jane Jacobs,[22] Fiorello La Guardia,[23] and Harold Washington,[24] understood the potential for cities not as mere "laboratories of democracy," but as powerful democratic and governance ends in themselves. Although cities, their governments, and their law offices do not have unlimited powers,[25] they are increasingly discovering the powers they do have. One example is the focus of this chapter's next topic: The rise of cities in public interest litigation.

[21] Schwarz, *supra* Note 17 at 386.

[22] Jane Jacobs was a brilliant Twentieth Century urban scholar and activist whose books included *The Death and Life of Great American Cities* (1961); *The Economy of Cities* (1970); and *Cities and the Wealth of Nations* (1984). Jacobs' work was most recently celebrated in Richard Schragger's book *City Power: Urban Governance in a Global Age* (2016), and the documentary *Citizen Jane: Battle For the City* (Altimeter Films 2017).

[23] Fiorello La Guardia was a three-time mayor of New York City whose "greatest accomplishment" by his own reckoning was battling "corruption and special privileges" and setting a persuasive national example of "efficiency and honesty in municipal government." *La Guardia Is Dead; City Pays Homage To 3-Time Mayor*, The N.Y. Times (Sept. 21, 1947), https://archive.nytimes.com/www.nytimes.com/learning/general/onthisday/bday/1211.html?scp=1&sq=laguardia%2520is%2520dead&st=cse. For a full history of Fiorello La Guardia's mayoral career, *see* Thomas Kessner, *Fiorello La Guardia and the Making of Modern New York* (1989).

[24] Harold Washington was the first African American mayor of Chicago. He confronted "the Democratic machine's patronage system by appointing professionals, minorities and women to city positions." Robert Davis, *The Death of Mayor Harold Washington*, Chicago Tribune (Jan. 3, 2008), www.chicagotribune.com/news/nationworld/politics/chi-chicagodays-haroldwashingtondeath-story-story.html. For a full history of Harold Washington's mayoral career, *see* Gary Rivlin, *Fire on the Prairie: Chicago's Harold Washington and the Politics of Race* (1992). For an excellent radio program about Harold Washington, *see Harold*, This American Life (Nov. 21, 1997), www.thisamericanlife.org/84/harold.

[25] The most powerful threat to city power is the shadow their own states cast by threatening to enact preemptive legislation. Most states have near-plenary authority to override city regulations, even when their state constitutions guarantee a degree of local home rule. *See* Richard Briffault et al., *The Troubling Turn in State Preemption: The Assault on Progressive Cities and How Cities Can Respond*, Issue Brief, American Constitution Society for Law & Policy (Sept. 28, 2017), https://acslaw.org/sites/default/files/ACS_Issue_Brief_-_Preemption_0.pdf. *See also* Graham, *supra* Note 10 at A1 (describing city–state tensions on multiple social issues).

The Rise of Cities in Public Interest Litigation

As we have seen, city governments operate both as public corporations and as units of representative democracy enacting and enforcing local laws. Until relatively recently, law offices for cities have focused overwhelmingly on advising the public corporation and enforcing and defending city ordinances in court.

To perform these two functions, city lawyers advise the corporation on the acquisition, sale, and use of property; oversee public contracting; oversee local taxation; advise city officials on the constitutionality of local ordinances and policies; enforce local ordinances; and defend city policies and actions against court challenges by private and public entities. Engaging in these activities requires a city's legal team to master local, state, and federal laws addressing federalism and localism; federal and state preemption; federal and state constitutional law; state and local open meetings law; federal, state, and local environmental and land use law; private and public contract law; family law; property and real estate law; federal, state, and local tax law; labor and employment law; tort law; energy law; telecommunications and privacy law; and the law of economic development and municipal finance. This is a formidable range of lawyering activity. As cities grow, their law offices must grow and increase in sophistication.[26]

Until relatively recently, most city law offices have not engaged in the kinds of public interest cases taken up by state attorneys general, civil rights organizations, labor and employment firms, and plaintiffs' firms. But in the past decade or so, city attorneys have been embracing a broader role as champions of the public interest.[27] I personally became involved in such an effort in San Francisco, beginning in 2003. That year the (then and current) San Francisco City Attorney, Dennis Herrera, hired me to serve as a deputy city attorney in his office. Soon afterward, city clients asked Herrera to challenge two statutes – a federal statute restricting abortion access and a state statute limiting marriage to opposite-sex couples – on constitutional grounds. I was assigned a lead role in both cases.

Over the next few years, Herrera and his deputies began to understand the value a city attorney's office can add to public policy debates playing out in open court. We began to think more broadly about whether and how our office could build out its

[26] The City of New York, with a population of 8.5 million, has the largest city law office in the nation, employing approximately 760 lawyers. San Francisco, with a population of less than one million, employs approximately 200 lawyers. For a description of New York's public law office, *see* William E. Nelson, *Fighting for the City: A History of the New York Corporation Counsel* (2008), and Schwarz, *supra* Note 17 at 376 (reviewing Nelson's book).

[27] New York was the first city to pursue public interest litigation. *See* Schwarz, *supra* Note 17 at 391–93. In more recent years, many cities have begun engaging in public interest litigation. *See* Kathleen S. Morris, Cities Seeking Justice: Local Government Litigation in the Public Interest, *in How Cities Will Save the World* 189 (Raymond Brescia & John Travis Marshall eds., 2016) (describing and providing examples illustrating the more recent shift in city attorneys' offices across the United States).

institutional capacity to engage more systematically in constitutional and other public policy litigation.[28] In 2006, Herrera asked me to lead the effort to consider that question. That same year, I heard Yale Law Professor (now Dean) Heather Gerken speak at a conference, where she called on law students and young lawyers to get involved in local government.[29] Gerken and I began to discuss how law students could support San Francisco's public interest litigation efforts. We ultimately co-founded a collaborative project through which Yale Law students worked with San Francisco deputy city attorneys to investigate, research, and litigate public interest cases. Eventually, Herrera added and staffed up an active affirmative litigation unit within the city attorney's office, and Yale's informal reading group grew into a full-fledged clinic known as the San Francisco Affirmative Litigation Project, which still thrives today.[30]

Our original approach to developing cases was to team each of a dozen deputy city attorneys with a few law students, and have each lawyer–student team focus on an issue affecting economically and socially vulnerable San Franciscans (we focused on poor and working class people and neighborhoods, senior citizens, children, and immigrants). Each team would conduct an investigation of its assigned problem and consider whether the city would make sense as a plaintiff in a litigation effort. Our first cases focused on predatory lenders, wage theft, unlawful advertising aimed at children, and unsafe housing. In the dozen years since we founded the project, Herrera's office has tackled an astonishing range of government and corporate injustices.[31]

The expansion of the city attorney's role is neither universal nor uncontroversial.[32] Yet the election of Trump as President has, if anything, lit a fire under city attorney's offices already inclined to pursue cases vindicating the interests of their constituents.

[28] San Francisco City Attorney Louise Renne, who was in office from 1986–2001, was the first elected city attorney to engage in affirmative litigation on behalf of that city. Herrera's contribution was to move away from an ad hoc approach to bringing public interest cases and toward a permanent, organized institutional commitment to creating a unit focused on bringing affirmative litigation in the public interest.

[29] I later discovered that Gerken had published an article discussing San Francisco's role in the marriage equality debate. *See, e.g.*, Heather K. Gerken, *Dissenting by Deciding*, 57 Stan. L. Rev. 1745, 1749 (2005) (discussing San Francisco's challenge to California's marriage laws).

[30] This history is recounted briefly at https://law.yale.edu/yls-today/news/sfalp-clinic-celebrates-10-year-anniversary. A description of the clinic in its current form can be found at https://law.yale.edu/studying-law-yale/clinical-and-experiential-learning/our-clinics/san-francisco-affirmative-litigation-project.

[31] San Francisco's public interest litigation is set forth on the City Attorney's website, www.sfcityattorney.org.

[32] *See* Gerken, *supra* Note 29 at 1749 (approving San Francisco's challenge to California's marriage laws as appropriate to the city's role in democracy), and Kathleen S. Morris, *The Case for Local Constitutional Enforcement*, 47 Harv. C.R.-C.L. L. Rev. 1, 41–42 (2012) (disputing critics of San Francisco's role in the constitutional litigation). *Cf.* David J. Barron, *Why (and When) Cities Have a Stake in Enforcing the Constitution*, 115 Yale L. J. 2218, 2222–23 (2006) (disapproving San Francisco's constitutional litigation as outside a city's proper role).

Cities and counties are increasingly pursuing constitutional, labor and employment, civil rights, environmental, and consumer protection cases.[33] In 2017 alone, cities have filed lawsuits on both sides of the so-called sanctuary cities issue in immigration law;[34] sued energy companies for spreading false information about climate change;[35] and sued to protect online consumers' private information.[36]

The Rise of Cities in Legal Scholarship

The economic, political, and legal position of cities has drawn the attention of an ever-increasing number of legal scholars, fueling the rise of cities in legal scholarship. In 1980, Gerald Frug published *The City as a Legal Concept*,[37] founding the modern field of state and local government law. Between 1980 and 2000, a small group of pioneering legal scholars – including Joan Williams,[38] Clayton Gillette,[39] Richard Briffault,[40] Richard Ford,[41] David Barron,[42] and Rick Hills[43] – continued to break ground in the field.

[33] *See* Morris, *supra* Note 27 at 189 (describing a wide range of city-filed "public interest" cases active across the nation as of the date of publication). The institution leading the effort to build out this work is the Public Rights Project (www.publicrightsproject.org), a nonprofit organization Jill Habig founded in 2017.

[34] *See Seattle Is Sixth Local Government to Sue Trump Over Threats to Sanctuary Cities*, Yes Magazine (Mar. 31, 2017) (describing multiple city challenges to federal immigration policy), www.yesmagazine.org/peace-justice/cities-suing-trump-for-executive-order-punishing-sanctuary-cities. *See* Hillary Davis, *Newport Beach Is the Latest City to Fight California 'Sanctuary State' Law*, The L.A. Times (Apr. 11, 2018) (describing plans by multiple California cities to fight the State's "sanctuary state" law in court), www.latimes.com/local/lanow/la-me-newport-sanctuary-20180411-story.html.

[35] *San Francisco and Oakland Sue Top Five Oil and Gas Companies Over Costs of Climate Change*, San Francisco City Attorney (Sept. 19, 2017) (describing city suits against energy companies contributing to a harmful rise in sea levels), www.sfcityattorney.org/2017/09/19/san-francisco-oakland-sue-top-five-oil-gas-companies-costs-climate-change/.

[36] *Herrera sues Equifax over Data Breach*, San Francisco City Attorney (Sept. 26, 2017) (describing city suit against a data company that failed to alert consumers that its computer systems had been hacked and their private information stolen), www.sfcityattorney.org/2017/09/26/herrera-sues-equifax-massive-data-breach/.

[37] *See* Gerald E. Frug, *The City as a Legal Concept*, 93 Harv. L. Rev. 1059 (1980).

[38] *See* Joan C. Williams, *The Constitutional Vulnerability of American Local Government: The Politics of City Status in American Law*, 1986 Wis. L. Rev. 83 (1986).

[39] *See* Clayton P. Gillette, *Plebiscites, Participation, and Collective Action in Local Government Law*, 86 Mich. L. Rev. 930 (1988).

[40] *See* Richard Briffault, *Our Localism: Part I – The Structure of Local Government Law*, 90 Colum. L. Rev. 1 (1990), and Richard Briffault, *Our Localism: Part II – Localism and Legal Theory*, 90 Colum. L. Rev. 346 (1990).

[41] *See* Richard Thompson Ford, *Geography and Sovereignty: Jurisdictional Formation and Racial Segregation*, 49 Stan. L. Rev. 1365 (1997).

[42] *See* David J. Barron, *The Promise of Cooley's City: Traces of Local Constitutionalism*, 147 U. Pa. L. Rev. 487 (1999).

[43] *See* Roderick M. Hills, Jr., *Dissecting the State: The Use of Federal Law to Free State and Local Officials from State Legislatures' Control*, 97 Mich. L. Rev. 1201 (1999).

Since 2000, an accelerating number of law professors have taken an interest in the rise of cities in law and policy. Taken together, legal scholars across subject matter areas have taken on an incredibly wide range of local government-related topics, including the promise of localism;[44] the legal and political barriers to localism;[45] the relationship between state constitutions and local power;[46] the relationship between localism and federalism;[47] the need to re-theorize localism;[48] the rise in local policymaking;[49] the threat of state preemption;[50] localism and foreign affairs;[51] localism and immigration;[52] localism and race discrimination;[53] affordable housing and land use;[54] gerrymandering and urban

[44] *See* Bruce Katz and Jeremy Nowak, *The New Localism: How Cities Can Thrive in the Age of Populism* (2017).

[45] *See, e.g.*, Gerald E. Frug and David Barron, *City Bound: How States Stifle Urban Innovation* (2008). *See also* Richard C. Schragger, *The Limits of Localism*, 100 Mich. L. Rev. 371 (2001).

[46] *See, e.g.*, Michael Libonati, *Local Government Autonomy*, 62 LA. L. REV. 97 (2001).

[47] *See, e.g.*, Heather K. Gerken, *Foreword: Federalism All the Way Down*, 124 HARV. L. REV. 4 (2010), Heather K. Gerken, A *New Progressive Federalism*, DEMOCRACY (Spring 2012), https://democracyjournal.org/magazine/24/a-new-progressive-federalism/. *See also* Nestor Davidson, *Cooperative Localism: Federal-Local Collaboration in an Era of State Sovereignty*, 93 VA. L. REV. 959 (2007).

[48] *See, e.g.*, Morris, *supra* Note 32 at 41–42; *see also* Kathleen S. Morris, *Uncooperative Localism* (Apr. 19, 2018) (unpublished manuscript) (on file with author).

[49] *See, e.g.*, Richard Schragger, *City Power: Urban Governance in a Global Age* (2016). *See also* Richard Briffault, Local Leadership and National Issues, *in Why the Local Matters: Federalism, Localism, and Public Interest Advocacy* 67.

[50] *See, e.g.*, Kenneth Stahl, *Preemption, Home Rule and Local Democracy*, 44 FORDHAM URBAN L.J. 133 (2017). *See also* Matthew J. Parlow, *Progressive Policy-Making at the Local Level: Rethinking Traditional Notions of Federalism*, 17 TEMP. POL. & CIV. RTS. L. REV. 371 (2008).

[51] *See, e.g.*, Judith Resnik, *Foreign as Domestic Affairs: Rethinking Horizontal Federalism and Foreign Affairs in Light of Translocal Internationalism*, 57 EMORY L.J. 31 (2007). *See also* Judith Resnik, New Federalism(s): Translocal Organizations of Government Actors (TOGAs) Reshaping Boundaries, Policies, and Laws, *in Why the Local Matters: Federalism, Localism, and Public Interest Advocacy* 83.

[52] *See, e.g.*, Cristina Rodriguez, *The Significance of the Local in Immigration Regulation*, 106 MICH. L. REV. 567 (2008). *See also* Matthew Parlow, A *Localist's Case for Decentralizing Immigration Policy*, 84 DENV. U. L. REV. 1061 (2007); John De Stefano, Jr., Cities and Immigration Reform: National Policy from the Ground Up, *in How Cities Will Save the World* 137.

[53] *See, e.g.*, Michelle Wilde Anderson, *Mapped Out of Local Democracy*, 62 STAN. L. REV. 931 (2010); Michelle Wilde Anderson, *Colorblind Segregation: Equal Protection as a Bar to Neighborhood Integration*, 92 CAL. L. REV. 841 (2004). *See also* Risa Goluboff, Civil Rights History Before, and Beyond, Brown, *in Why the Local Matters: Federalism, Localism, and Public Interest Advocacy* 11.

[54] *See, e.g.*, Robert Solomon, How to Increase Our Affordable Housing Stock, *in Legal Scholarship for the Urban Core: From the Ground Up* (Rashmi Dyal-Chand & Peter Enrich eds. 2019). *See also* Roderick M. Hills, Jr., *Saving Mount Laurel?*, 40 FORDHAM URBAN L.J. 1611 (2013); Christopher Serkin & Leslie Wellington, *Putting Exclusionary Zoning in Its Place: Affordable Housing and Geographical Scale*, 40 FORDHAM URBAN L.J. 1667 (2013); Matthew J. Parlow, *Unintended Consequences: Eminent Domain and Affordable Housing*, 46 SANTA CLARA L. REV. 841 (2006).

power;[55] localism and economics;[56] local public finance and budgeting;[57] municipal bankruptcy;[58] local economic development;[59] firearms localism;[60] local prevention of natural disasters and cities' role in post-disaster recovery and relocation;[61] localism and climate change;[62] local cultural preservation;[63] local responses to predatory lending;[64] local constitutional and civil law enforcement;[65] energy localism;[66] public health localism;[67] localism and clean air;[68] the local response to drought;[69] local efforts in education;[70] and transportation localism.[71]

As they grow, cities will find themselves faced with ever-more complex law and policy questions; so, we can expect interest in cities to grow among legal scholars. As the next section will discuss, we can also expect lawyers and law students to be in greater demand at the local sites of American democracy.

55 *See, e.g.*, Diller, *supra* Note 9 at 287; Paul A. Diller, *Reorienting Home Rule: Part 2 – Remedying the Urban Disadvantage through Federalism and Localism*, 77 LA. L. REV. 1045 (2017).

56 *See, e.g.*, David Schleicher, *The City as a Law and Economic Subject*, 2010 U. ILL. L. REV. 1507 (2010).

57 *See, e.g.*, Darien Shanske, *Local Fiscal Autonomy Requires Constraints: The Case for Fiscal Menus*, 25 STANFORD LAW AND POL'Y REV. 9 (2014). *See also* Celina Su, Renegotiating the Constituent's Role in Urban Governance: Participatory Budgeting in New York City, *in How Cities Will Save the World* 233.

58 *See, e.g.*, Michelle Wilde Anderson, *Dissolving Cities*, 121 YALE L.J. 1364 (2012), Michelle Wilde Anderson, *The New Minimal Cities*, 123 YALE L.J. 1118 (2014).

59 *See, e.g.*, Peter Pitegoff, Community Development Finance and Economic Justice in *Legal Scholarship for the Urban Core*.

60 *See, e.g.*, Joseph Blocher, *Firearm Localism*, 123 YALE L.J. 82 (2013).

61 *See* Debbie M. Chizewer & A. Dan Tarlock, *New Challenges for Urban Areas Facing Flood Risks*, 40 FORDHAM URBAN L.J. 1739 (2013). *See also* Marla Nelson & Renia Ehrenfeucht, Moving to Safety? Opportunities to Reduce Vulnerability through Relocation and Resettlement Policy, *in How Cities Will Save the World* 65.

62 *See, e.g.*, John Travis Marshall, Assessing Metropolitan Resiliency: Laying the Foundation for Urban Sustainability, *in How Cities Will Save the World* 33.

63 *See, e.g.*, Ryan Rowberry, Avoiding Atlantis: Protecting Urban Cultural Heritage from Disaster, *in How Cities Will Save the World* 49.

64 *See, e.g.*, Ray Brescia, Cities and the Financial Crisis, *in How Cities Will Save the World* 11.

65 *See, e.g.*, Paul Diller, *The City and the Private Right of Action*, 64 STANFORD L. REV. 1109 (2012). *See also* Kathleen S. Morris, *Expanding Local Enforcement of State and Federal Consumer Protection Laws*, 40 FORDHAM URBAN L.J. 1903 (2013); Kaitlin Ainsworth Caruso, *Associational Standing for Cities*, 47 CONN. L. REV. 59 (2014).

66 *See, e.g.*, Hannah J. Wiseman, *Urban Energy*, 40 FORDHAM URBAN L.J. 1793 (2013).

67 *See, e.g.*, Paul A. Diller, *Why Do Cities Innovate in Public Health? Implications of Scale and Structure*, 91 WASH. U. L. REV. 1219 (2014).

68 *See, e.g.*, Scott L. Cummings, *Preemptive Strike: Law in the Campaign for Clean Trucks*, 4 UC IRVINE L. REV. 939 (2014).

69 *See, e.g.*, Sarah B. Schindler, Exploring Options for Urban Sustainability in an Era of Scarce Water Resources: A Possible Ban on Lawns, *in How Cities Will Save the World* 97.

70 *See, e.g.*, John A. Lovett, Can Charter Schools Save Cities? Social Capital and Urban Public Education, *in How Cities Will Save the World* 159.

71 *See, e.g.*, M. Becht Neel & Julian Conrad Juergensmeyer, Financing Urban Transportation Infrastructure: Old and New Approaches for Funding Urban Regeneration and Resiliency: The Atlanta Example, *in How Cities Will Save the World* 253.

THE ROLE(S) OF LAWYERS IN AMERICAN DEMOCRACY

Legal Scholars on Lawyers in Democracy

Lawyers have been at the center of public life in America from its inception. Of the fifty-six signers of the Declaration of Independence, twenty-five were lawyers.[72] Almost sixty years after that document was signed, the historian and political scientist Alexis de Tocqueville praised the omnipresence of lawyers in US leadership and government as a singularly stabilizing force:

> In visiting the Americans and studying their laws, we perceive that the authority they have entrusted to members of the legal profession, and the influence that these individuals exercise in the government, are the most powerful existing security against the excesses of democracy.[73]

At least one legal scholar has argued that the rise of capitalism in the nineteenth century eroded the cultural idea of the lawyer-as-public-figure.[74] Yet, as an empirical matter, lawyers have continued to play a significant role in government. Twenty-five of the forty-five presidents of the United States (including two of the last four) have been lawyers.[75] Lawyers are also heavily represented in Congress[76] and the state legislatures.[77] As for public lawyers, not including judges, one-eighth of all lawyers in the United States work for a federal, state, or local public entity: 37,300 lawyers work for the federal government, and 90,200 work for a state or local government.[78]

[72] *See* National Archives, The Declaration of Independence: Signers Factsheet, www.archives.gov/founding-docs/signers-factsheet (last visited Jul. 8, 2017).

[73] Alexis de Tocqueville, *Democracy in America* 271 (1835) (Henry Reeve, trans.) (George Adlard, 1839).

[74] *See* Russell G. Pearce, *Lawyers as America's Governing Class: The Formation and Dissolution of the Original Understanding of the American Lawyer's Role*, 8 U. Chi. L. Sch. Roundtable 381, 381, 392–93, 410–11 (2001) (describing how the de Tocquevillean model of lawyers-as-governing-class waned in the latter part of the twentieth century, as the model of lawyer-as-businessperson overtook it). *See* Kenneth M. Rosen, *Lessons on Lawyers, Democracy, and Professional Responsibility*, 19 Geo. J. Legal Ethics 155, 155 (2006) (arguing that law schools do and should play a major role in teaching students to understand and support democratic institutions).

[75] Chelsea Beran, *Before They Were Presidents...They Were Lawyers*, Law Technology Today (Feb. 15, 2016), www.lawtechnologytoday.org/2016/02/before-they-were-presidents-they-were-lawyers/.

[76] *See* Bill Lucey, *113th Congress by the Numbers*, Huffpost (Apr. 23, 2013), www.huffingtonpost.com/bill-lucey/113th-congress-by-the-num_b_2737382.html.

[77] *See* Jen Fifield, *State Legislators Have Fewer Farmers, Lawyers; But Higher Education Level, in* Unrepresentative: The Demographics of State Legislatures, Pew Charitable Trusts (Dec. 10, 2015), http://pewtrusts.org/en/research-and-analysis/blogs/stateline/2015/12/10/state-legislatures-have-fewer-farmers-lawyers-but-higher-education-level.

[78] Stephen M. Sheppard, *The American Legal Profession in the Twenty-First Century*, 62 Am. J. Comp. L. 241, 260 (2014).

The overrepresentation of lawyers in government means that American law schools have always been better positioned than perhaps any other collective institution to influence and support democratic leadership. The most influential scholarly work addressing the close relationship between American law schools and democracy is arguably Paul Carrington's *Stewards of Democracy*.[79] In it, Carrington argues that because a legal education is a privilege afforded few Americans, those lucky enough to study law should be intentionally trained to act as thoughtful mediators among the public and private forces that comprise democracy and society. He argues, further, that lawyers are morally obligated to facilitate self-government and national cohesion by "mediating between the ruling democratic majority" and "minorities who may at times be found in opposition to the majority."[80]

Carrington predicted, presciently (in 1999), that as a result of the technological and free trade revolutions, the nation would face ever-deepening class divides that would threaten the survival of American democracy. In this moment, he argued, lawyers have a special "responsibility to shelter and nurture the institutions of self-government."[81] He urged law students to focus, in particular, on becoming stewards of state and local governments:

> In state and local governments, to borrow a phrase from architecture, political power can be exercised on a human scale, that is, within the limits of our understanding and prudence ... Some of the attention of academic lawyers, our "ministers without portfolio," might usefully be redirected to the work of legislative bodies and government agencies, even those of state and local governments. Such devolutionary changes would require lawyers and even law professors to spend more time with people owning conventional moral and political values and less with intellectuals and word processors.[82]

Two years later, Mark Jones published the first in a trilogy of articles about American law and legal education.[83] Jones echoed Carrington's claim that the roles lawyers

[79] *See* Paul D. Carrington, *Stewards of Democracy: Law as a Public Profession* (1999).

[80] *Id.* at 1; *see also id.* at 224 ("the judiciary and the profession [should] recognize that they are commissioned not to rule the Republic, but to mediate between the forces seeking to do so."). Rebecca Roiphe and Bradley Wendel have echoed Paul Carrington's view that all lawyers act as mediators between the public and private sectors. *See* Rebecca Roiphe, *Tilting at Stratification: Against a Divide in Legal Education*, 16 NEV. L.J. 227, 228 (FALL 2015) (explaining that all lawyers, not just government lawyers, negotiate "private interests with shared social norms," and in this way serve a "beneficial role" in democracy); W. Bradley Wendel, *Government Lawyers, Democracy, and the Rule of Law*, 77 FORDHAM L. REV. 1333, 1341–49 (2009) (asserting that all lawyers serve as public and private sector go-betweens).

[81] Carrington, *supra* Note 79 at 219.

[82] *Id.* at 220–21. In a 2017 panel at the national conference of the American Constitution Society ("ACS"), Yale Law School Dean Heather K. Gerken made a similar point. *See Professor Gerken Discusses Progressive Federalism at ACS Event*, YALE LAW SCHOOL (June 20, 2017), https://law.yale.edu/yls-today/news/professor-gerken-discusses-progressive-federalism-acs-event.

[83] The first article in the Jones trilogy includes a comprehensive bibliography of writings in legal education and society, and introduces an original taxonomy that divides law into six

play in public life stretch far beyond public lawyering, and called on law schools to intentionally focus on producing citizen-leaders:

> Historically, lawyers have served in a wide variety of leadership roles, ranging from positions of national importance, such as President or member of Congress, to positions of state and local importance, such as state legislator, board of education chair, and corporate CEO. Lawyers are not the only citizens who lead, of course, but lawyers have always been central in leading the Republic throughout its history. This was true during the first phase in the historical development of legal education, and it is true today ... I believe that legal educators owe a responsibility to society to prepare practically wise citizen leaders, as well as practically wise legal practitioners, who possess the particular ensemble of substantive knowledge, practical skills, and qualities of character needed for such leadership.[84]

Rebecca Roiphe, Deanell Reece Tacha, and Kenneth Rosen have also written of the need in a democracy for law schools to educate all of their students – not just public interest and public sector law students – on the fundamentals of democracy and governance. Rosen, a business law scholar, wrote that the lawyer's calling to serve democracy should not be seen as an *aspiration*, but a professional *obligation*:

> Law schools are *professional* schools. As such, we must prepare students to fulfill their *professional* obligations, and ranking among an American lawyer's greatest professional responsibilities is the duty to understand and to support democracy. In part, what characterizes the legal profession is its members' supposed expertise in the mechanics and principles of our polity. Such knowledge enables lawyers to make a difference in our polity and brings with it special responsibility to our democracy. Accordingly, emphasis on this "democratic duty" in our law schools is essential.[85]

Rosen explains that to fulfill this professional responsibility, lawyers must do two separate things: They must (1) study and understand not just some, but *all of the intricacies of representative democracy* and (2) function as lawyer-citizens by serving the greater society and supporting democracy their entire professional lives.[86] Rosen embraces Edmond Cahn's 1961 insight that, by fulfilling their duty to democracy,

fundamental dimensions: substantive, structural, practical, social, cultural, and transnational. *See* Mark L. Jones, *Fundamental Dimensions of Law and Legal Education: A Theoretical Framework*, 26 OKLA. CITY U. L. REV. 547, 562 (2001). The second article reviews the first one hundred years of American legal education, to provide an historical lens through which to review his proposals on law school pedagogy. *See* Mark L. Jones, *Fundamental Dimensions of Law and Legal Education: An Historical Framework – A History of Legal Education Phase I: From the Founding of the Republic until the 1960's*, 39 J. MARSHALL L. REV. 1041 (2006). The third article proposes changes to law school pedagogy that would successfully teach law students the fundamental dimensions of law. *See* Mark L. Jones, *Fundamental Dimensions of Law and Legal Education: Perspectives on Curricular Reform*, 63 MERCER L. REV. 975 (2012).

84 Jones, *supra* Note 83 at 1051–52 (footnotes omitted).

85 *See* Rosen, *supra* Note 74 at 158–59 (emphasis in original).

86 *Id.* at 162–63.

lawyers can bolster the reputation of the profession while simultaneously acting as democracy's "watchmen":

> Ultimately, American lawyers are American citizens. It is not easy to be a citizen in a democracy. One of the paradoxes of democracy is that if the polity's actions are based in consent, all citizens might be held responsible for society's actions, including its miscues ... Lawyers have a greater capability than most to be America's watchmen. The hours they invest in such a venture may be long, but are part of fulfilling their natural calling.[87]

Rebecca Roiphe and Deanell Reece Tacha have also defended the importance, to the health of both the legal profession and American democracy, of educating *all* law students, not just *some*, on the basics of democracy and governance. Roiphe has explained that:

> Lawyers are a critical component of a modern democracy because their training, experience, or devotion to the law situates them to direct private passions and particular interests towards a socially productive goal, which will benefit everyone in the end ... By definition, lawyers bring government into the interstices of individual lives. As such, they can shape the way individuals interact with the public, while making sure that the agencies of government do not overstep their bounds as well.[88]

In 2004, Tacha, who was then a federal court of appeals judge, gave a speech providing a view of legal education from the bench. In that speech, Judge Tacha placed "promoting a healthy democracy" *among the top three most important teaching goals* of American law schools.[89] Tacha stated that a healthy democracy requires lawyers to be well educated in law and government, and to educate non-lawyers about how law and government work.[90] In light of recent reports on the

[87] *Id.* at 168 (citing Edmond Cahn, *The Predicament of Democratic Man* 14–15, 94–98, 110–11 (1961)).

[88] Rebecca Roiphe, *Redefining Professionalism*, 26 U. Fla. L.J. & Pub. Policy 193, 230 (2015). *See also* Rebecca Roiphe, *A History of Professionalism: Julius Henry Cohen and the Professional as a Route to Citizenship*, 40 Urban L.J. 33 (2012) (reviving the discussion of the relationship between professional legal identity and modern democracy); Rebecca Roiphe, *Tilting at Stratification: Against a Divide in Legal Education*, 16 Nev. L.J. 227, 227 (2015). In the third paper, Roiphe engages, and disagrees with, the argument that American law schools should create higher and lower tiers of legal education in which full research professors educate higher-tiered law students in all aspects of the law, while lower-tiered law students focus on taking skills classes.

[89] *See* Deanell Reece Tacha, *Refocusing the Twenty-First Century Law School*, 57 S.M.U.L. Rev. 1543, 1550–51 (2004). Tacha argued that at a minimum law schools should teach their students: (1) how to think like lawyers; (2) how to communicate well; and (3) how to actively promote a healthy democracy through civic education and service.

[90] Drawing on Carrington's work, Tacha argued: "Lawyers, students, and faculty have to step forward en masse throughout the nation to educate the public on civil affairs. You have a duty to help the general public learn the basics about the law and government to which we have devoted so much of our professional lives ... Help us train the next generation of lawyer-

American public's ignorance of basic civics,[91] Tacha's warning is more urgent today than when she gave the speech.[92]

Lawyers in Local Democracy and Government

Public and private lawyers working within cities fulfill all of the democracy-enhancing roles these legal scholars identified. Lawyers working both inside and outside local government mediate between public and private interests; educate their friends, families, and community about law and democracy; and commonly serve in leadership roles in the public and private sectors. And as we have seen, lawyers who work inside city and other local governments conduct a wide range of complicated law and policy work. It bears emphasis that, as a group, our nation's local public law offices provide two particular, unique services to American democracy.

First, local governments "run" the state and federal constitutions day to day. City lawyers and officials regularly interpret dozens of state and federal constitutional provisions that apply to police departments, sheriffs' departments, and executive agencies. They do this in order to decide which of their actions are constitutional, and also whether the state or federal governments have overstepped their bounds vis-a-vis city constituents. As the political scientist Alec Ewald has observed, local public officials and their lawyers "reduce [the constitutions'] grand principles to practice by their actions both routine and extraordinary."[93] Since very often "no bright line or policy" dictates the answer to many of our constitutional questions, and official determinations are

citizens to serve and promote the democratic values upon which this nation was founded." *Id.* at 1550–51. *See also* W. Bradley Wendel, *Lawyers and Fidelity to Law* 210 (2010) (explaining that, in modern democracy, the institution of law is the closest Americans come to having a set of common, agreed-upon values).

91 *See, e.g., Americans Know Literally Nothing about the Constitution*, CNN (Sept. 13, 2017), 4:39 p.m., www.cnn.com/2017/09/13/politics/poll-constitution/index.html. *See also* Deroy Murdock, *Civic Ignorance Threatens American Liberty*, THE CATO INSTITUTE (Jun. 30, 2000), www.cato.org/publications/commentary/civic-ignorance-threatens-american-liberty; Jonathan R. Cole, *Ignorance Does Not Lead to Election Bliss*, THE ATLANTIC (Nov. 8, 2016), www.theatlantic.com/education/archive/2016/11/ignorance-does-not-lead-to-election-bliss/506894/.

92 Legal scholars have also written on a closely related issue, which is the need for law schools to incorporate into legal education courses the fundamentals of leadership. *See, e.g.*, Robert E. Matthews, *The Lawyer, the Law Schools and Responsible Leadership*, 25 ROCKY MTN. L. REV. 482, 488 (1953) (urging law schools to teach leadership); Deborah Rhode, *Developing Leadership*, 52 SANTA CLARA L. REV. 689, 724 (2012) (urging law schools to join business schools in providing leadership education); Donald J. Polden, *Educating Law Students for Leadership Roles and Responsibilities*, 39 U. TOL. L. REV. 353 (2008) (same); Michael Coper, *Educating Lawyers for What? Reshaping the Idea of Law School*, 29 PENN. STATE INT'L L. REV. 25 (2010) (arguing that law schools should teach not only technical competence but also leadership, citizenship, and service).

93 *See* Ewald, *supra* Note 19 at 160 n. 10 (quoting John Rohr, *Civil Servants and Their Constitutions* 141 (2002) (internal quotation marks omitted)).

relatively rarely challenged in court, local officials and their lawyers collectively exercise significant (yet often overlooked) constitutional authority.[94]

Second, city law offices frequently act as the first-rung of public service for lawyers who later seek public office. Frequently, today's city lawyers become tomorrow's mayors, city council members, district attorneys, and state and federal legislators. A tradition in both major political parties is for political aspirants to work in local government and then seek local government office, before running for state or federal offices. Accordingly, one natural first step for law graduates with political ambitions is to try to join a city attorney's office. I bore anecdotal witness to this city-law-office-to-politics dynamic as a deputy city attorney in San Francisco. When I joined that office in 2003, my fellow deputy city attorneys included Kamala Harris, Scott Weiner, and Rob Bonta. Harris was later elected as the San Francisco District Attorney, the California Attorney General, a US Senator from California, and is now a candidate for President. Weiner was later elected as a San Francisco Supervisor, then a California State Senator. Bonta was later elected to the Alameda City Council, then the California State Assembly.

Because lawyers play a central role in democracy and government, and because cities are growing in strength, law schools are in a unique position to influence and strengthen democracy and government from the ground up by plugging into cities. The final section will suggest the steps they can take to do so.

HOW LAW SCHOOLS CAN PLUG INTO THE GROWING ENERGY IN CITIES

The Governance Gap in American Law Schools

The overwhelming majority of our nation's legal institutions – its laws, public offices, and courts – operate at the state and local level. We have not one but fifty-one constitutions that design our tri-level democracy. Our state constitutions in particular are such a ripe potential source of individual and group rights that, as far back as 1986, US Supreme Court Justice William Brennan wrote an article calling on the nation's law schools and lawyers to unpack and invoke them.[95]

94 *See* Schwarz, *supra* Note 17 at 376 (making this point) (internal citations and quotation marks omitted). As I have explained elsewhere, based on my own experiences in San Francisco: "[M]ayor's offices routinely announce time, place, and manner restrictions to rally requests. Sheriff's offices develop strip search policies to be applied to pretrial detainees. Public hospitals determine whether patients are entitled to abortions. Police chiefs develop policies on the permissible use of force during an arrest. Public contracting agencies evaluate the constitutionality of programs designed to remedy race discrimination. Legislative aids draft ordinances in the shadow of the Supremacy Clause. And for their part, local public law offices routinely help their clients make [all of these] constitutional determinations." Morris, *supra* Note 32 at 41–42.

95 *See* William Brennan, Jr., *The Bill of Rights and the States: The Revival of State Constitutions as Guardians of Individual Rights*, 61 N.Y.U. L. Rev. 535 (1986). For a comprehensive

Yet, thirty years later, law schools continue their passive insistence on a kind of federal parochialism. Most American law schools require their students to learn the structures and functions of the federal constitution and government, but few or none require them to also learn the structures and functions of state and local governments. They teach federal (but not state) constitutional law, federal (but not state) courts and evidence, federal (but not state) civil and criminal procedure, and so on.

Many law schools also have a blind spot when it comes to preparing students for jobs in public leadership, law, and policy. Perhaps due to market forces, law schools have gradually evolved into institutions that prepare students for legal jobs in one of three areas: private corporate law, private nonprofit law, and criminal law. Thus, even though (as discussed in Section II) law graduates can be expected to continue being overrepresented in all levels of government, law schools do not prepare them to govern. The good news is that any law school can begin to close the governance gap by taking the modest steps below.

Closing the Governance Gap

Add a Full-Time State and Local Government Scholar to the Faculty

Any law school that wants to help strengthen democracy and government should begin by hiring a state and local government scholar onto the full-time faculty. Doing so is critical for at least two reasons. First, tenure-track hires signal a subject matter's importance and bolster its prestige. Since law students and lawyers are highly sensitive to prestige, tenure-track hiring is critical to signaling the subject matter's importance.

Here I offer a personal anecdote. When I went on the law teaching market in 2012, an interviewer from a law school ranked in the top 20 told me in all candor that the legal academy does not view my scholarly interests – state and local government law, state constitutional law, and localism – as intellectually worthy. Accordingly, he believed, most law faculties would view me as intellectually unserious. He explained that other subjects (like race, gender, immigration law, and the like) had gone through a similar period of "un-seriousness," and that like those subjects, my subject would eventually rise to the level of being equally worthy. This moment in American politics and democracy should, I hope, convince all law schools that the time has come to treat sub-federal democracy as a serious and intellectually worthy subject.

Second, state constitutional law and state and local government law are overdue for an infusion of intellectual energy. At present, the United States has 204 American Bar Association-accredited law schools,[96] but probably fewer than 20 dedicated state

treatment of the rights and protections of state constitutions, *see* Robert F. Williams, *The Law of American State Constitutions* (2009).

96 *See* ABA-Approved Law Schools, American Bar Association, www.americanbar.org/groups/legal_education/resources/aba_approved_law_schools.html (last visited Apr. 29, 2018).

and local government scholars.[97] Over the past one hundred years, law schools have poured enormous intellectual energy into understanding the structure and functions of the US constitution, the federal government, and federal law, which together make up a fraction of our law and governance structures. Yet law graduates have a relatively sparse understanding of the structure and functions of state and local governments.[98] This strikes me as the rough equivalent of America's medical schools teaching anatomy classes that cover the largest bones, muscle groups, and organs, but leave out the small bones and muscle groups, connective tissue, and the entire nervous system. Legal scholars have yet to fully unpack and understand the structural and substantive features of sub-federal democracy, including the fifty state constitutions, innumerable city and county charters, and the multiplicity of appointed and elected entities at the state and local levels. Legal scholars also have yet to connect these state and local features to federalism, which would allow for a fully integrated picture of American democracy. The scale of this immensely complicated work is vast yet hardly begun.[99]

Imagine how much more deeply judges and lawyers might comprehend our tripartite democracy if every law school made a commitment to infusing state and local government law and policy with fresh intellectual talent and energy. Even if the market does not currently demand it, one could make a strong case that the health of our democracy demands it. And ultimately, law schools can seek to recoup the expenditure involved in making a state and local government hire by marketing their commitment to democracy to prospective students, foundations, and private donors.

Require (or at Least Offer) a Course in State Constitutional Law, State and Local Government Law, and Public Lawyering

Since state and local governments and laws are central to democratic functioning and public and private lawyering, law schools should probably move toward requiring all students to take a survey course that introduces them to state constitutional law, state and local government law, and public lawyering. At the very least, every law school should offer such a course.

If a law school wants to go on to develop a specialty in public leadership and lawyering, it should consider adding courses that address a broader range of topics,

[97] This estimate is based on attendance at the annual state and local government scholars conference, a small-but-hardy group that regularly includes scholars from the law schools at Buffalo, Chapman, Columbia, Golden Gate, Harvard, New York University, Stanford, Texas, Toronto, U.C. Davis, Virginia, Willamette, and Yale.

[98] *See* Heather K. Gerken, *supra* Note 47 at 13 (noting this analytical gap and calling on legal scholars to develop a vision of federalism that accounts for the wide and complicated world of local public entities).

[99] *See id.*; *see also* Kathleen S. Morris, *Uncooperative Localism* (Apr. 19, 2018) (unpublished manuscript) (on file with author) (suggesting next steps in this essential work).

including: (1) leadership and management (so they can run public law offices and departments[100]); (2) civil law enforcement (to learn how public entity platforms enforce labor, consumer, environmental, civil rights, and other civil laws); (3) the fundamentals of public policy research (through which they can gain a baseline level of familiarity with the vocabulary and analysis that drives policy discussions[101]); (4) state and local taxation, public finance and assets, and public contracts (so they have a basic grasp on how public funds are acquired and managed at the city and state level); and (5) law and technology (because technology has become so central to running the democracy and corporations, including public corporations); (6) lawyering and public engagement (through which they can learn about law and organizing, working with citizen groups, and managing public communication around legal issues); and (7) drafting and enacting legislation and regulations.

Offer a Practical Seminar or Clinical Course That Tackles the Law and Policy Challenges of a City, County, or District

Law students and local governments have complementary needs. Most law students are required and/or wish to engage in some form of clinical work and to work on an upper-division research and writing project. Most local governments and their law offices lack sufficient staff to research the potential of law and policy innovations. Law schools are ideally positioned to connect smart, public-minded students and local public servants. And in my own experience, it is surprisingly easy to do so.

I created two such projects: The San Francisco Affirmative Litigation Project at Yale Law School,[102] and the Cities Law and Policy Project at Golden Gate Law School. Both projects started as simple reading groups, and eventually grew into formal two- or three-unit seminars.[103] In the reading group format, the students conducted original, supervised research in response to complex law and policy questions, and produced an upper-division paper at the end of the semester that satisfied the upper-division writing requirement. In the seminar format, the students conducted research projects while also reading and discussing scholarly papers and foundational cases in state and local government law. In the case of the Golden Gate Law and Policy Project, the school intends to publish the students' work so that it will serve as a publicly available owner's manual for innovative city government. Both projects were easy to create and run, and both resulted in gratified law students and local governments.

[100] A number of legal scholars have stressed the wisdom of teaching leadership in law schools. *See* citations, *supra* Notes 79–92.

[101] For an excellent discussion of how law schools can better prepare their students to engage in public lawyering by teaching them the basics of policy analysis, *see* Peter Schuck, *Lawyers and Policymakers in Government*, 61 WTR Law & Contemp. Probs. 7 (1998).

[102] *See supra* Note 30 and accompanying text.

[103] The Yale Law project ultimately grew into a clinic. *See id*. The Golden Gate Law project is still a seminar.

Who Will Benefit if Law Schools Plug into Cities?

In my own personal experience, when a law school plugs into the energy in city government, benefits flow to multiple stakeholders. Students find doing the actual work of democracy to be deeply meaningful and often thrilling. Scholars whose research interests are guiding them toward state constitutions and state and local government law relish having an expert in the building to help them anchor their research. Ambitious city governments obtain the research support that is indispensable to their being able to actually pursue initiatives that might otherwise lie fallow. City constituents benefit from the student research along with their cities. Law graduates who understand the full range of public law are in a much stronger position in the private and public law markets, because they have a solid understanding of the governments and courts with whom they are most likely to come into contact. In the long range, if all American law schools took these simple steps, our lawyers would have a wider and deeper appreciation of our democratic institutions, which would strengthen the democracy itself.[104]

CONCLUSION

What collective American institution is better positioned than law schools to strengthen democratic institutions from the ground up? Every law school in the nation can do so at least in part by plugging into America's rising cities. In my own experience, the law schools that do so stand to energize faculty and students, intrigue pro-democracy foundations and other donors, and generate goodwill in state and local governments and their surrounding communities.

[104] *See supra* Notes 79–92 and accompanying text.

8

Education and Social Justice

Urban Schools and Law Schools

*Peter Enrich**

This chapter – like the book of which it is a part – addresses the intersection of two challenges, one about the urban core and one about the legal academy. In the case of this chapter, both challenges concern education. One challenge is the continuing failure of the schools serving the children of the urban core to meet the needs of those children and to equip them for full participation and opportunity in our economic and civic life. The other challenge is the struggle of legal education to forge a pedagogy and a curriculum that can effectively introduce law students, not only to legal doctrine and argument, but to the complexities of what lawyers do and to law in its full social context.

Of course, the challenges of urban schools spring from a wide range of causes, only a fraction of which can be attributed to or addressed through lawyerly tools. And of course, legal education has a great many topics and tools to cover, only a fraction of which relate to issues connected to the problems of urban schools. But this chapter will discuss the example of one program at one law school – the Social Justice Projects program at Northeastern University School of Law – that has sought to expand the tactics and topics of legal education by putting first-year law students to work in addressing issues of urgent social concern, including (although by no means limited to) the challenges of urban schools. The results, I will suggest, are positive in addressing both challenges – transformative in the impacts on the first-year law school experience, and at least modestly helpful in advancing progress on specific issues affecting urban schools (and an array of other societal concerns).

* Professor, Northeastern University School of Law. I am grateful for the research assistance provided by Tessa Anderson, Rachel Cilibraise, Andrew Farrington, ShanShan Guo, and Rachel Uemoto. I am also indebted to helpful comments from many of the Northeastern University School of Law faculty who have been involved in building and leading the Social Justice Program that is the focus of this chapter, as well as from representatives of several of the program's partner organizations, and from Rashmi Dyal-Chand. I, however, am solely responsible for the characterizations and assessments of the program discussed in this chapter.

The chapter will proceed in three stages. The first section will offer an introduction to each of the educational challenges of concern, with little effort to connect the two. The second section will introduce Northeastern's Social Justice Projects program and describe three examples of projects undertaken through the program that focused on issues affecting schools serving the urban core. A final section will offer some reflections on the promise – and the challenges – of the program and of the three examples, both for legal education and for urban schooling, and some tentative thoughts about the relevance of this story for legal scholarship.

THE CHALLENGES

Schools Serving the Urban Core

As Chief Justice Warren famously observed in *Brown* v. *Board of Education,*

> Today, education is perhaps the most important function of state and local governments. Compulsory school attendance laws and the great expenditures for education both demonstrate our recognition of the importance of education to our democratic society. It is required in the performance of our most basic public responsibilities, even service in the armed forces. It is the very foundation of good citizenship. Today it is a principal instrument in awakening the child to cultural values, in preparing him for later professional training, and in helping him to adjust normally to his environment. In these days, it is doubtful that any child may reasonably be expected to succeed in life if he is denied the opportunity of an education.[1]

Nonetheless, more than six decades later, the schools that we provide for children in our urban cores and other poor communities are often squalid. They are inadequately equipped, class sizes are typically unmanageable, and teachers are often underqualified, under-supported, and unable to meet the educational needs of their students. As Robert Putnam vividly portrays in his powerful recent book, *Our Kids,* the schools serving children from poor communities often provide little more than custodial care and behavior management; academics are at best an after-thought.[2]

The results for the students are stark. In the words of a 2013 report from the Department of Education's Equity and Excellence Commission, "Ten million students in America's poorest communities ... are having their lives unjustly and irredeemably blighted by a system that consigns them to the lowest-performing teachers, the most run-down facilities, and academic expectations and opportunities considerably lower than what we expect of other students."[3] Indeed, for many

[1] *Brown* v. *Board of Educ.*, 347 U.S. 483, 493 (1954).

[2] Robert Putnam, *Our Kids: The American Dream in Crisis* 154 et seq. (2015).

[3] U.S. Department of Education, *For Each and Every Child – A Strategy for Education Equity and Excellence* 14 (2013) www2.ed.gov/about/bdscomm/list/eec/equity-excellence-commission-

students, these failing schools, with their inability to provide meaningful educational opportunity and their emphasis on managing behavior through harsh discipline, are less pathways to opportunity than way-stations on the cradle-to-prison pipeline that devastates these communities.

Comparisons between the conditions and outcomes for schools in poor communities and for those in neighboring, better-off communities underscore the depths of the problem. A recent analysis of a massive national database of student test scores finds not only that most states show significant gaps in scores from district to district, but that those gaps are biggest in the states with the highest levels of racial and economic segregation among districts. The gaps get larger as students advance through school, and the gaps grew dramatically over the years covered by the analysis.[4] Putnam's book is only the latest in a vast literature documenting the stunning differences in the educational opportunities offered by poorer and richer communities.[5] Further comparative evidence can be found in the records developed in the litigation challenging these disparities that has been pursued, with varying outcomes, in almost every state.[6]

Differences in class sizes, teacher preparation and qualifications, course offerings, availability of modern textbooks and technology, and conditions of physical facilities are shockingly wide. And student outcomes, measured by graduation rates, reading levels, and scores on standardized tests, display similarly stark disparities. In short, the educational opportunities of America's children differ dramatically depending on the communities in which they live. And, while the most commonly discussed

report.pdf. To take just one statistic from the report, "In reading . . . although U.S. children in low-poverty schools rank at the top of the world, those in our highest-poverty schools are performing on a par with children in the world's lowest-achieving countries." *Id.* at 12.

4 *See* Erin M. Fahle and Sean F. Reardon, *How Much Do Test Scores Vary among School Districts? – New Estimates Using Population Data, 2009–2015* (CEPA Working Paper No.17–02, 2017, retrieved from Stanford Center for Education Policy Analysis: http://cepa.stanford.edu/wp17–02). *See also* Sean F. Reardon, The Widening Academic Achievement Gap between the Rich and the Poor: New Evidence and Possible Explanations, *in Whither Opportunity? – Rising Inequality, Schools, and Children's Life Chances* 91 (Greg J. Duncan & Richard P. Murnane, eds., 2011) ("The achievement gap between children from high- and low-income families is roughly 30 to 40 percent larger among children born in 2001 than among those born twenty-five years earlier.").

5 *See* Putnam, *supra* Note 2 at 135–90; *see also, e.g.*, Duncan & Murnane, eds., *supra* Note 4; Jonathan Kozol, *Savage Inequalities* 101–160 (1991).

6 For a few examples from the voluminous case law, *see, e.g.*, *William Penn Sch. Dist.* v. *Pa. Dept. of Educ.*, 170 A.3d 414, 428–31 (Pa. 2017) (reversing dismissal of state constitutional challenge to education funding system and remanding for fact finding); Class Action Complaint, *Gary B.* v. *Snyder*, 2016 WL 4775474 (E.D. Mich.) (No. 2:16-cv-13292) (challenging Michigan's funding of Detroit schools under federal Constitution for entirely depriving students of an education), *dismissed*, 2018 WL 3609491, *appeal pending*; *Hancock* v. *Driscoll*, 2004 WL 877984 (Mass. Sup. Ct.) (report to the state's Supreme Judicial Court by Special Master Margot Botsford, detailing disparities between poorer and richer school districts in state constitutional challenge to education funding system), *reviewed and decided sub nom. Hancock* v. *Comm'r of Educ.*, 443 Mass. 428 (2005). For a current catalogue of the state school finance cases, *see* 110 A.L.R.5th 293 (originally published 2003).

disparities are between neighboring school districts, similar gaps can often be found between schools in richer and poorer neighborhoods of a single urban school system.[7] As Putnam convincingly demonstrates, the parlous state of schools in poor neighborhoods is a key contributor to America's widening divide between rich and poor and to the rapid decline in intergenerational socioeconomic mobility.

The causes underlying these failings and disparities are complex and contested. For many years, the primary focus – particularly in the legal literature and the litigation that has been its focus – has been on the wide disparities in funding that result from the school finance system's heavy reliance, in most states, on local property taxation and from the extreme variations in per-student property wealth between richer and poorer communities. Those fiscal gaps persist as sources of wide funding differences in many jurisdictions.[8] And, although Putnam suggests that the funding gaps are shrinking in many places, he emphasizes that the funding available to schools in poor communities continues to fall far short of what those schools would need to provide educational opportunities comparable to those in wealthier communities.[9]

Equal funding cannot suffice to address the complex array of challenges facing schools that serve poor communities. Poor students come to school with multiple burdens, often grounded in long histories of discrimination and neglect. They frequently arrive at school undernourished and often have significant untreated health problems that limit their capacity to participate and perform. For many, English is a second language. Housing is often unstable, with the result that many poor children must make frequent, disruptive transitions from school to school. Parents are often less available, and less capable, to provide support to student engagement and learning than their wealthier and better educated counterparts. And poor children experience a far higher frequency of traumatic events – from family disruption to encounters with violence – than their better-off peers, while a growing body of evidence documents the impact of repeated traumatic experiences on cognitive function and ability to learn. By high school (and even by middle school), economic demands and the high visibility of economic and social

7 *See* Lauren A. Webb, *Educational Opportunity for All: Reducing Intradistrict Funding Disparities*, 92 N.Y.U. L. Rev. 2169, 2173 (2017); Terrance L. Green et al., *Communities and School Ratings: Examining Geography of Opportunity in an Urban School District Located in a Resource-Rich City*, 49 Urb. Rev 777 (2017).

8 *See, e.g.*, Ivy Morgan and Ira Amerikaner, *Funding Gaps 2018 – An Analysis of School Funding Equity across the U.S. and within Each State* (Education Trust 2018) https://edtrust.org/resource/funding-gaps-2018/; U.S. Dept. of Education, *supra* Note 3 at 15 ("The common situation in America is that schools in poor communities spend less per pupil – and often many thousands of dollars less per pupil – than schools in nearby affluent communities."); Laurie Reynolds, *Full State Funding of Education as a State Constitutional Imperative*, 60 Hastings L.J. 749, 754–61 (2009) (detailing recurring funding inequities even in states where funding litigation and reform have succeeded).

9 Putnam, *supra* Note 2 at 166–68; *see also id.* at 179–81.

alternatives centered on drugs and related criminal activity draw students away from school, especially when they recognize that their needs are not being met there.

The challenges faced by individual children are compounded in urban core schools that serve populations of concentrated poverty. Extensive evidence establishes that the socioeconomic status of one's classmates is one of the strongest predictors of academic success. For schools that serve high proportions of students from poor families, not only do the teachers face a heightened frequency and intensity of the multiple obstacles to learning catalogued earlier, but the students also lack the support, the modeling, and the expectations that better-off students and their families bring to the classroom. The obstacles facing these urban core schools are daunting, and it is perhaps unsurprising that repeated waves of reform have produced only scattered examples of significant accomplishment.

Legal Education

In many respects, law schools are at the opposite end of the educational continuum from the schools serving the children of the urban core. Despite some recent challenges, most are reasonably – and many are quite generously – resourced. Their faculties are extraordinarily qualified and often gifted. They attract students with strong skills and high levels of commitment, and they are able to channel most of those students into successful professional careers.

Yet there is growing concern, coming from a wide range of voices (including some of the same voices that are troubled by the state of legal scholarship), that law schools, and the pedagogy that has predominated in them for the past century and a half, are failing in their primary function of preparing new lawyers for their professional roles.[10] Much of this concern has focused on the question of whether law schools are teaching students the things they actually will need in their new roles – whether they are equipping them with the knowledge and the skills that practicing lawyers actually use. Another dimension of concern asks about the effectiveness of the tools preferred by the legal academy, and particularly the dominant case-based, "Socratic" pedagogy, as a way to introduce students into their future profession.

In almost all American law schools, the primary curricular focus remains on a familiar set of "doctrinal" courses, designed to introduce students simultaneously to core elements of the legal rules and principles governing major areas of lawyerly endeavor and to the standard analytic and argumentative strategies that lawyers use

[10] *See, e.g.*, Harry T. Edward, *The Growing Disjunction between Legal Education and the Legal Profession*, 91 MICH. L. REV. 34, 34 (1992); Robin West, *Teaching Law: Justice, Politics, and the Demands of Professionalism* 7–11 (2014); *Amer. Bar Ass'n Sect. of Legal Educ. & Admission to the Bar, Legal Education and Professional Development – An Educational Continuum* 3 (1992) (*MacCrate Report*).

in applying the law to factual settings.[11] This focus is particularly pronounced in the largely mandatory first-year curriculum, which is in many respects the most impactful phase of students' legal education – in framing their understanding of the law and lawyering, in titrating their future career opportunities, and in holding their close attention before other activities and interests diminish their focus on classes in the subsequent years of law school.

While many of the professors teaching these courses have adopted a variety of strategies to expand the range of materials, activities, and skills addressed, the courses continue to focus primarily on study of appellate cases (often heavily edited) and on the use of "Socratic" discussion interspersed with faculty lecture to unpack these materials.[12] The primary task of the students in these courses is to develop the ability to extract possible rules and principles from the cases (and from other "primary" authorities, such as the Federal Rules of Civil Procedure or the Uniform Commercial Code) and to frame arguments about the application of those rules and principles to varying fact patterns. Student performance is primarily evaluated on the basis of a single final examination, predominantly designed to assess the students' success in learning the relevant rule structure and argumentation about its application.

This familiar pedagogy is arguably quite effective, at least for many students, in introducing them to significant doctrinal content and in developing their skills in the extraction and manipulation of those doctrinal materials ("thinking like a lawyer," in the familiar, if problematic, parlance). But, as students of legal education have increasingly observed, it also neglects or undervalues much of what an emergent lawyer needs to learn and much of what employers of beginning lawyers need them to know. And it also has a range of troubling impacts on the way students come to perceive the legal system and their place within it.

In recent years, arguments that legal education must become more focused on engaging and training students for the actual work that lawyers do and more attentive to the social and ethical roles of law and lawyers have gained increasing prominence.[13] The central argument of the 2007 Carnegie Report, which has become a centerpiece of contemporary discussion of the challenges of American legal education, is that effective professional training should include a balanced

[11] *See, e.g.*, A. Benjamin Spencer, *The Law School Critique in Historical Perspective*, 69 Wash. & Lee L. Rev. 1949, 1958 (2012); Jamie R. Abrams, *Reframing the Socratic Method*, 64 J. Legal Educ. 562, 563 (2015).

[12] Compelling evidence of the continuing dominance of the Socratic method, drawn from sociolinguistic study of multiple law-school courses, is provided in Elizabeth Mertz, *The Language of Law School* (2007).

[13] The most prominent recent statement of this argument came in the so-called Carnegie Report. William M. Sullivan et al., *Educating Lawyers: Preparation for the Profession of Law* (2007). *See also, e.g.*, Beverly Petersen Jennison, *Beyond Langdell: Innovating in Legal Education*, 62 Cath. U.L. Rev. 643 (2013). For a suggestion that these concerns have a lengthy history in legal education, *see* Spencer, *supra* Note 11.

mixture of three crucial "apprenticeships," whereas current law school education concentrates predominantly on just one of those apprenticeships.

In the Carnegie Report's framing, the first apprenticeship, the intellectual or cognitive apprenticeship, focuses on the subject-area knowledge and the modes of thinking and analysis that are appropriate to the particular profession. The second, the apprenticeship of practice, moves from theory to application; it involves learning from expert practitioners how the cognitive content and methods of the profession are used in effectively addressing the needs of actual or simulated clients. Finally, the apprenticeship of identity and purpose, or the apprenticeship of professionalism, which, like the second apprenticeship, draws on experiential engagement in the practice of the profession, focuses on the values that guide the profession and the ethical and societal norms that inform community expectations of the members of the profession.[14]

The Carnegie Report's primary critique of legal education, in line with those of many other critics, is that law schools, unlike many other graduate professional schools, focus almost exclusively on the cognitive apprenticeship, tossing in only occasional (and often marginalized) nods to the other apprenticeships. But in fact, the problem is even deeper than that, because law schools, in their almost exclusive reliance (especially in the crucial first year curriculum) on appellate cases as the sources of legal knowledge, limit the cognitive apprenticeship to only a particular subset of the cognitive content that underlies legal practice, a subset that prioritizes doctrine and application of law to facts as the essential content and method for the profession.

One of the most troubling aspects of the prevailing law school pedagogy is that it not only fails to provide students with the full range of competencies (or even a recognition of that full range of competencies) needed for effective practice of law, but it also presents them with a distorted and unrealistic conception of what law is and of how the legal system operates within the larger societal structure of which it is one important part. In consequence, the dominant pedagogy leads many students to experience law and lawyering (or at least law schools' conception of them) as out of touch and disconnected from the world as they experience it and from their expectations about their future professional roles.

A primary goal of the case law method is to teach students how to move from the specific factual setting of a particular case to the rules – or, more typically in the post-realist legal academy, to the range of possible rules – that can be extracted from the case and applied to different factual settings. Central to this process is the stripping away of the specific factual and social context of the particular case (much of which has, of course, already been stripped away in the judicial process that leads to the

[14] *See* Sullivan et al., *supra* Note 13 at 28 (defining the three apprenticeships with reference to professional education in general).

appellate opinion on which the class focuses).[15] Then, once the possible rules have been distilled from their context, another central goal is to familiarize students with a range of argumentative strategies for deploying those rules (applying them, distinguishing them, extending them, etc.) to support various possible outcomes in new factual situations, in which process those new factual situations likewise must be stripped of much of their factual and social context.

Of course, many contemporary professors put considerable time and energy into "problematizing" this decontextualized focus on rules and arguments. We repeatedly remind students of the social context, of the features that are submerged in the cases, of the practical consequences of and limitations on judicial interventions. And we invite students to consider the policy implications and the political underpinnings of choices of rules and applications of them. But, as Elizabeth Mertz has carefully documented, these discussions of societal context and policy implications are consistently presented in a way that implicitly signals their secondary importance for the students' learning.[16] And a host of cues inform the students that these dimensions of the class will not be significantly tested on the final exam or weighed in the evaluation of students' performance. Students quickly learn that they're supposed to be focusing on "the rules" and their manipulation, not on context or "policy."

What lessons do students take away from the pervasive focus on rule distillation and application? Several responses are natural and common, each of which can contribute to students' experience of law school's version of the legal system as alien from their prior observations and their aspirations.

For one, the emphasis on the identification and manipulation of rules characterizes the law as formal and abstract, and the work of lawyers as predominantly analytical and logic-based. Appeals to values and societal consequences are relegated to a secondary role that can leave students wondering where (or whether) law derives its moral authority. For Langdell and the early practitioners of the case law method, this disconnection was central to uncovering the objective, "scientific" character of the law.[17] But even for post-realist and critically oriented teachers of recent decades, who wish to expose the rules as indeterminate, inconsistent, and manipulable, the primary focus is on the argumentative moves and countermoves.

More concretely, the reasoning in the cases, and the modes of argumentation that students are guided toward, seem systematically decoupled from the dynamics of power, class, race, and gender that students recognize as crucial determinants of

[15] *See* Mertz, *supra* Note 12 at, *e.g.*, 5, 131–33. *See also* Oliver W. Holmes, Jr., *The Path of the Law*, 10 Harv. L. Rev. 457, 457–58 (1897) (observing the centrality in "legal thought" of "eliminating all the dramatic elements with which [the] client's story has clothed it, and retaining only the facts of legal import").

[16] *See* Mertz, *supra* Note 12 at, *e.g.*, 75–79 (discussing the marginalization of social and policy concerns); *id.* at 115–24 (discussing the marginalization of aspects of identity and of ethical norms).

[17] *See* C. C. Langdell, *Selection of Cases on the Law of Contracts* viii–ix (1879). *See generally* Morton J. Horwitz, *The Transformation of American Law 1870–1960* at 9–20 (1992).

actual legal outcomes in the real world around them. Whether and how rule manipulation can actually affect these practical power relationships (and how the actual power relationships infiltrate the rule systems) remain largely an undiscussed mystery. Many students find themselves perplexed about how law as they're learning it in their classes relates to law as it operates in everyday life, and about what they, as lawyers, will be expected to do to help clients to use the law to navigate in the world.

For a substantial number of students, especially those who have not grown up or worked among lawyers, the disconnection between the focus of their classes and their prior exposure to the legal system results in disorientation and confusion.[18] Rarely are faculty deliberately seeking to disorient or confuse their students, but these effects are far from an accidental feature of the Socratic method. Indeed one of the reasons that the pedagogy of law school classes is called "Socratic" is surely its sharing of the Socratic perspective that rigorous questioning leads to knowledge only by first producing a recognition of the student's (and perhaps even the teacher's) deep ignorance.[19] One of the implicit goals of the accepted pedagogy is to reveal to students how little novices understand about the nature of the law and about what lawyers do, and thus to cleanse them in preparation for their initiation into the mysteries of the profession.

The alienating effects of law school pedagogy are often particularly pronounced for students of color and other students from societally marginalized groups, and similarly for students who come to law school seeking opportunities to advance social justice.[20] These students are particularly likely to have encountered examples of the ways that the law, in practice, is influenced by dynamics of power, race, and class, and are particularly likely to be perplexed or frustrated by a pedagogy that discounts these influences. And these students are often particularly susceptible to a sense of not belonging or not being fully accepted in the elite atmosphere of professional education, feelings that are easily triggered by the Socratic techniques that discount the understandings of and experiences with the legal system that entering students bring to law school.

Thus, the prevailing approaches of contemporary law schools fall short in at least two respects. First, they introduce students to only a restricted range of the skills and knowledge that students will need to become effective attorneys. And second, even in the areas of knowledge and skills on which they do focus, their pedagogy presents

[18] Mertz provides both vivid examples and careful explication of the mechanics behind this disorientation. *See* Mertz, *supra* Note 12 at, *e.g.*, 7–11, 133–35.

[19] Meno famously compared the effect of Socrates' questioning to the numbing produced by the sting of a poisonous fish. Plato, *Meno* at 12 (trans. J. Holbo & B. Waring 2002). *See also* Mary Joe Frug, *Re-Reading Contracts: A Feminist Analysis of a Contracts Casebook*, 34 AM. U. L. REV. 1065, 1106 (1985) (describing the disorienting and alienating effects of starting the Contracts course with the study of remedies).

[20] Mertz, in her sociolinguistic study of first-year Contracts classes, provides both a helpful summary of the evidence of the alienating effects of the law school experience on minorities and women and rich insights into the pedagogical elements that contribute to it. *See* Mertz, *supra* Note 12 at 174–203.

students with a narrow and distorted view of the ways that law actually functions within the larger societal contexts that clients will expect their lawyers to help them navigate. In part, these shortcomings reflect legal education's narrow emphasis on learning legal rules and their application. In part, they result from over-reliance on appellate decisions as the primary focus, when only a tiny fraction of the work lawyers actually do will ever end up in an appellate court. And in part, they derive from the continuing dominance of Socratic dialogue as the paradigm for student learning. Together, these pedagogical choices, remarkably persistent since the days of C. C. Langdell, leave too many students frustrated by their law school experiences and inadequately prepared to enter their chosen profession.

NORTHEASTERN'S SOCIAL JUSTICE PROGRAM

Northeastern's development of its program of Social Justice Projects as a signature element of its first-year curriculum was designed to respond to these shortcomings of legal education. The projects themselves have ranged over a wide array of issues and interests. But a substantial number of them, over the years, have addressed the challenges faced by schools serving the urban core, while many others have targeted a range of the other challenges that bedevil poor and marginalized urban communities and populations. The impact of the program on legal education at Northeastern has been profound. The impact on the challenges of the urban core, and particularly of schools serving the urban core, has, unsurprisingly, been modest, but in many respects positive.

Origins and Goals

Northeastern's Social Justice Program is the product of a gradual (and continuing) evolution over the past quarter-century. But it had its origins in student dissatisfaction with the first-year curriculum, which crystallized, early in the 1990s, in a student boycott of one of the first-year criminal law courses, organized by a coalition of students of color in response to their perception that the course was systematically disconnected from the racial and social realities dominating the criminal justice system and lurking – but largely unexamined – just beneath the surface of the cases the course studied. Among the students' demands was that the first-year curriculum be augmented to ensure closer attention to the social dynamics that interpenetrate the workings of the legal system in the real world.

The faculty response was the introduction of a new course into the mandatory first-year program, called "Law, Culture and Difference," whose goal was to supplement the more traditional first-year doctrinal and skills courses with some focused attention on the ways that societal realities, and particularly power differentials among different social groups, influenced and were influenced by law's content and application. In its early years, the course went through a series of experiments, drawing on guest presentations, faculty lectures, and small group discussions, largely drawing on examples of law reform challenges related to one or more of the traditional first-year substantive courses. But none of these experiments met great success in moving the program's concerns beyond a relatively marginal place in the first-year experience, until the innovation of adding real-world projects on behalf of community-based client organizations to the program, an innovation that, from the outset, was a topic of much faculty controversy, both about the capacity of first-year students to take on such representational responsibilities competently and about the costs of diverting student attention from the more traditional foci of the first-year program.

With the introduction of these social justice projects, which initially were only one element in the Law, Culture, and Difference program's broader (and pedagogically more traditional) curriculum, the program took a quantum leap in its efficacy and perceived importance.[21] Over the ensuing years, the projects have taken on an increasingly central role in the program, and the project-based social justice program has emerged as a signature element of Northeastern's first-year curriculum.[22] The social justice projects provided a critical energy and focus that finally gave life to the piece of the curriculum whose absence had been the target of the earlier student protests.

In the course of its evolution, the Social Justice Program has sought to serve a wide and shifting set of goals, all tied to the concerns behind the precipitating student protests, about the disconnection between the law school classroom and the social realities with which practicing lawyers (and their clients) are engaged. But, over the years, the key goals have gradually clarified, and, a few years ago, a group of faculty connected to the program came up with a statement that distilled out a set of three primary and three supporting goals of the Program, as follows:

A. Primary Goals:

1. Placing/keeping the law in its social context through detailed engagement with a single complex legal problem that can expose students to how legal issues are embedded in a rich array of social institutions and relationships.

[21] Primary credit for the concept of the social justice projects and for implementation of the concept belongs to Northeastern's dean at that time, David Hall, and to Professor Susan Maze-Rothstein, who for nearly two decades managed the program, first as a part-time instructor and subsequently as a full-time faculty member and program director. A number of other Northeastern faculty have contributed importantly to the growth and development of the program over the years, including Lucy Williams, James Rowan, Lois Kanter, Mary O'Connell, Hemanth Gundavaram, Gabriel Arkles, Margaret Hahn-Dupont, and the author of this chapter. As I discuss later, the program is now in the able hands of a dedicated team of seven faculty, for whom the integrated first-year skills program is their primary teaching responsibility.

[22] To see how Northeastern depicts the program on its website, visit Northeastern University School of Law, Legal Skills in Social Context, www.northeastern.edu/law/experience/lssc/index.html (last visited Oct. 9, 2018).

2. Introducing students to facets of the lawyer's representational role and the dynamics of lawyering as a service to a client.[23]
3. Providing the opportunity to develop and practice emerging legal skills – problem definition, issue identification, research (both legal and factual), reasoning, analysis, written and oral presentation – in a collaborative experiential setting.

B. Supporting Goals:

4. Appreciating law's social impacts, and law's reflection of social power dynamics, with particular attention to the impacts on marginalized populations.
5. Exploring the strengths and weaknesses of law as an instrument of social change.
6. Developing and reflecting on the skills needed to manage a complex project as part of a diverse team.

The most significant recent development in the continuing evolution of the Social Justice Program has been the integration of the program with the other, more traditional elements of Northeastern's first-year skills program, into a single Legal Skills in Social Context course. In this current iteration, a member of the program's seven-person faculty guides each section of first-year students through a range of both simulated and real-world assignments that introduce the students both to the customary skill set of first-year skills courses (legal research, analysis, and both objective and persuasive legal writing) and to the challenges of working as a team to address the situational needs of an external organizational partner.

The Program's Design

Throughout the evolution of the Program, one element has remained at its core: focusing the students' work around an actual societal/legal problem brought to the program by an outside organization seeking the Program's assistance. Over the years, the Program has developed relationships (some limited to a single project, others extending to multiple projects over multiple years) with a wide range of partner organizations, drawing on our alumni, faculty networks, and Northeastern's network of cooperative employers.[24] A few examples include the Lawyers' Committee for

[23] In fact, while the program does pay close attention to the dynamics of lawyering as a service to the client, it pays particular attention to the role of lawyers in social change efforts and to the particular dynamics involved in working with organizations that seek systemic reform for marginalized communities.

[24] Under Northeastern's cooperative (or coop) system, all law students spend four academic quarters during their second and third years working full-time for a legal employer. While some of these placements are arranged individually by students, the law school maintains

Civil Rights and Economic Justice, Greater Boston Legal Services, the Innocence Project of New Orleans, and the Massachusetts Department of Public Health.[25] Many partner organizations are from New England, but others are located around the country, and in several cases around the world. They include organizations that provide legal services to marginalized communities, a wide range of advocacy and policy-focused organizations, and some governmental agencies. Some primarily do legal work, while others have no attorneys on staff. What they have in common is that they come to the Social Justice Program with an issue that has a significant legal dimension that they need assistance in addressing, and that significantly impacts an underserved or marginalized group.

Projects are selected for each year by the Program's faculty, on the basis of proposals submitted by potential partner organizations. The proposals include a brief description of the proposed project, of how it relates to the organization's work, and of the work the organization has done on the issue to date. Program faculty often spend considerable time working with potential partner organizations to sharpen the focus of the proposal to better fit the program's capabilities and to ensure a good match with the program's pedagogical objectives.[26] Because the projects are conducted by first-year students, albeit with intensive support and supervision, the program does not undertake projects that involve the rendering of legal advice or representation to individual clients. Rather, the projects generally involve more general issues or policies, often involving systemic reforms, that will help the partner organization in performing its functions (which in many cases do involve legal representation of individuals).

In the next section, I will provide some detail about three recent projects dealing with issues of urban schools. But, more generally, typical projects have included, among others, research and analysis in support of contemplated or pending impact litigation, review of best practices and/or strategic options for addressing a particular issue, development of popular education materials about legal rights in a field, and development of legislative or regulatory proposals.[27] To date, the program has completed more than 300 projects, covering a broad range of issue areas,[28] although, as part of the recent integration of the program into a comprehensive legal skills

ongoing relationships with some 1,500 coop employers, including a wide range of public interest, nonprofit, and governmental organizations.

25 For a more extensive listing of partner organizations, *see* www.northeastern.edu/law/pdfs/experience/lssc/orgs-2018.pdf.

26 In recent years, Northeastern has introduced an upper-level seminar course, Dynamic Lawyering for Systemic Change, which serves as an incubator for project proposals that need significant further development and analysis before they are sufficiently focused for adoption as social justice projects.

27 For a typology of projects, see the pie chart at www.northeastern.edu/law/experience/lssc/index.html.

28 For brief descriptions of a representative sampling of the projects undertaken in the program to date, *see* www.northeastern.edu/law/experience/lssc/abstracts.html.

course, each faculty member in the program is planning to concentrate primarily on projects in a particular field, to enable development of supporting simulations and exercises relating to that field that can be used consistently over a number of projects.

Incoming first-year law students are divided into small sections, referred to as "law offices," typically with about a dozen students in each. The entire first-year skills curriculum is conducted in these law-office sections, and each law office undertakes a particular social justice project. Until a couple of years ago, the more traditional skills curriculum was delivered by dedicated skills faculty, while the social justice project portion of the program was primarily led by competitively selected upper-level students ("lawyering fellows") who were themselves closely supervised by the program director together with several general law-school faculty who took on aspects of the supervisory role as part of their overall teaching package. Over the last few years, we have recruited a new team of faculty for the program, each of whom is responsible for the entire skills curriculum for two law offices, integrating the usual legal skills components with the work on the project, while student lawyering fellows continue to provide significant support for the students' work.[29]

While some elements of the skills curriculum involve each student doing her or his own work and being individually assessed on it, the social justice projects are explicitly structured as team projects, to be conducted by the full law office or to be divided among subgroups of the office. This team-based structure was dictated largely by the practical limitations on supervisory capacity, while having the entire first-year class involved in producing real work for real partner organizations. But the opportunity to support students in learning how to function effectively as parts of a diverse team managing a complex project has proven to be one of the significant benefits of the program.

Students are introduced to their projects, typically by means of the project proposal and some materials about the partner organization, at the very beginning of the fall semester. Early in the fall, after some modest initial background research, the law office meets with one or more representatives of the partner organization to initiate what will typically become an ongoing discussion between law office and partner about the specific goals and scope of the project. The law office then collaborates in designing, implementing, and iteratively refining a research agenda for the project, with the support of the office's faculty, its lawyering fellows, and often other faculty, library staff, or outside advisers with subject-matter expertise. The research typically includes both typical legal research, focused on cases, statutes, regulations, and legal secondary sources, and factual research into the real-world conditions being addressed by the project, drawn from a diverse range of sources, from nonlegal academic writings to field observations and interviews. This emphasis on combining "legal" research with factual research is one of the distinctive features

[29] The three projects described all pre-date this transition.

of the program, and serves both to expose students to a wider range of the skills that lawyers will use in practice and to ensure that students experience the connection between their law school work and the real-world contexts in which the law operates.

As the research continues, the law office frequently discovers the need to revise the framing of the project to respond effectively to the partner organization's goals (which themselves often are evolving, whether in response to changing external circumstances or to the information being gathered by the law office) and to fit the capacity of the team and its timelines. The resulting interactions between organizational partner and law office are another opportunity for a kind of student learning and engagement that only such a real-world project can provide. Often, this phase of the project work provides opportunities for students to produce, both individually and in small groups, a variety of written products to memorialize and share their work.

Over the course of the year, intermingled with the project work (in addition to the simulation-based work on the standard repertoire of legal skills) are a range of readings, discussions, and activities designed to allow students to reflect on the challenges they are encountering and the skills they are developing though the project. During the years when the social justice program was largely being delivered by upper-level students, these elements were uniform for all of the law offices. In the current program, individual faculty select materials to fit their own projects and approaches. Among the topics frequently addressed are the challenges of lawyer–client communication, especially across boundaries of social difference;[30] alternative approaches to representational roles (client-centered, cause-focused, etc.);[31] the roles of imagery and story-telling in legal argumentation;[32] the impact of societal power distributions on the practical operation of "neutral" legal rules; and strategies for addressing such non-neutrality.[33]

[30] For some examples of readings used for this theme, *see* Lucie E. White, *Subordination, Rhetorical Survival Skills, and Sunday Shoes: Notes on the Hearing of Mrs. G.*, 38 Buff. L. Rev. 1 (1990); Nelson P. Miller, *Beyond Bias: Cultural Competence as a Lawyering Skill*, 87 Mich. B.J. 38 (2008).

[31] Examples include Betty Hung, *Movement Lawyering as Rebellious Lawyering: Advocating with Humility, Love and Courage*, 23 Clinical L. Rev. 663 (2017); William P. Quigley, *Revolutionary Lawyering: Addressing the Root Causes of Poverty and Wealth*, 20 Wash. U. J. L. & Pol'y 101 (2006); Charles Elsesser, *Community Lawyering: The Role of Lawyers in the Social Justice Movement*, 14 Loy. J. Pub. Int. L. 375 (2013).

[32] Examples include Lucy A. Williams, *Race, Rat Bites, and Unfit Mothers: How Media Discourse Informs Welfare Legislation Debate*, 22 Fordham Urb. L.J. 1159 (2011); Keith Cunningham-Parmeter, *Alien Language: Immigration Metaphors and the Jurisprudence of Otherness*, 79 Fordham L. Rev. 1545 (2011).

[33] Examples include Ian Haney Lopez, *White by Law: The Legal Construction of Race* (1996); Marc Galanter, *Why the "Haves" Come Out Ahead: Speculations on the Limits of Legal Change*, 9 Law & Soc'y Rev. 95 (1974).

At the beginning of the spring semester, Northeastern sets aside several days, before other classes commence, as a social justice project intensive period, during which law offices devote full-time to moving the project forward. As the spring semester proceeds, law offices, while typically continuing some aspects of their research, increasingly focus on producing successive drafts of what will result, by mid-semester, in a final written product for the project. These final products almost always include a detailed, and carefully documented, report for the partner organization (often running to over a hundred pages), but they also often include a variety of other materials, such as popular education materials, web-site content, draft legislation, training manuals, etc. Each of these products is refined through multiple drafts, with extensive review and feedback both from peers in the law office and from faculty, lawyering fellows, outside advisers, and, in some cases, representatives of the partner organization.

Particularly in the program's early years, many faculty (myself included) had grave doubts about the appropriateness of delivering first-year student work to outside organizations (including many without substantial legal capacity of their own) who were going to rely on that work in guiding their own conduct. Were we modeling appropriate standards for professional responsibility, we worried. But experience has largely laid these concerns to rest (at least for me). With only occasional exceptions, the quality of the work produced by the law offices has been remarkable – highly responsive to the partner organization's concerns, carefully researched, intelligently analyzed, thoroughly documented (and fact- and cite-checked), and at least reasonably well presented. And in the cases of the occasional exceptions, we have been able to deliver the materials to the partner organizations with appropriate caveats, and in some cases with supportive follow-up. The somewhat surprising quality of these final products reflects several factors – the intelligence and skills that the students admitted by a competitive law school bring with them on arrival; the intensive supervision and support that the program provides; and, most intriguing to me, the extraordinary ways in which the diverse skills of a group of students, at least a group with appropriate support in learning to function effectively as a team, allow it to far outperform any of its individual members.[34]

As a final program capstone, each law office, a few weeks after completion of its written product, produces an hour-long oral presentation to representatives of the partner organization, interested members of the law school community,[35] and,

[34] For those who, like me, are intrigued by this capacity of teams to outperform their members by drawing on the diverse abilities of those members, a fascinating, non-human example of these dynamics can be found in Jennifer Ackerman, *The Genius of Birds* 247–53 (2016) (describing how variations among its members enhance a bird flock's ability to respond effectively to environmental changes).

[35] Actually, as one of the program requirements, each first-year student is required to attend the presentations of at least two other law offices. The presentations are also publicized to, and often attended by, law school faculty and staff and upper-level students.

where the organizational partner deems it appropriate, interested members of the larger community as well. These presentations, typically supported by increasingly sophisticated audio-visual technology, often provide a valuable opportunity for the law office to step back and place its work in a broader, less technical setting, and also support the development of students' oral and presentation skills. At the conclusion of the presentation, the law office, the representatives of the partner organization, faculty, and other project advisers spend an additional hour debriefing the project and assessing the experience from the perspectives of both the students and the partner organization.

Three Examples

To put a bit more flesh on this bare-bones description of the program, and to give some sense of what difference the projects can make, what follow are brief descriptions of three recent projects (all of which I supervised) addressing various dimensions of the challenges facing schools that serve students from the urban core.

Expanding Access to Vocational/Technical Education

In Massachusetts, high school students are supposed to have the choice of whether to attend a regular academically focused high school or a vocational/technical program, which integrates the state's academic requirements with training in a chosen career path. Vocational/technical education is primarily provided through dedicated vocational high schools, operated either by individual school districts or by regional consortia of local districts. However, in recent years, thousands of students who sought to attend their districts' vocational schools were unable to enroll in them, with many placed on wait-lists because of insufficient capacity in their district's or region's vocational school. The preponderance of the students unable to pursue vocational/technical education came from at-risk populations – minority students, students from low-income families, students whose first language is not English, and students who live in the state's poor cities. For many of these students, the inability to attend a vocational school contributed to academic failure and lost economic opportunity.

This problem was brought to the Social Justice Program by the Massachusetts Communities Action Network (MCAN), a recurrent partner organization in the program. MCAN is the umbrella organization for a network of faith-based community organizations working for economic and social justice through community organizing. Its affiliated organizations are situated in seven of the state's poor, urban centers.[36] The issue about access to vocational education emerged as a pressing concern for members of a number of MCAN's local affiliates, and MCAN's

[36] For more background on MCAN, see its website at www.mcan-pico.org/about-mcan.

leadership had started to build relationships in the vocational education community to explore the dimensions of the problem and possible solutions, but they needed assistance in more fully understanding the legal dimensions of the issue.

During the 2013–14 academic year, MCAN's project was assigned to one of the Program's law offices. I was the faculty supervisor for the project, working together with two lawyering fellows who had both been educators before law school (and both of whom have gone on into careers on the boundaries between law and urban schools), as well as another faculty member with expertise in education law.

In its initial project proposal and the early discussions about project scope, MCAN asked that, to the extent possible, the law office research several topics: the scope of the existing gap between available vocational school opportunities and student demand; factors contributing to the gap, including an analysis of the state funding mechanisms for vocational schools; possible legal claims challenging the present situation, based on the state's obligations under the federal "No Child Left Behind" law; best practices for the provision of vocational education in other states; and proposed changes in Massachusetts law and policy to address the gap. This was a dauntingly broad agenda. And, as the students began their research, they quickly identified at least two more legal arguments, which appeared at least as promising as the No Child Left Behind law argument – the state's obligation, under the Massachusetts constitution's education clause, to meet the educational needs of all children, and a possible violation of Title VI of the federal Civil Rights Act of 1964 if the state's policies had the effect of providing more limited vocational educational opportunities to minority students.

So, while it conducted its initial background research, the law office worked with MCAN to sharpen the focus of its work, in order to best match the students' capacities with the organization's needs. This process is a common feature of many social justice projects, and one of the respects in which the program introduces students to a critical dimension of legal work rarely explored in law school courses. Even at the end of this winnowing process, the law office's agenda remained an ambitious one, including the following components:

- Analyze and explain the state's system for funding vocational education, and identify ways the funding system contributed to the capacity gap in poorer districts.
- Conduct a survey of vocational schools, working in collaboration with the state association of vocational school administrators, to define the size and composition of wait-lists for admission.
- Analyze and assess the three possible grounds for a legal challenge to the limits on access to vocational education (state constitution, federal civil rights law, federal education law).
- Identify possible changes in state law and policy to address the inadequate access to vocational schools for children from poor districts.

Over the course of the year, the law office achieved remarkable success in addressing each of these items. Along the way, the students had the opportunity to develop and refine a wide array of research skills. For each of the threads (although only minimally for the exploration of possible legal challenges), they needed to identify and build constructive relationships with a wide range of stakeholders and experts and to conduct effective interviews with them. They gathered and analyzed large bodies of factual information, both in designing, conducting, and analyzing the wait-list survey and in exploring and explaining the state education department's voluminous data on vocational school funding. They researched and analyzed a wide range of more traditionally legal sources, including state and federal statutes and constitutions and case law interpreting them, regulations (particularly in the Title VI research, where federal Department of Education regulatory materials were of primary importance), and sub-regulatory materials (particularly in the No Child Left Behind research, where the state's elaborate waiver agreement with the Department of Education was the primary operative source of law).

Applying this massive body of research to MCAN's objectives provided additional rich opportunities for learning. Each of the three more narrowly legal issues raised complex questions both about the strength of the legal arguments and about the procedural paths available for pursuing them, points on which the law office at times had to grapple with conflicting guidance from their faculty and other expert advisers. Identifying realistic reforms for MCAN to pursue required nuanced assessment not only of the likely effects of potential reforms but also of the political environment and of the barriers to change. The program encourages law offices to think, not only about the legal arguments but also about how to identify and address the challenges of framing and social setting that often impede reform. For example, this law office identified the frequent tendency to distinguish "vocational education" from "regular education" as an impediment to increased support for the vocational "alternative," and, in its report, reframed the non-vocational alternative as "college-centric education," while including vivid stories and descriptions about the benefits and efficacy of vocational schools. And, of course, the work on numerous preliminary memos and multiple drafts, with iterative feedback both from peers and from supporting faculty and lawyering fellows, provided the students ample opportunities to develop their writing and editing skills.

The end result was a rich, careful, and meticulously documented seventy-page white paper, accompanied by multiple appendices with supporting detail. MCAN has used the report both to clarify its work on this issue and to raise its prominence in Massachusetts policy discussions. The law office's documentation of the size of the wait-lists was the focus of a major story in the *Boston Globe*,[37] and the vocational school wait-list has now become a prominent and persistent topic of policy maker

[37] *See* Megan Woolhouse, *Schools' Wait Lists Called a Drag on the Economy*, BOSTON GLOBE, Sept. 15, 2014 at B1.

and advocate attention. Drawing on the law office's report, which MCAN shared widely with stakeholders and advocates, MCAN has taken a leadership role in building an umbrella of interested groups, the Alliance for Vocational Technical Education, which is pressing for legislative and regulatory changes to address the issues.[38] Although no steps have been taken to pursue the legal challenges analyzed in the report, the possibility of a state constitutional challenge or of engagement with the Department of Education's Office of Civil Rights over the Title VI claim continue to be topics of conversation within the advocate community.[39] While the law office's work has not yet contributed to meaningful reforms, it has played a significant role in raising the prominence of the issue and in shaping the discussion of it.

Funding Extended-Day Programming

The students attending schools in the urban core commonly arrive at school far less ready to learn than their peers in wealthier communities. Many of them have limited English-language skills, are dealing with challenges in their health, housing, nutrition, and family stability, and have had far less exposure to experiences that prepare them for success in school.[40] These gaps only grow wider as their education continues. During their school years, students from upper-income families spend far more time each year engaging with caring adults and participating in enriching experiences outside of the classroom than do children from low-income households.[41] Upper-income families spend some $6,600 annually on out-of-school enrichment opportunities for their children, some nine times more than lower income families can.[42] These disparities in opportunities contribute significantly to the gaps in achievement, both in school and beyond.

One widely recommended strategy to address these gaps is to provide expanded learning opportunities to the children in poor schools, whether by extending the school year, by extending the regular school day, or by offering enrichment opportunities that extend beyond regular classes. Citizen Schools is a nonprofit organization that organizes and manages extended learning opportunities in selected urban schools in a number of states. It focuses on middle schools, where it believes the

[38] The Alliance's website is at: http://allianceforvoceducation.org/.

[39] The third legal argument assessed by the law office, grounded in the state's obligations under the federal No Child Left Behind law, was deemed the least promising in the report's analysis, and, in any case, has been rendered moot by the replacement of No Child Left Behind in 2015 by the Every Student Succeeds Act, Pub. L. No. 114–95, 129 Stat. 1802 (2015).

[40] *See, e.g.*, PUTNAM, *supra* Note 2 at 135–90 (2015); Matthew Desmond, *Why Work Doesn't Work Anymore*, N.Y. TIMES (Sept. 16), 2018, at 36.

[41] *See, e.g.*, Neeraj Kaushal et al., How Is Family Income Related to Investments in Children's Learning?, *in Whither Opportunity?* (Duncan & Murnane, eds.) at 187, 187–88; Pamela R. Bennett et al., *Beyond the Schoolyard: The Role of Parenting Logics, Financial Resources, and Social Institutions in the Social Class Gap in Structured Activity Participation*, 85 SOCIOLOGY OF EDUC. 131, 131–57 (2012).

[42] PUTNAM, *supra* Note 2 at 125.

opportunity for impact is greatest. Its programs, which operate at the end of the school day, rely on adult volunteers, drawn from businesses and professions, who draw on their interests and knowledge to provide ten-week-long experiential educational programs that help students build skills while exposing them to career opportunities and models of professional success.

Citizen Schools, like other providers of extended learning opportunities, depends on a mix of philanthropic support and public funding, and limited resources have constrained the number of schools and students it can reach. So, in the 2014–15 academic year, Citizen Schools proposed a social justice project to analyze state funding of education in the seven states where the program was in operation[43] and to identify strategies for Citizen Schools and its allies to advocate for increased state funding for extended learning time programs in those states. The primary goal for the project was to research and explain the funding formulae used in each state to determine state support of school districts and to identify ways to adapt those formulae in order to target funding for extended learning opportunities. Citizen Schools also was interested in identifying legal and political arguments and analogies in each state – including possible arguments deriving from litigation concerning state constitutional rights to education – that could advance legislative or administrative action to increase funding for extended learning opportunities.

The students in the law office divided into sub-groups, each of which took responsibility for two or three of the seven states, so that all of the students would be exposed, not only to detailed research on specific states but also to comparisons between them. Education funding formulae are often the tangled results of long and complicated histories, and both researching and explaining them were challenging tasks, drawing on statutes, regulations, sub-regulatory guidance and administrative materials, secondary literature, and interviews with local experts. In addition, many of the seven states had comparably long and complex histories of litigation involving the state constitutional right to education. Although Citizen Schools was clear that it had no interest in pursuing litigation, it was interested in arguments about possible rights to extended learning time that students in disadvantaged schools might assert under existing or potential judicial decisions, which required both close reading of the case law and creative exploration of possible arguments developing or expanding on the reasoning in the cases.

As work on the project advanced, it became increasingly evident that the structures of the states' education funding formulae were not well suited to revisions that would meet Citizen Schools' goal of providing dedicated funding for extended learning opportunities. So, in consultation with Citizen Schools' leadership, the law office expanded its state-by-state research to include several other dimensions: identification of state grant programs, operating independent of the basic funding

[43] The seven states were California, Illinois, Massachusetts, New Jersey, New York, North Carolina, and Texas.

formula, which might provide funds for extended learning or which might provide models for new grant programs for that purpose; analysis of other areas of educational innovation (such as expansion of early childhood education) for which the state had provided dedicated funding, again as possible models for securing funds for extended learning and for the arguments that had proven politically effective; and assessment of each state's current fiscal condition and political environment. The overall goal was to identify the most promising strategies, in each state, for seeking new funding sources for extended learning programs.

Work on the project provided the students with rich opportunities, not only to develop a wide array of research and communicative skills but also to focus on the ways that legal tools, analysis, and argumentation operate in the context of legislative, administrative, and political decision making. In addition, one of the most rewarding aspects of the project grew from the comparative nature of the work, in which students came to appreciate the powerful impacts of different histories, legal frameworks, and political contexts in the different states on the plausible strategies to pursue in each. These comparisons helped the students to gain a nuanced appreciation of the ways in which legal strategies and opportunities must be responsive to their broader social and political contexts. The strategies that the law office prioritized in its final report varied widely from state to state, reflecting these contextual differences. For example, in a couple of the states, the focus shifted away from ways to affect state funding and instead to ways to influence local school district priority setting and resource allocation, and additional research and analysis were undertaken on that front.

The law office's final product was a white paper, which began with an overview discussion of varying approaches taken toward the design and funding of extended learning opportunities in the seven states and a comparative description of the range of strategies appropriate to advancing the issue in the varying contexts. The report then included ten- to fifteen-page chapters on each state, which filled in the specifics about each state's funding system, its litigation history, its approach to other educational innovations, and its political and fiscal environment, and then used that information to suggest potential paths for advocacy to increase public funding for extended learning opportunities. The report aimed to provide information and strategic advice that would be accessible to nonlegal staff and allies of Citizen Schools to guide them in their strategic planning and advocacy work.

Citizen Schools found that the report provided them with a valuable tool for their efforts to expand funding. The program's executive director wrote, "Their detailed work is thoughtful and insightful. This important research will serve as a key foundation for future work in these seven states ... This research will be utilized by leaders in these states for years to come."[44] To share the law office's work more widely, Citizen Schools invited a member of the law office to deliver a presentation

44 *See* www.northeastern.edu/law/news/announcements/2015/colin-lssc.html.

of the project at a national "summit" conference in the spring of 2015 about extended learning opportunities in low-income communities, and reported that the presentation was very favorably received by the conference participants.

Addressing the Impacts of Traumatic Experiences

One of the particular challenges facing schools that serve the urban core is the high proportion of their students who have been exposed to severely stressful experiences outside of school, and whose behavior and readiness to learn bear the impacts of those experiences. In recent years, research across a range of fields has demonstrated the dramatic impacts of such traumatic experiences on school performance.[45] And the prevalence of what have come to be known as "Adverse Childhood Experiences (ACEs)" among children from disadvantaged backgrounds is extreme. The stress from such experiences in childhood has been shown to have significant consequences on neurological development, and hence on behavior management and learning capacity.[46] The resulting close correlations between frequency of ACEs and a wide range of difficulties in school and in later life are a natural outcome. And in schools with a large number of students with high levels of ACEs and resultant traumatic responses, the functioning of the entire school is inevitably impacted.

Southern Legal Counsel (SLC) is a small, not-for-profit, public interest law firm in Florida, which has turned to Northeastern's social justice program for a number of projects on varying topics. SLC pursues institutional reform, largely through impact litigation, in several fields, including employment discrimination, rights of the homeless, and educational rights, with a particular focus on special education. In the 2015–16 academic year, SLC asked the social justice program to work with them on a new project, focused on the need for a trauma-informed approach to educational services in Florida. Aware of the growing body of evidence about the impact of childhood trauma on students' and schools' performance, SLC sought help in exploring potential legal strategies for ensuring that affected students received services that were responsive to their conditions. SLC staff were aware of a growing body of successful experience, in several states, school districts, and organizations, with "trauma-informed" educational strategies,[47] and sought

[45] *See, e.g.*, Yael Cannon & Andrew Hsi, *Disrupting the Path from Childhood Trauma to Juvenile Justice: An Upstream Health and Justice Approach*, 43 Fordham Urb. L.J. 425, 426 (2016).

[46] *See, e.g.*, Charles A. Nelson III & Margaret A. Sheridan, Lessons from Neuroscience Research for Understanding Causal Links between Family and Neighborhood Characteristics and Educational Outcomes, *in Whither Opportunity?* (Duncan & Murnane, eds.) at 27, 35–36; Lois A. Weithorn, *Developmental Neuroscience, Children's Relationships with Primary Caregivers, and Child Protection Policy Reform*, 63 Hastings L.J. 1487, 1522–23 (2012).

[47] The leading national examples of state-level efforts to implement trauma-informed models of public school education at the time were Washington State and Massachusetts. *See* Mass. Dept. of Elem. & Secondary Educ., *Safe and Supportive Schools*, www.doe.mass.edu/sfs/safety/ (describing implementation of the Mass. Safe & Supportive Schools Act of 2014); Ray Wolpow et al., *The Heart of Learning and Teaching: Compassion, Resiliency, and Academic Success* 81–125 (2011) (describing Washington State's trauma-informed education system). *See generally*

assistance in identifying ways to advance the implementation of such strategies in Florida schools.

SLC's initial focus was on possible litigation strategies grounded in federal disabilities rights laws – the Individuals with Disabilities Education Act (IDEA), Section 504 of the Rehabilitation Act of 1973, and the Americans with Disabilities Act (ADA) – and their Florida law counterparts. They sought an analysis of the relationships between childhood trauma and disability, of the research on effective educational responses to the impacts of trauma, and of the ways that disabilities law could be used to obtain appropriate accommodations for trauma-affected students, whether through representation of individual students or through impact litigation, perhaps modeled on a pending class-action suit pursuing such a strategy in California.[48] They also wanted the law office to draft a know-your-rights handout for parents, informing them of the need for schools to respond constructively to the impacts of trauma on students and of students' rights to accommodation under the disabilities statutes.

The team's research, however, rapidly shifted the project's focus. Exploration of the extensive literature on the impacts of childhood trauma on students' functioning in schools and on the emergence of effective trauma-informed approaches to education revealed that the most promising approaches to the problem were school-wide reforms, rather than individualized accommodations. Several states, most notably Washington and Massachusetts, had recently adopted legislation to guide and support reform efforts in their school systems, with encouraging early results. On the other hand, the challenges in employing existing disability rights law, either on an individualized or a more systemic basis, were daunting, both because of the mismatch between the effects of trauma and the recognized categories of disabilities and because of the mismatch between the remedial approaches available under disabilities law and the effective systemic approaches to trauma-informed schooling.

While SLC, in response to this information, did not see practical value in exploring a legislative strategy in Florida, they were receptive to a widening of the project's scope to include, not only a critical assessment of the short-comings of reliance on disabilities law but also discussion of the need to focus on systemic

Susan F. Cole et al., *Helping Traumatized Children Learn: Supportive School Environments for Children Traumatized by Family Violence* (Mass. Advocates for Children 2009) (describing design of trauma-informed educational models). SLC was also aware of initial steps toward addressing the need for trauma-informed education in its home community, Alachua County, Florida, under the leadership of a local coalition, Peace4Gainesville. *See* www.peace4gainesville.org/.

48 *P.P.* v. *Compton Unified Sch. Dist.*, 135 F. Supp. 3d 1098 (C.D. Cal. 2015). A few weeks after the students began work on the project, the court issued several preliminary rulings in the case, declining to dismiss the named plaintiffs' claims, but denying class certification and withholding any preliminary injunctive relief. *See also* 135 F. Supp. 3d 1126 (2015) (denying injunctive relief); 2015 WL 5752770 (Sept. 29, 2015) (denying class certification). There have been no subsequent reported decisions or developments in the case.

reform and development of advocacy tools and strategies for pursuing such reform. This led the law office, not only into more focused analysis of the intricacies of disability law but also into more thorough exploration, through both library research and interviews with experts, of state-of-the-art approaches to trauma-informed schooling. They also delved into the legal and administrative structures governing educational policy making at the state and district level in Florida, and into the kinds of advocacy that could be effective in those settings. The scope of the research that the law office undertook – multiple complex areas of disability law, cutting edge issues of child development and educational policy, field research into actual practices and reforms across multiple states – was remarkable, as were the complexity and sophistication of the discussions of law, strategy, and advocacy, both within the law office and with SLC and other allies.

The law office's ultimate written work-product consisted of three components, intended for three different audiences: a 100-page legal memorandum, providing SLC both with a detailed analysis of the possible applicability (and the limitations) of the three areas of disabilities law and with a guide to Florida law and practice relating to school governance; a forty-page policy brief, directed to potential allies, advocates, and decision makers, explaining the educational impacts of trauma, emerging approaches to trauma-informed schooling, and the arguments for a focus on school-wide systemic reform; and a one-page tri-fold flyer, directed at parents, educators, and other potential allies, laying out the basics of the problem, the preferred solution, and ways to get involved in advocating for reform.

The quality of the work produced by this law office was extraordinary, even by the high standards that we have come to expect in the program. Nonetheless, given how far the project had shifted away from SLC's litigation focus, I was skeptical about how much use they would have for it and how much practical impact it would have. But in fact, over the ensuing two years, SLC's work has been profoundly influenced by the law office's work, and they have used it in numerous contexts, both to achieve actual reforms in Florida schools and to share the law office's information and approach widely among advocates and allies across Florida and beyond.

Drawing on the law office's work, SLC has adopted advocacy for trauma-informed services for children as one of the primary focuses of its work, and incorporated it as an important element in the children's legal services grant that it receives from Florida's IOLTA program. They have focused on representation of children with high levels of ACEs and, in those cases, have sought opportunities to educate school personnel about the emerging understanding of trauma-informed schooling and have emphasized the importance of school-wide reforms. In several cases, they have achieved agreements from Florida schools, not only to provide individualized accommodations, but also to undertake school-wide training of all personnel (including not only classroom teachers but also school resource officers, cafeteria monitors, and other staff) to support trauma-sensitive approaches to student discipline and behavior management throughout the school.

At the same time, SLC has been working to share the law office's work and its recommended approaches to a wide range of constituencies. They have presented it to lawyers who advocate for children at both state and national conferences, including the special education bar, guardians ad litem, and juvenile public defenders, many of whom they report were unfamiliar with the growing literature on ACEs, trauma, and effective responses to them in educational and other institutional settings. They have also been providing training and support to groups of social workers involved in the schools and in the child welfare system, and are in the process of building a medical–legal partnership through which pediatricians are starting to screen their patients for ACEs and to draw on appropriate legal resources to address trauma-related issues. While this work remains in its early stages, it shows the promise of achieving meaningful changes in the capacity of schools and other Florida institutions to respond to children who have been impacted by trauma.

SOME TENTATIVE ASSESSMENTS

The Impact on Education in the Urban Core

No one would claim that these social justice projects, or the social justice program as a whole, have transformed urban schools or solved the problems of educating students from the urban core. But they have had real effects and have helped to empower their partner organizations to chip away at some of the important challenges besetting education for the children of the urban core.

Of course, not all of the program's projects succeed in producing results as substantial as those described here. But neither are the projects discussed in this chapter atypical. I am familiar with a number of other projects that are having real-world impacts on the needs of urban schools. One multi-year project designed and established a restorative justice approach to school discipline for a Boston public school, which has served as a model for similar restorative justice programs elsewhere in Massachusetts. Another provided critical factual and legal research in support of ongoing litigation challenging a voucher system that is diverting needed resources from urban school districts in Florida. Another provided legal analysis and empirical evidence that are providing needed support for efforts to renew litigation challenging Massachusetts' underfunding of its urban school districts. And beyond the issues around urban schools, the range of projects that have had powerful real-world impacts, whether in shaping legislation or regulations, in guiding and supporting impact litigation, in providing popular education materials to empower people interacting with the legal system, in equipping organizations with tools and information to support their organizing work, or in supporting the work of lawyers representing vulnerable populations, is too long to catalogue.

The key to the practical effectiveness of the social projects lies in the relationships with the program's partner organizations. They are the ones who actually put the law offices' research and analysis to work. Many organizational partners (like MCAN and Citizen Schools) have little or no legal capacity of their own. Others (like SLC), although staffed by (often highly skilled) attorneys, are stretched thin by the overwhelming demands of their current caseloads. The social justice program provides them with a depth of research and analysis that is otherwise unavailable to them. As one of SLC's lawyers put it, for a small, thinly staffed organization, the social justice program is "like having your own private think tank," whether to provide the careful detail needed to support an ongoing project or (as in the case of the trauma-informed education project) to provide a fresh, comprehensive look at a complex problem.

In many cases, a major element of the value that the program brings to a project is in helping the organizational partner to think creatively about, or to reconceptualize, how the law can help address their issue of concern. The scope and focus of most social justice projects evolve significantly over the nearly year-long process from project proposal to project completion. Often, partner organizations arrive with a relatively clear identification of the problem they want to address, but only tentative thoughts about the specific legal strategies to explore and pursue. Guided by the program's faculty, the upper-level lawyering fellows, and other project advisers, and grounded in the law office's research and analysis, the project's specific focus often evolves significantly, as the law office explores – in consultation with the partner organization – the range of ways, including but by no means limited to litigation, that law can advance social change.

In fact, one of the exciting features of the interactions between partner organization and project team is how the process allows both law students and activists to gain a more flexible understanding of the ways that law and lawyers can influence social change. Often both partner organization and law office initially focus on the potential for litigation as the key legal strategy. But, as in the examples discussed here, the year-long effort to truly understand the forces underlying the problem, the role that law plays in reinforcing those forces, and the ways that those patterns can be disrupted often leads to an emphasis on other ways – organizing campaigns, trainings of affected individuals and organizations, reform of statute, regulations, or administrative practices, information gathering and dissemination – of deploying legal tools to transform systems.

The Impact on Legal Education

While the practical impacts of the social justice program on urban schools (and on the other challenges the projects address) are incremental, and dependent on the capacity of the partner organizations, its impacts on legal education are far more direct and profound. At Northeastern, the social justice program has had a transformative effect on the first year of law school, both in its expansion of the range of skills to which students are introduced and in the messages it sends to students about what law is and what lawyers and legal education do.

From the first week of law school, students are focusing on the ways that the law impacts a specific societal problem, confronted by a real-world organizational partner and affecting real individuals or communities. They are continually confronted with a vivid example, not only of the practical consequences of law and lawyers but of the nuanced complexities that connect law and lawyering to social reality. They are constantly reminded both of the power of the law to change people's lives and of the difficulties of deploying law as a force for meaningful change. And they are not simply studying these dynamics; they are actively participating in them. This ongoing experiential engagement with law as an instrument of social change (and as an obstacle to such change) provides a powerful antidote to the alienation and disorientation that are so often the responses to the traditional first-year curriculum and pedagogy.

Substantively, the program ensures that, from the beginning of their legal education, students are alert to the complex roles that law plays in its social context. In coming to understand their partner organization's issue and its legal dimensions, they quickly recognize that the doctrinal rules are a part of the story, but not all (and often not most) of it, and that they need to understand the broader institutional settings in which those rules are applied and to appreciate the ways in which those institutional settings affect the practical import of the legal rules. The program specifically focuses attention on the ways that the legal system in its practical operation reflects and supports existing social hierarchies and power relationships, while, at the same time, it allows students to explore the ways in which the legal system's norms and principles can serve to advance social change.

The program's experiential orientation and its focus on issues with significant social impacts ensure that the program addresses a far broader range of competencies than the familiar law school curriculum. Recalling the Carnegie Report's complaint that law school focuses almost exclusively on the "cognitive apprenticeship," at the expense of the "practical" and "identity/purpose" apprenticeships, much of the social justice program's attention is on those neglected apprenticeships.

The projects immerse the students in the practice apprenticeship, by confronting them with the need to develop a project plan that responds to the situation of their organizational partner and by requiring that they interact repeatedly with the partner in using their emerging legal skills to meet the partner's needs. Although the students and the partner organization are not in a lawyer–client relationship, many of the key dynamics of professional service in furtherance of another's interests and agenda are present, and the program offers rich opportunities not only to experience but to reflect on the complexities of those dynamics, as reflected both in the law office's relationship with the partner organization and in the partner organization's relationship with the population that it serves. Issues of diligent representation, challenges of allocating responsibility for strategic and tactical choices, and complexities of communicating effectively across social differences, all are brought to the foreground of the students' attention. And likewise, with regard to the identity/

purpose apprenticeship, both the actual work on the projects and the reflective class discussions about that work draw students deeply into questions about the complicated relationships between the legal system and societal and individual ethical norms and about the complicated obligations of practicing lawyers to their own and to their clients' values and principles.

The program also trains the students in a far wider range of the skills needed by practicing lawyers than those that the familiar combination of doctrinal and research-and-writing skills courses address. Students learn how to take a complex, real-world problem and identify the potential legal issues that it entails. They learn to design, implement, and iteratively revise a multi-faceted research plan. They learn a wide range of research skills, beyond research in familiar primary and secondary legal sources, including expert interviews and, in many projects, a wide range of other types of field and library research. They develop communication skills, both written and oral, in a far wider range of contexts than in typical legal skills courses, ranging from informal email communications with partner organizations, experts, and advisers and explanatory materials for nonlegal audiences to richly documented white papers and formal oral presentations with audio-visual supports. And they learn to manage a complex project as part of a largely self-directed team, developing the needed communication, leadership, accountability, and conflict-management structures and tackling the challenges of working effectively across diverse backgrounds and skills.[49]

The program certainly has its challenges. Building the program around the real-world needs of organizational partners means that different law offices are focused on different skills, that changing circumstances at times disrupt a project or diminish its utility, and that some projects are more successful (both in quality and in impact) than others. Providing adequate support and supervision to ensure the professionalism of the work products requires a generous commitment of institutional resources. Conducting the projects in teams, while it has huge benefits in the development of collaborative skills and in the overall quality of outcomes, and while it is probably the only realistic way to manage the program with imaginable resources, means that different students have different responsibilities and are exposed to different skills, and is a frequent source of management challenges. The urgency and the reality of the project work can at times divert student attention from other important parts of their law school work.

But on balance, the educational benefits of the program are immense. It powerfully engages students in their new professional roles. It supports a rich and

[49] The rich range of skills that students acquire through the social justice program – many of which are further reinforced by the uniquely experiential design of Northeastern's second- and third-year programs, in which students spend almost a full year in full-time legal work settings – help to make our students unusually ready to enter the legal workforce on graduation. Many post-graduate employers observe that our students arrive a couple of years ahead of their peers from other law schools in their readiness to take on the full range of job responsibilities.

grounded understanding of how law and lawyering actually operate in their social setting. And it introduces students, in a compelling way, to a wide range of the skills that they will need as practicing lawyers. While some of these opportunities can also be supported by well-designed simulations,[50] many of the benefits of the program depend on its engagement with real-world organizations confronting real-world issues. The immediacy and reality of the project elicits a level of student engagement and a sense of professional responsibility that no simulation could generate. And even the richest simulation can never capture the multi-dimensional complexity and the fluidity of real-world problems and real-world lawyering. For a law school that is committed to preparing students for their professional roles and to fostering a commitment to law as serving the public good, this program makes irreplaceable contributions to the curriculum and the pedagogy.

Is There Legal Scholarship Here?

To acknowledge the obvious, this essay, although written for a book exploring the future of legal scholarship, is primarily about law school pedagogy, not legal scholarship. Of course, the interconnections between pedagogy and scholarship run deep in the legal academy, if perhaps less deep than in many other corners of academia. But what lessons, if any, might Northeastern's experience with its Social Justice Program have for our scholarship?

I will not argue that this chapter is an example of legal scholarship. At best, it may serve as a preface for the future scholarship that may arise from the Social Justice Program and from similar efforts elsewhere. But I do argue that the program is an exciting and important experiment in how we train future lawyers and what knowledge we seek to impart to them through their legal education. If so, then the projects themselves may be useful examples of what legal knowledge looks like, and hence of what legal scholarship should address. And the broader understandings that the program strives to develop – of how law contributes to social stasis and social change, of the complex potential roles of lawyers in advancing reform agendas, of the challenges of working as professionals across the boundaries of social difference – are topics that should be central to legal scholarship.

Nor will I argue that the work products generated by the social justice projects constitute legal scholarship, although many, if not most, of the final products include as a substantial element a law-review-style report that summarizes relevant areas of existing law and analyzes how they relate to the partner organization's objectives. While some of these papers approach the quality and the depth of

[50] Indeed, in the current iteration of the program, with its integration of the social justice projects with the rest of Northeastern's first-year skills training, faculty often rely on simulation exercises to prepare students for some of the challenges of the actual project work, or to provide opportunities to more fully explore and reflect on aspects of what they encounter in the project work.

published legal scholarship, they are primarily the work product of first-year law students, notwithstanding the supervision and support they receive from faculty, upper-level teaching fellows, and other advisers. For the most part, these products are better thought of as exercises in learning to produce legal scholarship or as preliminary drafts for such scholarship.

I do want to suggest, however, that the work being done in the Social Justice Program, both by the students and by the faculty, holds the promise of generating a rich vein of legal scholarship, or perhaps two distinct veins. The first vein would grow directly from the substantive work done for particular projects. Many of the projects, including, I would suggest, all three of the examples discussed earlier in the chapter, succeed in expanding our understanding of the legal dimensions of important social challenges and offer valuable insights into the strategic potential of law in facilitating societal change. With further refinement, perhaps in the hands of upper-level students working closely with faculty advisers, threads from these projects could easily give rise to polished articles, appropriate for publication, perhaps in a student-edited law journal, that would make important scholarly contributions to topics of interest both within and beyond the legal academy.

In some respects, such works would likely strain against some of the dominant norms in current legal scholarship. In many cases, doctrinal analysis would play only a peripheral or supporting role, while the primary topic would be explication of the practical settings impacting a partner organization's constituency, settings in which legal institutions and rules play a complex, but often limited, role. The focus would be less on clarifications of or proposed improvements in legal doctrine or procedure, and more on strategies for organizations on the ground to use in implementing change to advance their constituencies' interests. And these works would not take the dispassionate perspective of the objective observer, but would rather be oriented toward advancing a concrete agenda furthering the practical interests of an identified (and typically a disempowered) group. But perhaps these are precisely the features that a freshly relevant legal scholarship demands, features that are represented in a number of the examples of engaged, from-the-ground-up scholarship in this volume.

A second vein might focus, not on the specific issues that particular social justice projects tackled but on some of the issues of lawyering and law's role about which the social justice program seeks to educate its students. It might address, not the challenges of how to serve the needs of trauma-affected students but how lawyers can empower local organizing efforts; or, instead of exploring strategies for expanding access to vocational education, it might investigate the ways that the stories and images that dominate an area of policy and law can constrain the opportunities for reform in those areas, and how those stories and images can be adjusted to potentiate change. I would imagine this vein of scholarship being produced less by the students engaged in individual projects than by the program's faculty, who can bring the insight gained from repeated attempts to grapple with these issues in a variety of concrete situations. But I would anticipate that this scholarship, too, would delve deeply into specific examples and may offer more by way of rich stories than of broad generalizations or theories. Indeed, the boundaries between the two veins of scholarship may turn out to be so indistinct as to be meaningless.

Whether the focus is on a particular social problem and strategies for addressing it or on the broader questions of how the law and lawyers grapple with the challenges of systemic reform, the lessons to be learned from many of the program's projects offer fertile ground for exciting and provocative scholarship. Such scholarship could help expand understanding of the complex ways that legal rules and institutions shape some of our most pressing social issues, and of the paths, beyond the more familiar strategies of litigation or reform of legal rules, through which lawyers can contribute to addressing those issues. In its continuing evolution, I am hopeful that Northeastern's social justice program will find space and support to allow for the sharing of its work and its insights, not only with its students and its partner organizations but with the broader audiences for legal scholarship.

9

Conclusion

Legal Scholarship from the Ground Up

As we explained in the introductory chapter, our ambition for this volume is not only to showcase some rich examples of the ways that legal scholars are engaging with the issues that bedevil the urban core but also to explore these examples for hints of how legal scholarship can regain its relevance for a range of audiences who are interested in how the law can be understood and used in tackling societal problems and achieving social change. In this concluding chapter, we share some observations about some of the notable commonalities in the contributions to the volume, in hopes of identifying some of the characteristics that may distinguish such scholarship.

In particular, we focus here on three dimensions along which such distinguishing features stand out – their methodologies, their intended audiences, and their implicit epistemology, that is to say, their understanding of what counts as legal knowledge. On each of these dimensions, we can only begin to draw some tentative generalizations, and important questions about each dimension remain. But, taken together, these dimensions suggest that these chapters represent a shared approach to legal scholarship, one that is distinguished by the authors' engaged focus on the fine-grained details of particular institutions or processes on the ground, and that this approach, which we refer to as "from-the-ground-up" or, for short, "grounded" scholarship, shows promise for a rich vein of future legal scholarship.

Methodology

Looking collectively at the contributions in this volume, one of the striking consistencies that leaps out is the methodological approach, at least if methodology is broadly defined. All of our contributors have approached their chosen topics by concentrating their attention on one or a few concrete examples of phenomena, problems, or practices impacting urban cores and then asking what those examples might teach about the topic. As we will discuss more fully, some have done this by designing a formal case study or ethnographic study, while others have used more informal approaches grounded in personal involvement. Nevertheless, this range of contributions is remarkably consistent in this regard. There are no in-depth analyses of appellate opinions intended to explore a doctrinal development or mis-development. There are no economic formulas. There are no extended discussions of theoretical principles. While the analyses in this volume may well rely on certain theoretical, economic, or doctrinal foundations, their focus is decidedly qualitative and empirical in nature – even if sometimes quite informally so.

Even broadly described, as it must be to accommodate the range of styles and approaches evident in this volume, this methodology has several noteworthy features. Perhaps most obviously, our description of this approach as both qualitative and empirical is intended to capture our contributors' deep engagement with what they perceive to be one or a few important examples of issues they are interested in studying. Brito, Gordon, and Pate study the impact of the child support enforcement system not by reviewing appellate opinions, but rather by being present in child support enforcement proceedings, observing and recording events as they occur. Solomon considers expanding the availability of the Low Income Housing Tax Credit not by means of theoretical analysis or a broad survey of how such a change would affect a range of developers and developments, but by considering its value for a particular manufactured housing community that he has represented.

Breadth of example here is replaced by depth of inquiry into each example. Across the board, these scholars appear to revel in the details of their chosen cases of study. Cummings provides us with hundreds of details about individual lawyers and activists involved in his port trucking study. Pitegoff engages with the history of community development finance as it can be traced through a particular community development finance institution in coastal Maine. Each of the authors in this volume mines their cases for clues about what mattered in the specific context, and why.

Across this volume, the authors' descriptions of legal processes and phenomena operating in particular social contexts come to the fore in considering why law matters. In the process, the descriptions gain much more significance than that traditionally earned by "descriptive legal scholarship." The descriptions provided by these scholars about the effect of law in operation are a powerful form of "claim testing," as that term is defined and used in the qualitative empirical work of social science. Indeed, these scholars have designed their research to answer a broader set of questions than those traditionally answered by descriptive or normative legal scholarship. Their work is at times descriptive, normative, and predictive of legal outcomes in particular contexts. But it also tests (sometimes long-assumed) claims about how particular laws and regulations should work in particular contexts.

Moreover, "what matters" means something very different than in the typical statement of facts set forth in an appellate opinion, where the facts are distilled to only those relevant to application of narrow legal doctrines. Particularly in the more formal empirical projects, it seems almost as though the scholars have had to unlearn the lawyerly discipline of gleaning relevant facts. What matters in these examples includes the exact words, and word choices, of the participants involved in the studies or of the clients served. It includes how lawyers act and react in conversation with those individuals. It includes history and context; and context can involve such details as the room in which a hearing took place, the clothing the parties wore, and the tone of voice used. Perhaps most saliently, what matters in these studies is a question rather than a conclusion.

The result, in some of these analyses, is a very different perspective on why or how *law* matters in the particular cases. Cummings's discussion of preemption provides a compelling example. In developing the clean trucks campaign and joining forces with local environmentalists, the labor activists and lawyers in his case study did sophisticated analyses of the likelihood that the wage increases they proposed for drayage truck drivers would be preempted by federal law. In many respects, their efforts exemplified oft-used lawyering strategies: They analyzed the law as it was developed in recent court decisions, and then they devised a strategy to avoid certain applications of that law. But in telling the story of what happened next, Cummings reveals that such legal analysis could only go so far. Although law provided a powerful structure within which the "green–blue" coalition waged its clean trucks campaign, the strategic choices made by particular actors within and against that campaign at particular moments also had enormous consequences. Dyal-Chand's analysis of democratic participation in worker cooperatives teaches some of the same lessons. As her case study reveals, the legal question of how to structure a worker cooperative – including the drafting of its organizational documents – may depend quite precisely on the particular forms of voice, power, and control that workers in any given cooperative prioritize. Indeed, Dyal-Chand's chapter barely addresses the legal details of entity choice, focusing instead and deliberately on questions of institutional structure and organizational experience as antecedent to questions of law. In these studies, it appears that law frames, and sets context, but that it does not necessarily determine outcomes.

While these methodological features – qualitative, empirical, detail driven, relevance questioning, grounded in live context, claim-testing, and more generally "from the ground up" – are evident across this volume, it is also important to note that the different contributions formally represent a range of methodologies. These include formal case studies and ethnographic research on one end of the spectrum, and more informal narratives, some of which could aptly be described as "storytelling," on the other. As a comparison of these varied approaches reveals, each approach has unique functions, purposes, and advantages.

Consider first the more informal qualitative approaches employed by Solomon, Pitegoff, Morris, and Enrich. Each of these authors analyzes a legal question or conundrum by digging into a single or a few extended examples. In some respects, this is a relatively traditional form of legal scholarship, though these authors modify and extend the form in significant ways that align their methodologies more closely with formal qualitative empiricism than most legal scholarship would be. Most obviously, the "cases" that these authors examine are not appellate opinions, but rather cases in which they themselves have been involved, as lawyers, board members, advisors, teachers, or some combination of these roles. Also, in all but Morris's example, the cases are not defined primarily as lawsuits. Instead, even when these cases involve litigation, the authors often focus on a broader study of institutional arrangements that may involve transactional work, organizing campaigns, legislative strategizing, and a sweeping range of formal and informal norms and practices.

This twist on the traditional legal scholarly form provides a distinctive source of expertise: These scholars analyze the legal questions that arise in their cases not only on the basis of their knowledge and skills as legal thinkers but also on the basis of their experience with the facts, the individuals involved, the context, and the open questions – as they are unfolding. This is grounded (or applied) legal scholarship in its truest form. The scholars are able to evaluate legal issues not only through their abstract understanding of the relevant legal rules but by virtue of their own experience of the application of those rules to specific cases, clients, and contexts.

Because of their participation in the cases as they unfold, these scholars perform the vital lawyering skill of prediction fundamentally differently from scholars who are more distant from the cases they interpret. This matters perhaps most of all because of the difference in the scholarly interpretation and evaluation of risks and opportunities. The scholars in this volume have watched those involved in their cases adapt to risks and opportunities – to unpredictable changes as a case evolves. Their understanding of the relationship between risk and legal rules, and their corresponding ability to predict future risks and opportunities, is thereby sharpened. For example, both Pitegoff and Solomon share insights about the Low Income Housing Tax Credit on the basis of their extensive experience with this complex financing form, which in both authors' cases, includes transactions undertaken in clinics they have taught, and also by organizations they have served as board members. Pitegoff uses his knowledge in a wider discussion of the future potential and viability of community development finance. Solomon does so to propose very specific changes to the tax credit that could have enormous distributional consequences. Both sets of insights would be hard to discover without the experiences these authors have had with tax credit financing. This may be a particularly important advantage in the transactional context, in light of Ronald Gilson's insights about the connection between risk reduction and value added by transactional lawyers.[1]

[1] Ronald J. Gilson, *Value Creation by Business Lawyers: Legal Skills and Asset Pricing*, 94 Yale L.J. 239 (1984).

Moreover, by virtue of their involvement in the cases they study, the scholars in this volume can describe, and ultimately opine, on a broader range of issues. A prominent example of one such issue in CED scholarship is the role of *lawyers*, and not just of legal rules, in local economic development. Both Enrich and Morris provide compelling examples here. Both discuss the pedagogical value of teaching particular forms of public interest lawyering in law school. The examples that Enrich discusses explore the complex and disparate roles that legal advisers play in facilitating the efforts of groups seeking to exert local political power on behalf of disadvantaged communities. In her discussion of the development of a state and local law curriculum and pedagogy, Morris connects these issues to absolutely vital questions about the role of lawyers in a society experiencing deep democratic failures at the national level. In short, the scholars in this volume have created a much broader canvas on which to paint their predictions about the role and relevance of law.

The presence of legal scholars *in* the cases they study is profoundly relevant to the function, form, and purpose of their scholarship. It adds new and significant value to their analysis. Taken together, the work of these scholars provides a convincing argument for the centrality of this informal qualitative form of legal scholarship, which has at times been marginalized in favor of scholarship that has been viewed as more theoretical, doctrinal, or normative. To the contrary, such scholarship builds on theoretical, doctrinal, and normative analysis by adding the great value gained from experience, which, at least in the fields of urban studies and local economic development, is extremely valuable.

Toward the other end of the spectrum, Brito, Gordon, and Pate, Cummings, and Dyal-Chand represent a relatively recent – but growing – trend whereby legal scholars are deploying the formal methodologies of qualitative empiricism as such methodologies are used by sociologists, political scientists, and other social scientists. A principal reason for doing so is to reach a broader audience of social scientists interested in urban studies and local development, and this is something we take up in the next section. But it is also interesting to consider what these formal methodologies add to legal scholarship's scope and purpose.

It appears common to all three of the examples in this volume that the scholars employed formal qualitative methodologies because they sought answers about why the law was not working in a particular context. In Cummings's case, it is appropriate to define his inquiry more broadly as an examination of why *lawyers* were working with the law, and with other individuals who interacted with the law, in new and unexpected ways. Meanwhile, it is apt to describe the inquiry of Brito, Gordon, and Pate as a deeper questioning about the very purpose of child support enforcement, which in their study appears to achieve a new form of maldistribution rather than the intended form of basic redistribution.

As was the case for the other contributors to this volume, these three scholars could not find the answers to their questions by reading appellate opinions, statutes, and other sources of formal law. However, in contrast to the more informal qualitative studies, these scholars sought to fill their information gaps not on the basis of their own experience as participants in the cases they studied, but rather as interviewers and observers. Each was asking why and how legal institutions and actors function in unexpected ways. Their effort was to capture incisive glimpses into particular social – and legal – processes. Moreover, their inquiry was not necessarily intended to find a doctrinal answer, or even to develop any clear prescription. Rather their purpose was to understand deeper shifts or problematic patterns in social and legal behavior.

For such a purpose, it appears to have been important to each of these authors to gather a range of perspectives – in addition to their own – on the phenomena they studied. Because the goal partly was to see the dynamics and complexities in the subject(s) of their investigation, the multiplicity of voices, positions, and interpretations provided a more complete picture than could be assembled on the basis of one or a few interpretations of a legal question or failure. Even among this small group of three, there were likely important differences in positionality and goals. For example, in their chapter, Brito, Gordon, and Pate explore the question of how their research team's role as observers of administrative proceedings changed what took place. Meanwhile, Cummings discusses legal issues and transactions with which he has had deep experience as a practitioner.

In light of such goals, it thus seems appropriate for these authors to have used the instruments that social scientists originally borrowed from the lawyerly discipline of studying "cases," and then adapted for the purpose of achieving a more "objective" or "scientific" approach to the study of social phenomena. It may indeed be true that the greater formality of these studies resulted in a more scientific process of analysis than the more informal or personal case analyses in this volume. But it is undeniable that the techniques of rigorous recordation, the use of multiple and different sources of information, the interviewing of many individuals, the observation of many proceedings, the triangulation among different sources, and other aspects of formal qualitative methodologies are familiar to lawyers. Such techniques are some among a range of forms of the detailed digging that all of the contributors to this volume have prioritized in their research.

It is also worth considering the value gained from the use of these formal methodologies by *legal* scholars. Because these scholars are trained in interpreting the law, and explicating legal change, they can use the more formal qualitative analyses to inform our understanding about the connections between social behavior, social contexts, and law. Cummings teaches us something new about the law of preemption by studying how a complex campaign unfolded to manage that law. By observing a large number of child support enforcement proceedings, Brito, Gordon, and Pate reveal to us yet another legal arena in which the same law on the books nevertheless is used to maintain two distinct systems – one for people of color and those of lower incomes, and the other for those who are not. Dyal-Chand analyzes forms of democratic participation in a worker-owned business as a foundation for developing more granular legal mechanisms for achieving such participation. All three of the scholars who have employed formal qualitative approaches in this volume have described their work as laying a qualitative foundation for future qualitative and quantitative empirical work. The result should be a clearer path for future research, and ultimately for more well-grounded and accurate prescriptions for law reform and legal development. The work of these three scholars, and others employing formal empirical approaches, reveals that there is indeed much to be gained from using these methodologies to study the law.

Taken together, the spectrum of methodologies employed by all the authors in this volume inspire questions and conversations that we believe may be critical for the next generation of legal scholarship. For example, are some empirical methodologies on the spectrum evidenced here more appropriate for inquiries into operational questions of law, while others are more apt for systemic or institutional inquiries? Can legal scholars contribute to the development of blended methodologies that make use of both the more formal and the more personal approaches taken by our different contributors? Of what value are methodologies that aspire to objectivity and replicability to questions of normative legal scholarship? Certainly, the strength of the contributions made by scholars across this spectrum justifies a serious exploration of these questions.

Finally, it may be useful to pause over the question of why all the contributors to this volume have gravitated to using such a clearly (though broadly) defined methodology. Perhaps most importantly, it is apparent that the contributors to this volume are committed to learning from past mistakes and failures. As we have discussed, community economic development has been at times plagued by its cyclical tendency to develop bigger and more complex versions of solutions that have been attempted – and have failed before. Within CED's paradigm, we have seen mistakes repeated decade after decade. One consequence is the entrenchment of problems such as gentrification and re-segregation. Thus, one reason why the legal scholars featured here may have turned to a "from-the-ground-up" methodology is their own perception that it produces a more contextualized, detailed, and accurate prediction of risk and opportunity. This ought to be particularly useful in a field that seems prone to repeating the same mistakes over again.

But there is also a temporal aspect to this inquiry. While CED scholarship has always had a grounded or empirical sensibility, it is noteworthy that legal scholars of urban development have recently turned so definitively to qualitative, and increasingly formal, empirical methods. At the same time, a number of CED scholars have raised basic, even existential, questions about whether CED is still a useful paradigm for urban core transformation, whether we are in a "post-CED" world,[2] and whether we ought to be searching for other theories and paradigms for our work.

[2] We thank Scott Cummings for raising this question for us.

One interpretation of the confluence of an increasingly qualitative methodology and the existential questioning in this field is that the focus of legal scholars on particular cases is at least partly in aid of our search for new paradigms.[3] In the absence of a clearly workable paradigm in which to do our work, with which to frame our efforts, and through which to communicate to our audiences, it seems possible that many of us have turned to individual examples – both of success and failure – to explore why those examples matter. Our digging into the details of individual cases may not only be an attempt to avoid the mistakes of the past. It may also be an attempt to find new paradigms that reveal previously undiscovered paths forward.

At the same time, at least for some of us, there is a dawning recognition that the more deeply qualitative we go, the more productive the fit seems to be between methodology and the ability to develop meaningful answers to the many intransigent questions in this particular field of law. Thus, one question that the work in this volume inspires us to put on the table is whether the "from-the-ground-up" scholarship featured here is indeed the paradigm for which some of us are searching. A critical piece of the answer to this question relates to the puzzle of audience. Whom are we trying to reach? Who is best positioned to implement the legal changes we propose? Who can partner with us in avoiding the intransigent problems that have resurfaced from decade to decade in the urban core?

Audiences

Animating all of the contributions – and all of the contributors – to this volume is an interest in marshalling legal knowledge and legal skills to address the challenges confronting the disempowered communities of the urban core. But, unlike other generations and other veins of legal scholarship, they do not see impact litigation and the appellate courts as the primary means through which legal knowledge and skills will advance those goals. Instead, they focus on transactional work in support of housing or employment opportunities, reform of administrative and regulatory apparatus, policy advocacy, helping to build community power through local organizations, and support of individuals in low-level interactions with the legal system (for instance, in family court).

If these are the settings in which change is pursued, who are the audiences that these scholars seek to engage, the audiences that can help advance their goals? For more traditional scholarship, which sought progress through the improvement and deployment of legal doctrine, paradigmatically by influencing judicial interpretation and application of law, a primary intended audience, beyond the legal academy, has been the judiciary and the sophisticated litigators who advance creative legal

3 For the classic discussion of the role of paradigms and paradigm changes in scientific inquiry, *see* Thomas S. Kuhn, *The Structure of Scientific Revolutions* (1962).

arguments before them. But with a different set of expectations about how the law can achieve societal change, a different range of audiences – of potential change agents – becomes salient.

Particularly relevant are a wider range of legal practitioners, including those who provide transactional representation for entities engaged with urban core communities, those working in a range of governmental settings, and those who provide direct services to the urban poor. Also important are a wide range of the non-lawyers who can use legal tools to plan and implement social change, whether in guiding economic institutions in urban core communities, in organizing community power, or in developing or administering public programs and policies. And, as the primary focus of interest shifts away from the rarified worlds of appellate courts and federal policy making, it becomes important to connect with the general public, whose engagement is often crucial to on-the-ground change, and with law students, both to encourage their interest in addressing the challenges of the urban core and to equip them with the tools and perspectives that they can use to address them, even in the earliest stages of their professional careers.

Finally, as the locus for reform moves beyond the appellate courts and as the agency for change rests largely with the non-lawyer actors with whom lawyers interact, it becomes increasingly important, within the academy, for legal scholars to be in communication with scholars beyond the law schools, in a wide range of fields – from education to business to history to public health to sociology and beyond – that shed light on the workings and conditions of the urban core. Such interdisciplinary communication serves multiple purposes. It equips the nonlegal scholars with a deeper understanding of the ways that the law and lawyers impact, and can help to transform, the social phenomena on which they concentrate. Conversely, it offers legal scholars with richer understandings of the broader social contexts in which legal interventions can operate. And, from a methodological perspective, it offers models for how legal scholars can effectively explore the complex, multi-dimensional settings where they see law advancing social change, and invites reflection on the most constructive methodologies for such work. As noted in our discussion of methodologies, for these interdisciplinary conversations to thrive, it is valuable for legal scholars to draw on methodologies that are familiar and respected in the other disciplines with whom we wish to engage, at the same time that it is important for legal scholars to model variants on those methodologies that fit the nature of legal inquiry.

Some of the chapters in this book (for instance, Cummings' and Solomon's) provide examples of work that is designed to reach out to these broader audiences. Other chapters (for instance, those by Brito, Gordon, and Pate and Enrich) are intended less to exemplify than to explain and advocate for the development of scholarly work aimed at such audiences. But a recurrent thread throughout is the recognition that the challenges of the urban core reflect the interactions of the law with a complex web of institutions and actors, that the law can only serve as an instrument for social change through its use by a diverse range of institutional and individual actors, and that, as a result, legal scholarship can only be impactful if it reaches an audience extending beyond the legal academy and the elite bar.

In a number of ways, the scholarship exemplified and envisioned in these chapters is well suited to reaching these broadened audiences. Its richly descriptive methodology increases its accessibility to readers beyond the legal academy. Much of the work here is centered on stories, approachable narratives, which, even when they draw on complexities of legal doctrine or argumentation, can draw nonexpert readers into the issues and can introduce the complexities in specific applications that inform their meaning.

Moreover, in these chapters, law and lawyers are not at the center of the stories. Rather, they typically play supporting roles, in narratives where other players – community development corporations, local governments, nonprofit organizations, unions – are the central actors and in which dynamics and systems that are not narrowly legal are the primary focus of attention. In part, this reflects the authors' interest in describing real-world situations and transactions, in which the legal framework merely provides context and constraints and in which lawyers are primarily advisers and planners. And in part, it reflects the complex roles that legal doctrine, legal analysis, and legal experts play in the practical work most relevant to the challenges of the urban core. By situating the legal dimensions in their larger contexts, these discussions invite audiences other than lawyers (and likewise lawyers who are not experts on the legal issues) into the discussion by recognizing the roles that such audiences play in the issues under discussion.

Moreover, many of the scholars in this book do not play the role of objective, outside observers of the phenomena that they discuss. Instead, they are often participants, and their scholarship draws on, and is intended to advance, their work in support of individuals and organizations directly engaged in the challenges of the urban core. This engaged scholarship not only immerses the reader in the granular reality of the issues but injects an element of drama and of personal connection into the narrative, while also modeling the ways that legal scholarship can contribute to social change.

At the same time, it remains doubtful how deeply these chapters, largely crafted on the model of law review scholarship and published in a book from an academic press, are likely to penetrate a wide readership among these broader audiences. The genre these chapters reflect is primarily directed toward the legal academy and perhaps some other scholarly audiences. For that reason, a number of the authors in this volume are also turning to alternative paths to share their work.

Many of the authors of these pieces dedicate a significant portion of their time to work in law school clinics, and many of the chapters here grow out of work done in those clinics. That clinical work provides important additional channels for the dissemination of scholarly insights, both to students through formal instruction and collaborative clinical work and to the clients and organizations for whom they work.

When one of Prof. Morris's teams advises a city solicitor's office on how to construct a litigation plan, or when an economic development clinic designs a transaction for a development agency or for an emerging business, or when one of Northeastern's social justice projects provides a partner organization with strategic options for addressing an issue, academic research and analysis are being delivered to a relevant audience of change agents, whether or not we are accustomed to thinking of these products as scholarship.

Some of us are also exploring other forms of writing to share our work with wider audiences. Blogs, op eds, and perhaps even tweets provide shorter, less formal, more popularly oriented formats that are more likely to be read outside of the academy, although they sacrifice the detail and the complexity that longer forms accommodate. And, at the other end of the spectrum, several of our authors[4] have turned to full-length books to provide opportunity for the richly detailed descriptions and thorough explorations that can make their work accessible to wider, less technically oriented audiences. In all of these formats, these engaged legal scholars are seeking ways to reach a wider range of the change agents who can make a practical difference for the urban core, and for whom our scholarship can provide a helpful understanding of the ways that law and lawyering can support their work.

If legal scholarship is to make meaningful contributions to the work of those who effectuate social change on the ground, it is vital for legal scholars to present their work in more accessible, and more practically oriented, forms. We need to explore and develop new genres and venues for our work, which are far shorter, less formal, more concrete, and more engaging. But the call for such new scholarly forms is in tension with powerful norms and constraints in the legal academy. Tenure-track junior faculty are particularly susceptible to those constraints, because most institutions rest their tenure determinations almost exclusively on scholarship in the form of traditional law-review-type articles, and the expectations for productivity are so high that few senior mentors would encourage a junior colleague to devote much pre-tenure time to scholarship presented in other formats. And, even post-tenure, prevalent professional norms, and law schools' competition for scholarly "reputation," sustain law-review-style scholarship (along with academically focused books) as the path of least resistance and of greatest institutional support, although at least some law schools are increasingly encouraging faculty engagement in public discourse through op eds, blogs, and media commentary. Meanwhile, for the non–tenure-track faculty, who are often the people most directly involved in on-the-ground clinical and project work, scholarly productivity is often not a part of their job expectations, and their workloads often make any kind of scholarship a luxury. If the legal academy wishes to restore the relevance of its scholarship beyond the

[4] *See, e.g.*, Scott Cummings, *Blue and Green: The Drive for Justice at America's Port* (2018); Rashmi Dyal-Chand, *Collaborative Capitalism in American Cities: Reforming Urban Market Regulations* (2018).

academy, it will be important for law schools to give increasing recognition and support to more accessible forms of scholarly productivity.

Epistemology

So, what do the examples here teach us about the nature and the future of legal scholarship? What lessons can we draw from the subject matter, the methodologies, and the intended audiences and purposes of the works included in this volume, about the functions and the value of legal scholarship?

Presumably the core role of legal scholarship is to share knowledge about the law that has been acquired by students of the law.[5] But that brings us to the key question: What are we looking for when we seek "knowledge" about the law? What sorts of information constitute, and what sorts of activities generate, legal knowledge? Are we seeking clarity about the rules and principles that constitute the doctrinal substance of our legal regime, either in its existing or in its ideal state? Are we seeking descriptive accuracy about the practical operations of those aspects of social management that are assigned, at least in part, to the legal system? Are we seeking causal explanations, or perhaps normative justifications or critiques, of the connections between the legal system (either as a body of rules or as a system of institutions and practices) and other aspects of societal structure and organization?

Of course, as Jürgen Habermas has reminded us, knowledge is not a univocal concept. What counts as knowledge in different fields of human inquiry depends on the purposes that such knowledge is to serve and the human interests it is intended to advance.[6] And the methods for generating such knowledge and the standards for assessing its validity likewise reflect the functions that the knowledge is to serve. Thus, in the natural sciences, where the underlying goals of prediction and instrumental control of physical phenomena are generally acknowledged, the methodologies and standards for scientific knowledge are relatively clear and stable. But the ends to be advanced by knowledge of the law are more complex and more contested; so, it is perhaps unsurprising that uncertainty and debate surround the questions of what is to count as legal knowledge and of what we mean by "the law" when we seek knowledge about the law.

As noted in our introductory chapter, one dominant view, for which Robin West is a prominent and effective contemporary advocate, is that the law is the body of rules and principles that comprise law's substantive doctrinal content, and that legal scholarship's aim is the clarification and improvement of that body of doctrine,

5 *See Scholarship*, MERRIAM-WEBSTER.COM, www.merriam-webster.com/dictionary/scholarship (last visited Sept. 26, 2018) (defining "scholarship" as "a fund of knowledge and learning"); *Scholarship*, MACMILLANDICTIONARY.COM/US, www.macmillandictionary.com/us/dictionary/american/scholarship (last visited Sept. 26, 2018) (defining "scholarship" as "serious formal study and the knowledge you get from it").

6 *See generally* Jürgen Habermas, *Knowledge and Human Interests* (Jeremy Shapiro trans., 1971).

grounded in exploration of the normative principles that give that body of doctrine its claim on our respect and support. Meanwhile, critical legal scholars and their allies similarly take legal doctrine as the central object of attention, although the knowledge they seek concerns the tensions that lie at the heart of the doctrinal structures and the ways those structures reflect and reinforce underlying social dynamics of power and privilege. For the crits, legal knowledge understands legal doctrine in its broader social context, and their aim, like that of other practitioners of what Habermas denominates "self-reflective" or "critically oriented" science,[7] is to dissolve the normative force of "the law," and thereby to open up space for societal transformation.

In the chapters of this book, however, the role of legal doctrine is relatively peripheral. While legal rules are often a factor in the narratives presented, acting as constraints on available strategies or as potential tools in advancing them or as challenges to be managed, the primary focus is elsewhere, on the ways that local players seeking improvements in lived conditions work with and within the pertinent institutions to advance their agendas. What counts as law in these stories is not so much the content of doctrinal rules as the ways in which the salient institutions operate and the ways that they respond to the constraints and pressures that the legal system brings to bear on them. Some of those constraints and pressures have doctrinal origins, while others rest more on institutional design or on the ways that representatives of the legal system intervene in their operations. What counts as legal knowledge for the authors in this volume is less about doctrine than about the practical workings of the legal system within its larger institutional contexts, because their interest is in the ways to facilitate practical change in settings where appellate courts have only a limited role to play.

It might be suggested that the contextual, non-doctrinal focus of the scholarship here reflects the particular areas of law that are under discussion, areas that are transactional or bureaucratic and therefore are less accessible to interventions at the doctrinal level. Perhaps in other areas, such as constitutional law (which is West's primary area of substantive scholarship[8]), a different, more doctrinally oriented approach is more appropriate, while in other areas, such as antitrust or corporate law, the tools of economic analysis may offer the most constructive insights. Perhaps the moral is that different types of scholarship provide the different types of knowledge most salient to different areas of the law.

It is not our purpose to make hegemonic assertions about the universal appropriateness of the approaches exemplified here, and we certainly recognize the utility of different approaches and different types of knowledge about law in particular

7 *See, e.g.*, *id.* at 310. Habermas's paradigms for such self-reflective science are Marx and Freud.

8 *See, e.g.*, Robin L. West, *The Aspirational Constitution*, 88 Nw. L. Rev. 241 (1993); Robin L. West, *Constitutional Scepticism*, 72 B.U. L. Rev. 765 (1992); Robin L. West, *The Authoritarian Impulse in Constitutional Law*, 42 U. Miami L. Rev. 531 (1988).

contexts. Nonetheless, we would note, as Prof. Morris argues in her chapter, that, notwithstanding the importance of appellate litigation in defining and refining the operative legal principles in areas like constitutional law, the on-the-ground impact of those principles often rests far more heavily on the day-to-day operations of the institutions and practices that give them practical effect than on the carefully articulated details of the doctrinal declarations. And likewise, as the increasing focus in law-and-economics on "behavioral economics" suggests, the on-the-ground salience of economic analyses, even in areas to which it is best suited, often depend on the ways those concepts are filtered through the complexities of human and organizational behavior. Even in these areas, the question of whether legal knowledge is knowledge about the doctrinal declarations and analytic principles or rather about the on-the-ground operations of the legal system remains at least an open one.

There are obvious affinities between the orientation of much of the work in this volume and the approaches of the law and society movement. Both are more interested in the law in action than in the law on the books. So, both turn to the larger operational structures through which the legal system actually impacts lived arrangements, treating the question of doctrine's relevance as a contingent, empirical question, the answer to which will vary from situation to situation.

But, while much law and society scholarship aspires to the objective, observational stance of the empirical social sciences, the stance of many of the chapters here is more engaged and self-consciously perspectival. Many of the contributors to this book were active participants in the stories they tell, and most of the others tell their stories out of an interest in advancing the goals of particular parties in their narratives. Even for Dyal-Chand and Cummings, whose chapters aspire to carefully documented and objective observation, those chapters are parts of larger projects in which they are pursuing transformational agendas. The knowledge that these authors seek is not neutral; it is insight into how disadvantaged, disempowered, and marginalized groups can appropriate legal tools to advance their interests.

Thus, these works are, like West's doctrinally oriented model of scholarship, inherently normative. But unlike West's vision, the operative norms are not sought within the substantive content of legal rules and principles. Without disputing that legal doctrine derives from and aspires to important societal norms, the engaged scholarship here regards law's normative structures as simply one among many sets of facts about the paths and tools that comprise the legal system that activists must engage to pursue goals that find their justifications elsewhere. Certainly (and fortunately) those goals and values are, at times and to degrees, recognized by legal doctrine and by legal institutional arrangements, but so are antithetical goals and values. And while the paths to change sometimes involve efforts to bring legal rules into better alignment with the authors' motivating values, that is but one possible strategy that they explore.

In addition to being inherently normative and engaged, the scholarship in this volume is persistently granular. It tends to focus on very specific stories and situations, and it relishes detailed description of the idiosyncratic particularities of each one. Generalizations are relatively rare, and are frequently quite tentative. While the authors are certainly seeking to derive and share lessons from their stories, they appreciate the sensitivity of each story to the particular nuances of its players and circumstances, and a substantial portion of the knowledge to be gained is knowledge precisely about such situational sensitivity.

For many of the pieces included here, one of the central interests in this particularized description is the ways that the legal system is experienced by, and is managed or influenced by, the individuals and communities whose lives are affected by their encounters with that system. The authors recognize that an understanding of these encounters and of how they are experienced is crucial to an understanding both of where change is needed and of how change can be achieved. If a core function of legal knowledge is to advance social change, then understanding of these dynamics is a core component of legal knowledge. This focus drives not only the contextual, non-doctrinal orientation of these chapters but also their tilt toward granular description, which can strive to capture the complexities of lived experiences of encounters with the legal system.

Thus, the model of scholarship exemplified here is, at the same time, both richly descriptive and normatively focused, and those two threads are often inextricably intertwined. The on-the-ground description is in furtherance of understandings that can advance on-the-ground change, both in clarifying what it is that needs changing and in identifying strategies that can produce change. The authors here engage in their descriptive scholarship because of its utility in improving the conditions they observe, and they have little interest in categorizing the knowledge they produce as normative or instead as descriptive. If, for Prof. West, legal knowledge is normative all the way down, for these scholars, legal knowledge is engaged all the way down. Legal knowledge, for them, is inherently action-oriented.

Is these scholars' focus on detailed, engaged description, rather than on generalized explanation or normative theory, an inherent feature of the project these scholars pursue? Or is it a step along the path to a new paradigm of scholarship that can support a more "scientific" approach, more focused on generalizations or principles? As noted in our discussion of methodology, when old paradigms of scholarly inquiry break down, a retreat to more descriptive work may be a natural way-station on the search for a new theoretical framework that will ultimately support more structured work within a new paradigm.

Alternatively, not only with regard to methodology but with regard to the question of what to count as legal knowledge as well, this granular, descriptive attention to the nuances through which the use of legal tools succeeds or fails in achieving change for disempowered people may itself be the new paradigm. It may be the most meaningful way to provide change agents with the understandings that they need to be effective in their work. After all, theoretical bodies of generalizations, while powerful in the instrumental manipulation and prediction of the physical world that is the function of the natural sciences, are not the only way that scholarly undertakings can support human endeavors. Perhaps in this area, stories and learning grounded in detailed examples may be the very knowledge that law-oriented change agents need. And the infusion of those stories with values and aspirations may be a crucial source of their utility. The descriptive, qualitative, and engaged character of the approaches taken by the authors in this volume may be the very approaches that can generate the knowledge their intended audiences are looking for.

These hints at what may be the character of the legal knowledge sought by people interested in using law to change the world inevitably raise questions, not only about the nature of legal scholarship but also about the nature of legal pedagogy, and about the connections between our scholarship and our teaching. Many of the same criticisms that have been directed at the disconnection between legal scholarship and the real-world actors for whom the law matters have likewise been directed at a parallel disconnection between legal education and the world of practice.[9] And, while the focus of this volume has been on legal scholarship, a number of the contributions to it expressly address the relationships of legal scholarship to legal education.

If the examples in this book provide insight into what counts as legal knowledge for those interested in using the law as an instrument for social change, then those insights can inform not only our approaches to our scholarship but likewise our approaches to our teaching. In particular, these examples suggest that a central focus of legal education ought to be an exploration of actual examples of the roles that law plays in complex efforts to achieve change for disempowered groups and in the design and operation of structures that can advance their interests. Of course, law schools should introduce students to some of the basics of legal doctrine, to the mechanics of legal research and the standard forms of lawyerly communication, and to paradigmatic strategies of legal analysis and argumentation. But, if we really want to convey the knowledge that legal practitioners need, then at least as much emphasis should be dedicated to exploration of the actual ways that lawyers and non-lawyers use law and law-related institutions to advance change agendas in the real world. And, if we believe that a nuanced understanding of the experiences of those affected by the law and of the ways that they interact with the legal system are central to legal knowledge, then we should be ensuring that our students are placed in situations that enable them to understand these dimensions – and that equip them with the skills to pursue such understandings in the novel situations they will encounter in their practice lives.

It is unsurprising, then, that most of the scholars represented in this volume have dedicated portions of their academic careers to clinical teaching, and that many of

[9] Harry T. Edwards, *The Growing Disjunction between Legal Education and the Legal Profession: A Postscript*, 91 Mich. L. Rev. 2191, 2191 (1993); Robin West, *The Contested Value of Normative Legal Scholarship*, 66 J. Legal Educ. 6, 8 (2016).

their contributions to this volume grow out of that work. On the one hand, clinical teaching provides the opportunity for rich, and at least somewhat reflective, engagement with the real-world functioning of the legal system, and thus is a natural foundation for the scholarly approaches this book exemplifies. And on the other hand, clinical teaching provides the pedagogical space in which to equip students to acquire the engaged, particularized understandings of the law that they most need. The clinical work provides the material for our scholarship at the same time that it provides the venue to effectively pass the knowledge reflected in that scholarship to future lawyers.

Still, law school clinics are a remarkably labor-intensive and expensive component of legal education. It is unrealistic to imagine that they will come to be pervasive features of most students' educations. If the knowledge they can impart is so central to what law students must learn, then the legal academy will need to be creative in finding other ways to highlight these particularized, context-dependent understandings of the practical roles of law and lawyers, through use of simulations, case studies, team projects, or other strategies. Some of the scholarship presented or proposed in these chapters may provide useful materials to support such efforts.

Whether drawing on clinical work, case studies, ethnography, or more anecdotal sources and tools, the examples in this book suggest the value of particularized, engaged scholarly exploration of specific encounters between the legal system and the challenges of the urban core. Such from-the-ground-up scholarship may help change agents to arrive at a richer understanding of law's and lawyers' roles in their work. It may lead to a more nuanced and practical perspective on what counts as knowledge about the law, and it may rebuild bridges between legal scholars and the audiences, beyond the legal academy, who may benefit from their insights. We hope these examples will help to inspire further efforts along these lines, and further thought about the optimal paradigms for engaged legal scholarship.

Index